2649279

UNITED STATES
PROTOCOL

UNITED STATES PROTOCOL

The Guide to Official Diplomatic Etiquette

Ambassador Mary Mel French

Foreword by William Jefferson Clinton

ROWMAN & LITTLEFIELD PUBLISHERS, INC.
Lanham • Boulder • New York • Toronto • Plymouth, UK

Published by Rowman & Littlefield Publishers, Inc.
A wholly owned subsidiary of The Rowman & Littlefield Publishing Group, Inc.
4501 Forbes Boulevard, Suite 200, Lanham, Maryland 20706
http://www.rowmanlittlefield.com

Estover Road, Plymouth PL6 7PY, United Kingdom

British Library Cataloguing in Publication Information Available

Library of Congress Cataloging-in-Publication Data
French, Mary Mel
   United States protocol : the guide to official diplomatic etiquette / Mary Mel
French.
       p. cm.
   Includes bibliographical references and index.
   ISBN 978-1-4422-0319-8 (cloth : alk. paper)—
   ISBN 978-1-4422-0321-1 (electronic)
   1. Diplomatic etiquette—United States—Handbooks, manuals, etc. I. Title.
JZ1436.F74 2010
395.5—dc22   2009047918

⊗™ The paper used in this publication meets the minimum requirements of
American National Standard for Information Sciences—Permanence of Paper for
Printed Library Materials, ANSI/NISO Z39.48-1992.

Printed in the United States of America

DEDICATION

It is with great appreciation that I dedicate this book to the personnel who currently make up, and have made up, the Office of the Chief of Protocol, U.S. Department of State. The fine arts of diplomatic courtesy and etiquette are the foundations of the Office of Protocol; they provide the bedrock for officers working year after year to honor American and foreign traditions.

The work that keeps diplomatic protocol for the U.S. government up-to-date with internationally recognized standards requires countless hours, extraordinary dedication, and unparalleled professionalism. Protocol officers strive fervently to ensure that events—formal and informal, public and private—proceed seamlessly. Laboring quietly behind the scenes, officers' efforts often go unheralded. Those committed not just to doing protocol-related jobs but to maintaining the conviction necessary to do those jobs correctly deserve the spotlight.

Contents

Foreword

WILLIAM JEFFERSON CLINTON

ONE DECADE INTO THE NEW MILLENNIUM, we find ourselves immersed in an age of profound interdependence. The global economy and advancing technologies obscure borders and eclipse distances. Now more than ever, we must learn to live together, respecting our differences as we pursue our common goals.

Our greatest mission today is to strengthen the positive forces of interdependence while minimizing the negative ones. We must engage our neighbors in a constructive dialogue that will allow us to tackle questions of how to resolve the economic crisis and combat global warming, poverty, disease, and the lack of access to education; how we can increase our security and reduce religious, cultural, and ideological conflicts; and, in so doing, how we can restore the United States' standing and leadership in the world. All this requires immense international cooperation in which diplomacy will play a critical role.

Diplomacy, in theory, seems simple: by treating our neighbors with respect and dignity, we can work through our tensions and bridge our divides. In reality, it's a delicate art, and the prerequisites for its effective practice include tremendous discipline, acute cultural awareness, and mastery of a code of conduct known as diplomatic protocol.

The author of this book, Mel French, is a longtime friend. In the 1990s, she also became a skilled diplomat. Drawing upon the extensive experience she gained while serving as my administration's Chief of Protocol, she provides her unique insight into the intricacies of this important work and its significance to our foreign policy.

The ways in which we interact with one another have dramatically changed. Today's technology affords us unprecedented opportunities to exchange ideas freely and instantly. It also requires us to communicate at a frenetic pace, leading us to relax our standards of formality—in some cases, to our disadvantage. When we omit courtesies and context from our messages, we compromise the clarity of our objectives, leaving them vulnerable to misinterpretation. There is little margin of error within the realm of international relations, when seemingly minor missteps can have significant consequences.

The conventions of diplomatic protocol guide us in accurately expressing our intentions. Although the term may imply a rigid, old-fashioned sense of pomp and circumstance, it need not. Protocol evolves in step with our transition to interdependence. By upholding traditions, acknowledging customs, and maintaining appropriate formalities in our interactions with other nations, we convey respect and order, helping to create an environment conducive to mutual understanding and collaborative decision making.

To members of the Foreign Service and other employees of our federal government, the utility of Mel French's *United States Protocol* is self-evident. An authoritative user's manual for international relations, it promises to become an indispensible reference—not only for those in Washington but for all Americans in contact with people in other nations. If, as I believe, the future will require public-private partnerships working together to address our most pressing challenges, mastering diplomatic protocol will be everyone's first step to success.

President Bill Clinton
August 3, 2009

Author's Letter to Readers

A FEW YEARS AFTER MY TENURE AS Chief of Protocol for President William Jefferson Clinton, I picked up my precocious grandson, William, from kindergarten. His class had been studying the American presidents, and he got into my car full of questions and information.

His eyes large and full of innocent excitement, he asked, "Do you *remember* when you worked for the president?"

"I actually *do* remember that," I replied.

"Did you really like George Washington?"

I just couldn't burst his bubble. So I said, "Yes! I really did like him."

Protocol comes in many forms and often manifests itself when and where it is least expected. It consists of much more than knowing the correct place to put a fork or (as it concerns the government) knowing the proper place to seat an international guest of honor or foreign dignitary. At its root, protocol is about the establishment and maintenance of relationships, and it provides a framework for order whether between family members, friends, business associates, or world leaders.

When I answered my grandson's question, I had to call upon a few of my diplomatic abilities, and everything I knew about manners, in order to preserve his feelings. In the end, minus the George Washington part, my answer to him would have been the same: Yes, I remember working for the president. And yes, I liked working for the president. In writing this book, I have had the opportunity to reminisce not only about the more technical aspects of U.S. protocol but also about some of the entertaining mishaps and success stories that accompanied my job.

When man first realized he had an ego, protocol found its beginning. Early writings of the Egyptians show that they used rules to govern everyday rituals. Rituals developed through the centuries into what we now know as good manners.

Today, protocol is the accepted practice of international etiquette. "Protocol" is derived from the Greek terms *protos* (meaning "the first") and *kolla* (meaning "glue"). Protocol is therefore often considered the glue that holds everything together. Protocol is not political; knowing no party lines, it is a body of basic courtesies and rules that influence how people get along. Solid interpersonal and international relationships are the first step in global cooperation, and this book provides guidance for all who endeavor to initiate and maintain those relationships. This book should serve as a resource for many accepted practices in diplomatic protocol today and can be of use to those in government, business, and private sectors.

Those who work in the area of protocol, especialy in the Office of Protocol, challenge a world in which some consider etiquette outdated, manners old-fashioned, and tradition outmoded. We, on the other hand, recognize that protocol is no trivial matter; in fact, it is the undergirding of a strong nation and the outward signal of its vitality.

In a July 2009 speech at Delhi University in New Delhi, India, Secretary of State Hillary Rodham Clinton captured this sentiment for her audience. She said, "Not so long ago, the measure of a nation's greatness was the size of its military, or its economic strength, or its capacity to dominate its friends and adversaries. . . . But in this century—in the interconnected and interdependent world in which we live—greatness can be defined by the power of a nation's example."[1]

Respect and courtesy must be practiced throughout the diplomatic world. Both respect and courtesy matter; they are translated into everyday behavior and can either advance or destroy relation-

---

1. Glenn Kessler, "Clinton Hails India's Leadership, Discusses Arms Agreements," *Washington Post*, July 20, 2009.

ships between individuals and countries. The conduct not only of the government but also of the American public can make a difference in how America is viewed. Interactions between Americans and visitors to the United States from abroad, and likewise between foreigners and Americans traveling to foreign countries, create lasting impressions. Courtesy goes a long way, and knowing how to act and react in social or political situations shows respect for others. Thus, the guidelines of diplomatic protocol have the potential to enrich the status of our country on national and foreign soil. The United States should be a leader in universal decorum, influencing others to follow it in seeking solutions for the troubling dilemmas facing all nations.

United States Protocol includes aspects almost everyone can find interesting. The president, the president's spouse, employees of the U.S. and foreign governments, elected state and local officials, businessmen and women, and private citizens all have a stake in reading this book. It is informative and also provides amusing anecdotes and tales accumulated during my tenure as chief of protocol. Such stories help those carrying out their protocol-related responsibilities to smile a bit while executing more serious duties. The information in this book details how manners and civility function not only at the highest levels of American government but also in everyday lives.

Educating oneself about and heeding the rules of protocol can make the diplomatic world less stressful. Having an idea of what to expect during important social or political moments can provide a great deal of comfort. Protocol does not consist merely of *hard and fast rules*; the rules are flexible enough that they can be changed, if necessary, to provide for the organization and enhancement of behavior in this ever-changing world.

Acknowledgments

IN WRITING THIS BOOK, I have called upon a number of distinguished professionals who are among the elite in their protocol-related fields. Many answered my call, and I hope that the result accurately reflects their expertise as well as mine, including codification of those rules, forms, and standards specific to various facets of protocol. I am eternally grateful for the help and perseverance of these contributors, for it has taken a great deal of time and effort to put together a handbook of protocol information.

It is important and impressive to note that the contributors have crossed party lines to assist in building this book's infrastructure and in double-checking its accuracy. Thus, this book itself is a testament to, and an artifact of, bipartisanship.

All who contributed to this volume have assisted in creating a ready resource for government, business, and the public. From these contributions, readers will form an acute awareness of the crucial role of U.S. protocol, as well as the necessity for understanding its sociophilosophical underpinnings, in the promotion of international cooperation.

First, I want to thank Erin Pennington, editor, writer, and writing instructor at the University of Arkansas, Little Rock, and the Clinton School of Public Service. I could not have successfully concluded this book without her tireless assistance in editing drafts or her skills in assembling the final forms required by the publisher. I commend her for her devotion to the project and for her great personality and temperament. Erin and I spent the final months working on the book in Little Rock where I had tremendous support from many friends around the country who work in the fields relating to protocol.

During the book's early stages, I worked in Washington, D.C., with Larry Dunham, who generously contributed his vast knowledge for chapter 11, "Conduct of Diplomacy," which relates to the interworking of diplomatic and consular liaison from Larry's years as assistant chief of protocol for diplomatic affairs, U.S. State Department. Michelle Snyder Brady helped over many months, diligently tapping resources and accurately compiling documents. Michelle's father was a Foreign Service officer, and her experience growing up living all over the world added a helpful dimension to her advice and expertise. Laura Wills assisted with the foundational work at the beginning of this process and contributed knowledge gained from her position as a protocol gifts officer. Laura worked with me during the years I was part of the Office of Protocol and still confers her skills to the overall enhancement of protocol today. In the early days of assembling what I had worked on for months, Lauren Carey Daniels, a student at American University in the School of International Service, was a welcome and dependable young scholar who provided research for the book.

I do not have enough words to thank Rick Paulus, former State Department calligrapher and later White House calligrapher for many years, for editing and exhaustively reading and rereading chapter 5, "Titles and Forms of Address," and for offering much needed advice, which I have incorporated into that chapter.

During the writing of this book, I have consulted a number of people with considerable years and experience in the Office of Protocol, Department of State. I am deeply indebted to my associates and friends in the Protocol Office: Randy Bumgardner, April Guice, Tanya Turner, and Jessie Johnson.

Retired and former Office of Protocol personnel contributing background knowledge include Christine Hathaway, senior protocol visits officer, retired, whose vast knowledge of visits of foreign chiefs of state and heads of government is rivaled by none; Eve Wilkins, former visits officer for immigration and customs; and Carlos Elizondo, former protocol visits officer and presently the residence manager and social secretary for the vice president. Benedicte Valentiner, general manager of Blair House for over thirteen years, has been a valued consultant and has added enormous fun to the process.

Molly Raiser, former chief of protocol, read and reviewed each chapter of the book and has provided valued advice for changes.

Leslie Lautenslager, executive assistant to Gen. Colin L. Powell, USA Ret., and former assistant chief of protocol for ceremonials, State Department, has not only critiqued the manuscript but given critical advice gleaned from years of work experience with General Powell, for which I am very grateful.

For advice related to inclusion of information about the State Department, my thanks to Elaine Shocas, chief of staff to former secretary of state Madeleine K. Albright.

The complexity of the military information was daunting. I turned to Phil Fowler, chief of ceremonial activities, Military District of Washington (MDW), Fort Lesley J. McNair, Washington, D.C., for advice and fact-checking. I worked with Phil and with Tom Groppel, MDW, during my eight years in the Protocol Office. I have long valued their advice and commitment to working in this area.

I also thank John Miller, U.S. Secret Service, retired, for reviewing the information concerning security.

A number of people gave helpful insight as this project proceeded: Wayne Cranford of Cranford Johnson Robinson Woods (who gave generously of his time and editing expertise); Kaki Hockersmith, interior designer; Ron Maxwell, director, Arkansas Governors' Mansion; George H. Jensen, PhD, Mary Boaz, and Kathy Oliverio, University of Arkansas, Little Rock; and Micah McConnell, director of communications, Episcopal Diocese of Arkansas (whose knowledge is second to none in the area of religious communications). Buddy Carter, White House butler, provided direction concerning table settings and arrangements for state dinners. Several persons now retired from offices in the White House shared information concerning the areas in which they worked, including Ann McCoy, Office of the Social Secretary, and Denver Peacock, former White House advance. Also providing help were Betty Currie, presidential secretary; Janice Kearney, diarist; and Margaret Whillock, Visitors Office.

From the William J. Clinton Foundation, my thanks to Bruce Lindsey, chief executive officer and former assistant to the president and deputy White House counsel; Stephanie Streett, executive director and former presidential scheduler; and Nnenna Jemie, assistant to the foundation's chief operating officer in New York.

Candace Shireman, curator of Blair House, set me on the path to finding the right people to assist with photographs. Those people included Sara Garner, Center for Historical Buildings; Hillary Crehan of the White House Historical Association; and John Keller, audiovisual archivist at the William J. Clinton Presidential Library.

I have been blessed with ample friends and family who helped me tread through many months of long hours and difficult writing. My thanks to Beverly Lindsey, Gloria Cabe, Jill Indyk, Donna McLarty, Judy Green, Sara Erhman, Susan Berger, Barbara Roosth, Dena Benafield, Nancy Phillips, Nancy Vines, Carolyn McCrary, Sharon Edwards, Deborah Underhill, and Fahad Al-Otaibi. My thanks to my children, Mary Jane Roberts Redington, Julie Roberts McVicker, and William Dean Roberts. My grandchildren—Melanie, John, and William McVicker and Allie Redington—played parts by asking insightful questions that caused me to consider my responses carefully.

The publishing process was facilitated by Anna Jane Sitton Hays, publishing consultant and Stephens College friend, and by Sally Bedell Smith, author, who introduced me to my editor and publishing company.

Finally, I give heartfelt thanks to the publishing team at Rowman & Littlefield Publishers, namely, to Jon Sisk, editor, Darcy Evans, editorial assistant, and Elaine McGarraugh, production editor.

Chapter 1

Office of Protocol

President Clinton arriving at U.S. State Department with
Mary Mel French, Chief of Protocol. Author's collection.

FORMER ASSOCIATE CHIEF OF PROTOCOL Richard Gookin relayed the
comment of a former chief of protocol that Washington consisted of
one-third each alcohol, Geritol, and protocol. After being on the job
for a while, the chief said that he could avoid the alcohol, was young
enough to not to take Geritol, and was lucky enough to be responsible
for protocol.

CHIEF OF PROTOCOL

The chief of protocol serves at the president's direction and pleasure and traditionally has been a Presidential appointment. The chief of protocol advises the president, vice president, secretary of state, and high-ranking officials of the White House, departments, and agencies regarding the fulfillment of the U.S. government's obligations relating to national and international protocol. It is of utmost importance that the chief of protocol have connections and associations that lend credibility to the chief within the diplomatic world. Confidence in the chief's networking capabilities is especially important to foreign ambassadors who feel that diplomatic work is more easily accomplished when the chief of protocol has access to the president.

Broad questions of protocol from high-ranking officials of the White House or departments and agencies throughout the government may be directed to the chief of protocol to maintain, establish, and promote international relations between the United States and foreign countries.

The chief of protocol maintains contact with the White House and the Office of the Secretary of State in planning and arranging visits of foreign chiefs of state and heads of government. The chief of protocol receives distinguished foreign guests and chiefs of missions for the president and the secretary of state. The chief of protocol is responsible for protocol planning and preparation for presidential visits to foreign countries.

When the president invites a distinguished foreign dignitary to the United States, the chief of protocol acts, on the president's behalf, in welcoming that individual to the United States. At the secretary of state's request, the chief of protocol welcomes honored visitors on the secretary's behalf.

The direction of the protocol staff and the operation of Blair House, the President's Guest House, are under the umbrella of the chief of protocol. Activities related to official entertainment for the secretary of state fall under the chief of protocol's direction.

Accreditation of ambassadors and other diplomatic and consular officers assigned to foreign missions in Washington, D.C., permanent missions to the United Nations, and missions and delegations to the Organization of American States, along with registration of employees of these missions and delegations to the Department of State, are primary responsibilities of the chief of protocol.

It is of interest to note that a majority of foreign countries have a chief of protocol at the highest levels of their governments.

DEPUTY CHIEF OF PROTOCOL

The deputy chief of protocol serves as acting chief of protocol in the absence of the chief of protocol.

The deputy chief of protocol is responsible for implementation of presidential delegations and for credentialing ceremonies for newly appointed ambassadors to the United States.

The deputy chief of protocol has primary responsibility for management of the Office of Protocol and supervises the following individuals:

- Assistant chief of protocol for visits
- Assistant chief of protocol for ceremonials
- Assistant chief of protocol for diplomatic affairs
- Assistant chief of protocol for administration
- Assistant chief of protocol and general manager of Blair House, the president's guest house

ASSISTANT CHIEFS OF PROTOCOL

Assistant Chief of Protocol for Visits

The assistant chief of protocol for visits supervises the division that coordinates visits of chiefs of state and heads of government invited to the United States by the president and vice president. The assistant chief of protocol's office has the responsibility of planning, arranging, and executing detailed schedules for these visits. The assistant chief for visits is the protocol coordinator for summits in the United States hosted by the president and for protocol relating to state and official funerals. When the president, vice president, or secretary of state attends the United Nations General Assembly for bilateral, trilateral, and multilateral meetings with chiefs of state and heads of government, the assistant chief of protocol for visits facilitates these visits.

The assistant chief of protocol for visits is assisted by the protocol visits officer assigned to each visit to execute the day-to-day schedule with precise planning and detail. The protocol visits officer maintains a rigid schedule during a visit and is responsible for much of the success of the overall planning. This seasoned visits officer is often requested by a foreign embassy, a State Department official, or White House personnel to travel in the United States with visiting foreign dignitaries or to travel as a visits officer on a foreign trip. This particular visits officer is especially needed on these trips to coordinate schedules from the officer's professional experience, to add consistency with foreign groups with whom he or she has worked, and to nurture relationships and trust built with countries' dignitaries and staffs during previous work together.

The division handles foreign media for official visits of foreign dignitaries.

Appropriate selection of gifts to be given by the president, vice president, secretary of state, or their spouses is another responsibility of the visits chief.

Expedited port clearances for visiting dignitaries are also assigned to this office.

Assistant Chief of Protocol for Ceremonials

The assistant chief of protocol for ceremonials heads the Ceremonials Division staff that plan and execute arrangements for official functions hosted by the secretary of state.

The personnel in the division organize programs for certain public events where the diplomatic corps is involved, such as the inauguration of a U.S. president, state and official funerals, joint sessions and meetings of Congress, Democratic and Republican national conventions, and official functions hosted by the president, vice president, secretary of state, and high-ranking U.S. government officials.

The assistant chief and staff provide support for the secretary of state's participation in the General Assembly of the United Nations.

When the chief of protocol hosts receptions and briefings for the diplomatic corps, the ceremonials office coordinates the events.

Assistant Chief of Protocol for Diplomatic Affairs

The rights and immunities of embassy, consular, and other foreign-government personnel, as well as for employees of international organizations, are the basic focus of the Office of Diplomatic Affairs.

Responsibilities within the office include the following:

- Accreditation of ambassadors and chargés d'affaires
- Accreditation of diplomatic and consular officers assigned to foreign missions, to the permanent missions to the United Nations, to the delegations to the Council of the Organization of American States, and to other international organizations in the United States (including its territories and possessions)
- Determination of eligibility of diplomatic and consular officers and employees with respect to privileges and immunities
- Registration of other employees of foreign governments and employees of public international organizations in the United States, its territories, and possessions
- Issuance of appropriate credentials and handling of problems that arise in relations with foreign diplomatic missions

The office maintains the official records regarding the status of all diplomatic and consular officers of foreign governments accredited to or accepted by the United States, members of their staffs, and all other employees of public international organizations in the United States.

The *Diplomatic List* and *Foreign Consular Offices in the United States*, a list of consular offices in the United States, are published through the Office of Diplomatic Affairs.

Assistant Chief of Protocol for Administration

The assistant chief of protocol for administration heads the division, which is responsible for all budgetary, personnel, general-services, and administrative details in the implementation of all protocol programs.

Assistant Chief of Protocol and General Manager of Blair House, the President's Guest House

The general manager of Blair House manages the day-to-day operations of Blair House and welcomes arriving dignitaries to the guest house. The manager also provides a gracious atmosphere for those in residence at Blair House.

Acknowledgment of the Protocol Office

The officers and staff of the Office of Protocol provide tremendous support and organization for the president, the secretary of state, and foreign embassies. When all goes smoothly, most pay little attention to a job well done, but when there is a mistake, word is often disbursed: "It was protocol's fault." The personnel in the Office of Protocol work long hours and give freely of their immense institutional knowledge to ensure that every event is planned and executed for the enhancement of the president, vice president, secretary of state, and others involved, as well as of the United States as a whole.

Chapter 2

Order of Precedence Information

President Barack Obama at a bilateral meeting with President Vaclav Klaus and Prime Minister Mirek Topolanek, of the Czech Republic at Prague Castle, Prague. Attending the meeting, Secretary of State Hillary Clinton and National Security Advisor James Jones. Official White House Photo by Pete Souza.

GENERAL DISCUSSION

Overview

IN THE WORLD OF DIPLOMACY, the Order of Precedence is of supreme importance. Where government officials are represented, the Order of Precedence plays a significant role in the success of any event to function properly without confusion. One of the oldest diplomatic aids offered by the precedence list is its assistance with establishing the order or ranking of a country's government officials, military officers, and civic leaders for diplomatic, ceremonial, and social events at home and abroad. Therefore, the ranking of U.S. government officials dictates many aspects of official protocol for functions both domestically and abroad.

It is an insult not to recognize diplomats or highly elected officials by their proper rank. At public or private events, where officials are present, this sequence can be used in seating arrangements and receiving lines to facilitate order and lessen the likelihood of pandemonium.

WHO IS MOST IMPORTANT?
ORIGINS OF THE ORDER OF PRECEDENCE

The story goes that when leaders met for the Vienna Convention in 1814, each leader insisted he was the most important. Each gentleman argued that he should be the first to enter the room for the meeting and that he should have the principal seat.

To prevent any disputes, a round room was used and doors were cut around the room so that all could enter simultaneously and sit at a round table. If this story is true, use of a round room was a clever way to settle potential disagreements.

From that time forward, ambassadors' and leaders' ranks were established by the date and time they presented their credentials to a government, or were elected to office; this procedure is still used today. At least now, everyone knows where to sit and stand!

The international rules for the Order of Precedence were established by the Congress of Vienna in 1815. These rules determined the rank for diplomats of equal title according to the date and hour that they presented their credentials to the government that accredited them for service. These international courtesy rules are now well established and time-honored. Following them makes it easier for nations and people to work together by reducing the potential for disputes over rank. The rules represent a hierarchical standing of all present. This order is the generally accepted behavior in matters of state. A person's position is not necessarily an indication of his or her functional importance.

Who Uses This List

The White House, the Department of State, and other government agencies use the precedence list for official functions. It is extremely useful for private and business functions at which diplomats or high-ranking government officials are in attendance because it ensures that matters run seamlessly and successfully. It also gives hosts or hostesses an official reason for how and why they recognize and seat guests in a certain way.

Examples of Order of Precedence use (when diplomats and/or government officials are present) are*:

- Seating for White House, Department of State, government, and social functions
- Seating for any event at which diplomats and/or government officials are present
- Seating for state and official funerals
- Order of speakers and placement on stages at official functions
- Ranking for presidential announcements with other names or people included
- Order in receiving lines
- Ranking for presidential delegations
- Ranking for American ambassadors (at post or on state or official visit in the United States)
- Ranking for governors (in or out or their own state)

*This list is not exclusive and merely provides some examples.

The Order of Precedence establishes a way for government, businesses, and private citizens to easily organize a pattern for seating, receiving lines, and other functions within the guidelines of accepted practice commonly understood in the diplomatic world. One does not have to conform exactly to the pattern outlined and can make reasonable changes. An explanation of the changes should be provided when necessary.

Guidelines for Name Order

- High office, military rank, religious title, or hereditary title should precede lower office, rank, or title in the Order of Precedence.
- The person invited to an event should precede his or her spouse, escort, or guest in the Order of Precedence in a receiving line.
- For private citizens with shared surnames, the order should be "Mr." first, followed by "Mrs."
- For private citizens with different surnames, males should be listed first, or alphabetical order should be used.

RANKING INFORMATION FOR THE UNITED STATES

Secretary of State

To conform with international practice, the secretary of state ranks ahead of other members of the cabinet and ahead of foreign ambassadors in the U.S. Order of Precedence. This practice began in 1961.

Ambassador, Extraordinary and Plenipotentiary

An ambassador, extraordinary and plenipotentiary, ranks high on the precedence list as he or she is the highest-ranking diplomat representing his or her country.

In 1815, the Congress of Vienna set the standard for the Order of Precedence for nations by declaring that diplomats of equal title would be ranked according to the date and hour they presented their letters of credentials in the country to which they had been assigned. This precedence has nothing to do with the size or influence of the nation represented. The Ceremonials Division, Office of Protocol, Department of State, maintains the updated list of ranking for the Order of Precedence in the United States.

Members of Congress

Senators rank according to their length of continuous service. If several senators take office on the same day, they can be ranked by the date their state was admitted to the union or alphabetically by state.

House of Representatives members rank according to length of continuous service. Members who took office the same day can be ranked by the date their state was admitted to the union or alphabetically by state.

Governors of States

Governors, when in their own state, rank third on the Order of Precedence list, following the president and the vice president. When not in their own state, governors are ranked after U.S. senators by the date the governor's state was admitted to the union or alphabetically by state.

American Ambassadors

American ambassadors rank in the Order of Precedence when at post or when in the United States on state or official visits.

When an American ambassador is at post, as a courtesy in certain circumstances, he or she should relinquish his or her protocol position to the American secretary of state when the secretary is in the country.

Spouses of Ambassadors

The spouse of an American ambassador at post is considered a "distinguished visitor without rank" and is usually extended courtesies appropriate to the rank of the ambassador when the two are attending a function together. It is appropriate to abide by the protocol rules followed by the host country when the United States is not the host.

State and Local Officials

There is no fixed order of precedence within state and local governments for elected officials that is consistent from state to state. Therefore, it is advisable to check with the Office of the Governor for the local standing to be considerate of political significance.

Foreign Representatives

A foreign representative's position in the Order of Precedence is confirmed by the Ceremonials Division, Office of Protocol, Department of State, and is ranked accordingly. The Ceremonials Division is the custodian of the records establishing the dates on which accreditation has been given to a foreign government. The Ceremonials Division also keeps the U.S. Order of Precedence list up-to-date.

When in doubt regarding a question about the Order of Precedence, one should consult the Ceremonials Division, Office of Protocol, Department of State. This list is reviewed and revised periodically.

MEETINGS, DINNERS, AND LUNCHEONS

The rank of a diplomat or high government official from any country is very important and should be honored by those holding a meeting, luncheon, or dinner. It is appropriate to seat diplomats with others who have comparable rank and position in government and with those at their level of influence. There are many ways to overcome difficulties of rank. In seating, there can be several round or rectangular tables with a host and cohost at each so those of prominence can be seated appropriately.

Dinner Seating

Spouse of the President

When the president's spouse represents the president at an event, the spouse of the president (or a special representative from the president's family appointed by the president) is accorded the rank and courtesy that accompanies the presidency. A representative of other U.S. government officials is not accorded this same courtesy.

Spouses of Other Government Officials

Government officials' wives or husbands without rank are accorded the same rank as their spouse at official functions when they are attending together, and they are seated accordingly. This seating courtesy is the only ranking a spouse without title receives in the United

States. If, however, the spouse himself or herself holds an official position, he or she takes that official position when appropriate. The one exception is for widows of former presidents of the United States, who are provided their own rank in the Order of Precedence.

Guest of Honor

At seated meals, great care should be taken regarding the seating position of the guest of honor and the highest-ranking guest invited.

Highest-Ranking Guest

If the host feels that there could be a seating conflict because the highest-ranking guest should take the seating place of the guest of honor and the guest of honor should take the next-ranking place, the host should send the seating list, in advance, to the guest of honor so that any controversy may be resolved before the event. This situation could also be reversed if the highest-ranking guest is placed in the second-ranking place, giving the guest of honor the highest-ranking place. In that case, the seating list might be sent to the highest-ranking guest to avoid conflict. A wise host or hostess reviews his or her guest list for ranking order before completing the list and inviting guests.

CHANGES IN THE ORDER OF PRECEDENCE

The rules of protocol are subject to change occasionally, but changes should be made with utmost care. There must be a sound reason for change that can be explained without doubt. The president of the United States may alter the Order of Precedence within his or her own cabinet or government from administration to administration. Changes to the Order of Precedence must follow procedure. A request for change in rank must be submitted to the chief of protocol. A memo is sent from the chief of protocol to the White House chief of staff recommending or not recommending the change. The chief of staff makes a decision regarding the request and sends that decision to the chief of protocol. One should always check for the updated list in case the president has made changes to the order. The Ceremonials

Division, Office of Protocol, Department of State, is the custodian of the U.S. Order of Precedence.

Unofficial List

The U.S. government does not publish an *official* list of the Order of Precedence. The U.S. Order of Precedence listed in this book is considered *unofficial* but is as close as possible to the order that should be used as of the publication of this book.

Chapter 3

U.S. Order of Precedence

President Barack Obama delivers a health care address to a joint session of Congress at the U.S. Capitol in Washington, D.C., September 9, 2009. Official White House Photo by Lawrence Jackson.

ORDER OF PRECEDENCE

The president may make changes in the Order of Precedence for certain individuals' titles

1. President of the United States
2. Vice President of the United States
3. Governor of a state (when in own state)
4. Speaker of the House of Representatives
   Chief Justice of the United States

5. Former Presidents of the United States (by seniority of assuming office)
   American Ambassadors, extraordinary and plenipotentiary, to foreign governments (at post)
6. Secretary of State
7. President, United Nations General Assembly (when in session)
   Secretary General of the United Nations
   President, United Nations General Assembly (when not in session)
8. Ambassadors, extraordinary and plenipotentiary, of foreign governments accredited to the United States (in order of presentation of credentials)
9. Widows of Former Presidents of the United States
10. Associate Justices of the Supreme Court
    Retired Chief Justices of the United States
    Retired Associate Justices of the Supreme Court
11. Members of the Cabinet (other than the Secretary of State) according to date of establishment of the department and as added by the president, as follows:
    Secretary of the Treasury
    Secretary of Defense
    Attorney General
    Secretary of the Interior
    Secretary of Agriculture
    Secretary of Commerce
    Secretary of Labor
    Secretary of Health and Human Services
    Secretary of Housing and Urban Development
    Secretary of Transportation
    Secretary of Energy
    Secretary of Education
    Secretary of Veterans Affairs
    Secretary of Homeland Security
    Chief of Staff to the President*
    Administrator, Environmental Protection Agency*

* The President may make changes in his or her administration to the cabinet except regarding cabinet members who are cabinet by statute. These positions have cabinet status by administration:

Director, Office of Management and Budget*
U.S. Trade Representative*
Permanent Representative of the United States to the United Nations*
Chairman, Counsel of Economic Advisors*
12. President Pro Tempore of the Senate
Senators (ranked by length of service; when term of service is the same, by state's date of admission into the Union or alphabetically by state)
13. Governors of states—when outside own state (relative precedence among governors, all of whom are outside their own state, is determined by their state's date of admission into the Union or alphabetically by state)
14. Acting heads of executive departments
Former Vice Presidents of the United States or their widows
15. Members of the House of Representatives (ranked by length of service; when term of service is the same, by state's date of admission into the Union or alphabetically by state)
16. Delegates to the House of Representatives (nonvoting members) from Territory of American Samoa, District of Columbia, Territory of Guam, Commonwealth of Puerto Rico, and U.S. Virgin Islands (date of election of delegate determines their order of precedence in this list)
Governors of Commonwealth of Puerto Rico, Territory of Guam, Territory of American Samoa, U.S. Virgin Islands, and the Commonwealth of the Northern Mariana Islands (determined by territory's date of entering U.S. jurisdiction or alphabetically by territory)
17. Assistant to the President and Senior Advisor
Assistant to the President and Deputy Chief of Staff
Assistant to the President for National Security Affairs
Director of National Intelligence
Chief of Staff to the Vice President
Assistants to the President (ranked by seniority)
Director, Office of National Drug Control Policy
Chair, Council on Environmental Quality
Chief of Protocol (when at the White House or accompanying the President)

18. Chargé d'Affaires assigned to diplomatic missions in Washington, D.C.
19. Former Secretaries of State (by seniority of assuming office)
    Former Cabinet Members (by seniority of assuming office)
20. Deputy to Members of the Cabinet (according to date of establishment of the department and as added by the president), as follows:
    Deputy Secretary of State
    Deputy Secretary of the Treasury
    Deputy Secretary of Defense
    Deputy Attorney General
    Deputy Secretary of the Interior
    Deputy Secretary of Agriculture
    Deputy Secretary of Commerce
    Deputy Secretary of Labor
    Deputy Secretary of Health and Human Services
    Deputy Secretary of Housing and Urban Development
    Deputy Secretary of Transportation
    Deputy Secretary of Energy
    Deputy Secretary of Education
    Deputy Secretary of Veterans Affairs
    Deputy Secretary of Homeland Security
    Deputy Administrator, Environmental Protection Agency (EPA)
    Deputy Director, Office of Management and Budget (OMB)
    Deputy U.S. Trade Representative (USTR)
    Deputy Permanent Representative of the U.S. to the United Nations
21. U.S. Permanent Representative on the Council of the North Atlantic Treaty Organization (USNATO) (at post).
    Representative of the U.S. to the European Union (USEU) (at post)
22. Under Secretaries of State and the Counselor of the Department of State (as ranked by the department)
    Under Secretaries of executive departments and the Associate Attorney General (according to date of establishment of the department; if more than one from a department, as ranked within the department)
    Secretary of the Army
    Secretary of the Navy

Secretary of the Air Force
Postmaster General
Director, Federal Bureau of Investigation (FBI)
Chairman, Board of Governors of the Federal Reserve
Chairman, Export-Import Bank
Director, Central Intelligence Agency (CIA)
Administrator, Small Business Administration (SBA)
Administrator, Agency for International Development (AID)

23. Chairman, Joint Chiefs of Staff
Vice Chairman, Joint Chiefs of Staff
Retired Chairman, Joint Chiefs of Staff
Chief of Staff of the Army, Chief of Staff of the Air Force, Chief of Naval Operations, and Commandant of the Marine Corps (order based on chief's date of appointment)
Commandant of the Coast Guard

24. Lieutenant Governors (when in own state)

25. Permanent Representatives of foreign governments to the United Nations
Secretary General of the Organization of American States (OAS)
Chairman, Permanent Council of the United States to the Organization of American States (OAS)
Permanent Representatives of the U.S. and then of foreign governments to the Organization of American States (OAS)
Heads of international organizations, including International Monetary Fund, World Bank (International Bank for Reconstruction and Development), North Atlantic Treaty Organization (NATO)

26. Administrator, General Services Administration (GSA)
Administrator, National Aeronautics and Space Administration (NASA)
Director, Office of Personnel Management (OPM)
Administrator, Federal Aviation Administration (FAA)
Chairman, Nuclear Regulatory Commission
Director, Peace Corps

27. Deputy Director National Intelligence
Deputy Director, Office of National Drug Control Policy
Deputy Director, Central Intelligence Agency (CIA)
Deputy Administrator, Small Business Administration (SBA)

28. American Ambassadors (on state and official visits to the United States)
    Chief of Protocol (at the Department of State or at events outside the White House)
    Career Ambassadors
29. Chief Judges and Circuit Judges of the U.S. Courts of Appeals (by length of service)
    Solicitor General
    Chief Judges and District Judges, U.S. District Courts (by length of service)
    Chief Judges and Judges of the U.S. Court of Military Appeals for the Armed Forces
    Chief Judges and Judges of the U.S. Court of Appeals for Veterans Claims
30. Mayors of U.S. cities and the District of Columbia when in own city
31. American Chargé d'Affaires (at post)
32. Assistant Secretaries, Ambassadors at Large, Assistant Attorneys General, Counselors, and Legal Advisors of Executive Departments (according to date of establishment of the Department; if more than one from a Department, then as ranked within the Department)
    Deputy Assistants to the President (ranked by seniority)
    Deputy Administrator, Agency for International Development (AID)
33. Under Secretaries General of the United Nations
    Administrator, National Oceanographic and Atmospheric Administration (NOAA)
    Deputy Director, General Services Administration (GSA)
    Deputy Director, National Aeronautics and Space Administration (NASA)
34. Assistant Administrators, Agency for International Development (AID)
    Assistant U.S. Trade Representatives
35. U.S. Comptroller General
    Members of the Council of Economic Advisors (ranked alphabetically)
    Members of the Council for Environmental Quality
36. American Ambassadors-Designate (in the United States under normal orders or on leave)

37. Mayors of U.S. cities and the District of Columbia (when not in own city)
38. Under Secretary of the Army
   Under Secretary of the Navy
   Under Secretary of the Air Force
   Acting Deputy Secretaries of executive departments
   Acting Under Secretaries of executive departments
39. Four-Star military officers—General or Admiral (in order of seniority; retired officers rank with, but after, active officers)
   Assistant Secretary of the Army (by date of appointment)
   Assistant Secretary of the Navy (by date of appointment)
   Assistant Secretary of the Air Force (by date of appointment)
   Executive Secretary, National Security Council (NSC)
40. Three-Star military officers—Lieutenant General, Vice Admiral (in order of seniority; retired officers rank after active members)
   State Senators and Representatives (when in own state)
   Former American Ambassadors/Chiefs of diplomatic missions (in order of presentation of credentials at first post)
41. Acting Assistant Secretaries of executive departments
   President, Overseas Private Investment Corporation (OPIC)
   Treasurer of the United States
   Chairman, Federal Communications Commission (FCC)
   Other chairmen of bureaus, boards, and commissions not previously listed
   Librarian of Congress
   Vice Chairman and members of the Board of Governors of the Federal Reserve System
   Secretary of the Smithsonian Institution
   Chairman, National Endowment for the Humanities
   Chairman, National Endowment for the Arts
   Director, National Science Foundation
   Surgeon General, U.S. Public Health Service
   Heads of independent agencies not mentioned previously (by date of establishment of the agency)
42. Special Assistants to the president
   Chairman of the American Red Cross
   Deputy Chief of Protocol
   Commissioners (level IV executives)

43. Deputy Under Secretaries of executive departments (according to date of establishment of the department; if more than one from a department, then as ranked within the department)

Deputy Assistant Secretaries and Deputy Councils of executive departments (according to date of establishment of the department; if more than one from a department, then as ranked within the department)

44. Two-Star military—Major General, Rear Admiral (in order of seniority; retired officers rank with, but after, active officers)

Assistant Chiefs of Protocol

Consuls General of Foreign Governments

Deputy Assistant Secretaries of the Army, Navy, and Air Force (according to date of establishment of the Department; if more than one from a Department, then as ranked with the Department)

45. Chief Judge and Judges, United States (formerly Customs) Court of International Trade

Chief Judge and Associate Judges, U.S. Court of Claims

Chief Judge and Associate Judges, U.S. Tax Court

46. One-Star military—Brigadier Generals, Rear Admirals (in order of seniority; retired officers rank with, but after, active officers)

Members of bureaus, boards, and commissions

ORDER OF PRECEDENCE IN A STATE

This is a general model that many states follow. Some states follow the federal model, which ranks the members of the cabinet after the attorney general. *Check with each state to be certain of how officials are ranked.*

Governor
Lieutenant Governor
Attorney General
Secretary of State
U.S. Senators for the state by date of taking office
U.S. Representatives for the state by date of taking office
President of the state's upper house

Speaker of the state's lower legislative house: (State Assembly, House
  of Representatives, or House of Delegates)
Chief Justice of the State's Supreme Court
Former Governors by date of taking office
Active Justices of the State's Supreme Court
Retired Justices of the State's Supreme Court
Federal Judges
Widows of Former Governors by date of taking office
Members of the State's Upper House
Members of the State's Lower House
Members of the Cabinet
Judges of the State Court of Appeals
Judges of other state courts
Mayors by city population
Chairmen of Boards of Supervisors by jurisdiction population
Former Lieutenant Governors
Former Attorneys General
Appointed heads of a state department or institution
Chairmen of boards or of state departments or institutions
Executive Assistants to a Governor

Order of U.S. States Entering the Union (Chronological)

State	Date of Entry
1 Delaware	December 7, 1787
2 Pennsylvania	December 12, 1787
3 New Jersey	December 18, 1787
4 Georgia	January 2, 1788
5 Connecticut	January 9, 1788
6 Massachusetts	February 6, 1788
7 Maryland	April 28, 1788
8 South Carolina	May 23, 1788
9 New Hampshire	June 21, 1788
10 Virginia	June 25, 1788
11 New York	July 26, 1788

12	North Carolina	November 21, 1789
13	Rhode Island	May 29, 1790
14	Vermont	March 4, 1791
15	Kentucky	June 1, 1792
16	Tennessee	June 1, 1796
17	Ohio	March 1, 1803
18	Louisiana	April 30, 1812
19	Indiana	December 11, 1816
20	Mississippi	December 10, 1817
21	Illinois	December 3, 1818
22	Alabama	December 14, 1819
23	Maine	March 15, 1820
24	Missouri	August 10, 1821
25	Arkansas	June 15, 1836
26	Michigan	January 26, 1837
27	Florida	March 3, 1845
28	Texas	December 29, 1845
29	Iowa	December 28, 1846
30	Wisconsin	May 29, 1848
31	California	September 9, 1850
32	Minnesota	May 11, 1858
33	Oregon	February 14, 1859
34	Kansas	January 29, 1861
35	West Virginia	June 20, 1863
36	Nevada	October 31, 1864
37	Nebraska	March 1, 1867
38	Colorado	August 1, 1876
39	North Dakota	November 2, 1889
40	South Dakota	November 2, 1889
41	Montana	November 8, 1889
42	Washington	November 11, 1889
43	Idaho	July 3, 1890
44	Wyoming	July 10, 1890
45	Utah	January 4, 1896
46	Oklahoma	November 16, 1907
47	New Mexico	January 6, 1912
48	Arizona	February 14, 1912
49	Alaska	January 3, 1959
50	Hawaii	August 21, 1959

District of Columbia	July 16, 1790: Unofficially designated "Territory of Columbia" 1791: Named "Washington" in honor of George Washington May 6, 1796: Received official name "District of Columbia" June 1, 1871: Became District of Columbia by an act of Congress

Order of U.S. Territories Entering the Union (Chronological)

Commonwealth of Puerto Rico	1889
Territory of Guam	1898
(organized territory 1950)	
Territory of American Samoa	1899
U.S. Virgin Islands	1917
Commonwealth of Northern Mariana Islands	1978

Order of U.S. States Entering the Union (Alphabetical)

	State	Date of Entry
22	Alabama	December 14, 1819
49	Alaska	January 3, 1959
48	Arizona	February 14, 1912
25	Arkansas	June 15, 1836
31	California	September 9, 1850
38	Colorado	August 1, 1876
5	Connecticut	January 9, 1788
1	Delaware	December 7, 1787
27	Florida	March 3, 1845
4	Georgia	January 2, 1788
50	Hawaii	August 21, 1959
43	Idaho	July 3, 1890
21	Illinois	December 3, 1818

19	Indiana	December 11, 1816
29	Iowa	December 28, 1846
34	Kansas	January 29, 1861
15	Kentucky	June 1, 1792
18	Louisiana	April 30, 1812
23	Maine	March 15, 1820
7	Maryland	April 28, 1788
6	Massachusetts	February 6, 1788
26	Michigan	January 26, 1837
32	Minnesota	May 11, 1858
20	Mississippi	December 10, 1817
24	Missouri	August 10, 1821
41	Montana	November 8, 1889
37	Nebraska	March 1, 1867
36	Nevada	October 31, 1864
9	New Hampshire	June 21, 1788
3	New Jersey	December 18, 1787
47	New Mexico	January 6, 1912
11	New York	July 26, 1788
12	North Carolina	November 21, 1789
39	North Dakota	November 2, 1889
17	Ohio	March 1, 1803
46	Oklahoma	November 16, 1907
33	Oregon	February 14, 1859
2	Pennsylvania	December 12, 1787
13	Rhode Island	May 29, 1790
8	South Carolina	May 23, 1788
40	South Dakota	November 2, 1889
16	Tennessee	June 1, 1796
28	Texas	December 29, 1845
45	Utah	January 4, 1896
14	Vermont	March 4, 1791
10	Virginia	June 25, 1788
42	Washington	November 11, 1889
35	West Virginia	June 20, 1863
30	Wisconsin	May 29, 1848
44	Wyoming	July 10, 1890

Chapter 4

—————————◯—————————

Titles and Forms of Address Information

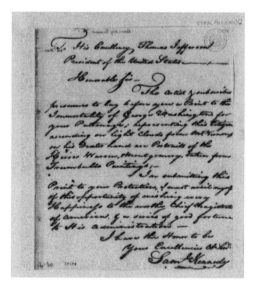

Letter to President Thomas Jefferson from Samuel Kennedy regarding a portrait of George Washington. Thomas Jefferson, U.S. president 1801–1809. (Library of Congress)

OFFICE OF PROTOCOL

IT IS IN GOOD TASTE AND COURTEOUS to address a person by his or her proper name and title. The following address forms are based on usage in the United States and internationally. The Ceremonials Division, Office of Protocol, Department of State, is considered the authority on formal and informal diplomatic correspondence and conversation; the Protocol Office should be contacted in the event of a question regarding titles and forms of address.

"THE HONORABLE"

The Honorable is a courtesy title distinction used in addressing high-ranking American officials who are in office or retired. Presidential appointees, federal and state *elected* officials, and mayors are included. Most other county and city officials are not addressed as The Honorable.

- Never use The Honorable when issuing or answering invitations or referring to oneself.
- Write The Honorable out in full whenever possible. It should appear on the line above or to the left of the full name.
- The Honorable sometimes must be abbreviated to The Hon. or T. H.
- "The" in front of honorable is not capitalized in the text of a letter or communication.
- Never use The Honorable in speaking to a person or in a salutation.
- The Honorable is sometimes used in platform introductions.
- The Honorable is the American spelling. An extra *u* indicates the British spelling: The Honourable.
- The Honorable is rarely used with a title; one or the other should be used. The *one exception* is when used on a social envelope with a principal and spouse of the same surname: Mr. and Mrs. Jones. In this context, The Honorable precedes the title.

Example: Social invitation only

The Honorable
The Secretary of Agriculture
and Mrs. (Jones)) or Mr. (Tom Jones)

Otherwise the correct form is as follows and may be used officially or socially:

The Honorable
(full name)
Secretary of Agriculture
and Mrs. (surname) or Ms./Mr. (full name)

American Officials Entitled to be Addressed as The Honorable

Executive Branch

President-elect
Vice president–elect
All members of the president's cabinet
Counselor to the president
Chief of staff to the president
Assistants to the president
The attorney general and deputy and associate attorney generals
Ambassadors, career and appointed
Deputy secretaries and assistant and deputy assistant secretaries
Undersecretaries and deputy and associate deputy undersecretaries
Representatives, alternates, and deputies of international organizations
Most appointees confirmed by the Senate
U.S. attorneys are appointed by the president

Defense Department

Secretary of an armed force
Undersecretary and assistant and deputy undersecretaries of an armed
    force

Diplomats

Ambassadors

Legislative Branch

SENATE

President of the Senate (Vice President of the United States)
President pro tempore
Senators
Senators-elect
Sergeant at arms

HOUSE OF REPRESENTATIVES

Representatives
Delegates
Representatives-elect and delegates-elect
Clerk of the House
Sergeant at arms

Government Agencies

Heads, assistant heads, and commissioners or members of equal rank
    appointed by the president and confirmed by the Senate

Other High Positions

Solicitor general
Postmaster general
Surgeon general
Comptroller general
Librarian of Congress
Public Printer of the United States

Judicial Branch

Associate justices of the U.S. Supreme Court who are retired
Chief judges, judges, and presiding judges of lower U.S. federal courts
The chief justice and associate justices of the Supreme Court *are not*
    addressed as The Honorable.
Judges of other courts

State and Local Government

STATE OFFICIALS

Governor, acting governor, and governor-elect
Lieutenant governor, acting lieutenant governor, and lieutenant governor–
    elect
Secretary of state
Attorney general

Treasurer, comptroller or auditor
Governor-appointed secretary of (portfolio)
Governor-appointed commissioner of a major state commission
President or speaker of a state assembly
State senator, state representative, or delegate to a state assembly
Clerk of the elected state assembly
Associate justice of a state supreme court
Chief judges, senior judges, and judges of lower state courts

Local Officials

Mayors (when an elected official)
Elected members of county boards of supervisors
Elected members of city and town councils
Sheriffs

Elected state and municipal officials are referred to as The Honorable.

It is always advisable to check with state and local officials for preferences in that state.

Addressed by Office or Title Only

In the United States, certain high officials are addressed by office or title only.

Only one person holds the following titles:

- President
- Vice President
- Speaker of the House of Representatives
- Chief Justice of the Supreme Court
- Members of the president's cabinet

Private citizens, doctors, and academics use basic honorifics: Mr., Mrs., Miss, Ms., Dr., Dean, Prof., and so forth.

The armed services use rank and name: General (full name or surname)

Clergy use hierarchical title or title and name: Reverend (full name or surname) or Reverend.

TITLE USAGE IN THIS BOOK

Ms.

Ms. is used as an honorific for a woman and does not specify marital status. Ms. is used professionally regardless of the title the woman uses outside her professional life.

Use of Ms. with a woman's name along with her spouse's name joined by "and" denotes that the couple is married.

Many unmarried women prefer to use Miss, and others (married, widowed, divorced) use the title Mrs.

All of these titles can be correct. It is advisable to inquire concerning the woman's preference.

Spouses

As the president or an official may be male or female, his or her spouse will be described appropriately. If a surname differs from that of the principal, this will be referenced.

Madam/Madame

Madam is used throughout this book to address a woman official. In some non-English speaking countries the term Madame may be used in place of Madam.

The President's Cabinet

Official and social addresses for members of the president's cabinet are basically the same. Use The Honorable followed by the full name, then title, then address.

When using the individual's name prior to his or her title, do not use the word "the" before the title.

Example:
The Honorable
George James
Secretary of Labor

On a *social* invitation, a title is used without the name when a married couple shares the same surname. This is the only time "the" precedes the title.

Example:
The Honorable
The Secretary of Commerce
and Mrs. (same surname)/Mr. (full name)

Spouses

For information regarding addressing spouses, see "Addressing Spouses" in chapter 5, Titles and Forms of Address.

Cabinet

For addresses, telephone numbers, and websites for cabinet members, see "Addresses for the President's Cabinet Agencies" in chapter 16, "Valuable Information."

Salutation

In an official salutation, a colon (:) follows the surname.

Example: Dear Senator Jones:

In a social salutation, a comma (,) follows the surname:

Example: Dear John,

White House Envelope Form

Indentions indicated below reflect appropriate form, either of which is correct usage. Typical tabbing is five spaces.

The President
　The White House
　　　Washington, DC 20500

or

The President
The White House
Washington, DC 20500

"HIS/HER EXCELLENCY"

His/Her Excellency are used for people entitled by a foreign government to that courtesy. Your Excellency is used to address a foreign official when he or she is entitled to that courtesy. An individual entitled to use this title may retain its use throughout his or her lifetime.

His/Her Excellency applies to a foreign chief of state (president), head of government (premier, prime minister, chancellor), foreign cabinet officer, foreign ambassador, or other foreign high official or foreign former high official.

American custom does not dictate the use of His/Her Excellency when addressing high officials of the U.S. government, although foreign government officials may occasionally address high-ranking American government officials by this title.

The Honourable

The Honourable is the title used in Australia, Canada, and the British Commonwealth.

In Canada and the United Kingdom, it is customary when addressing the prime minister or a cabinet officer to use The Honourable. Check for the correct honorific for every office. The prime minister takes the title The Right Honourable.

The prime minister and deputy prime minister of Australia are addressed as The Honourable. His Honour or Her Honour is a courtesy title in Australia.

Check for the correct honorific for every office in each country.

Chapter 5

---⚬---

Titles and Forms
of Address

Her Majesty Queen Elizabeth II and His Royal Highness The Prince Philip,
Duke of Edinburgh with President and Mrs. Bush. State Visit, May 2007.
Courtesy National Archives and Records Administration.

FEDERAL GOVERNMENT OFFICIALS
IN THE UNITED STATES

Executive Branch

President

Envelope: Official: The President
                              The White House
                              Washington, DC 20500

                              1600 Pennsylvania Avenue, NW is not
                              necessary; the White House has its own
                              zip code

               Social: The President
                              and Mrs. (surname)

                              The President
                              and Mr. (full name)
                              (The President is a woman)

                              The President
                              and Ms. (full name)
                              (spouse has different surname)

                              The President
                              and
                              (honorific) (courtesy title)
                              (full name)
                              (title)

                              The White House
                              Washington, DC 20500

Invitation, in envelope: The President

                              The President and Mrs. Ms. /Mr.
                              (surname)

The President of the United States of America (*use only when the President is abroad*)

Salutation:	Official:	Dear Mr. or Madam President:

Dear Mr. or Madam President:
Dear Mr. President and Mrs./Ms. (surname):
Dear Madam President and Mr. (surname):

Complimentary close: Respectfully,

Place card: The President *or*
The President of the United States of America (*use only when the President is abroad*)

Introduction: The President *or*
The President of the United States *or*
The President of the United States of America (*use only when the President is abroad*)

Announcement: *The President Alone*:
Ladies and Gentlemen: The President of the United States

The President with Spouse:
Ladies and Gentlemen: The President of the United States and Mrs. (surname)/Ms./Mr. (full name)

The President, Spouse, and Other Leaders:
Ladies and Gentlemen: The President of the United States and Mrs. (surname)/Ms./Mr. (full name) accompanied by

His/Her Excellency
(full name of leader)
(full name of country)
and Mrs. (surname)/Ms./Mr. (full name)

Receiving Line/Photograph:
The President, Guest, President's
Spouse, Guest's Spouse *or*
The President, Guest, Guest's Spouse,
President's Spouse

*Most appropriate: Guest of Honor to
President's right, then spouses'*
(See chapter 7, "Official Entertaining")

Conversation: Mr. President
                             Madam President

Spouse of President

Envelope: Official: Mrs. (surname) or Mr. (full name)
                             (White House address)

               Social: Mrs. (surname) or Mr. (full name)
                             (White House address)

                             Different Surnames:
                             Ms. (full name) or Mr. (full name)
                             (White House address)

Invitation, in envelope: Mrs./Ms./Mr. (surname)
Salutation: Dear Mrs./Ms./Mr. (surname):
Complimentary close: Sincerely,
Place card: Mrs./Ms./Mr. (surname)
Introduction: Mrs./Ms./Mr. (full name)
Conversation: Mrs./Ms./Mr. (surname)

Former President

Envelope: Official: The Honorable*
                             (full name)
                             (office address)

Social:+	The Honorable (full name) (address)
	As a Couple: The Honorable (full name) and Mrs. (surname) (address)
	The Honorable (full name) and Ms./Mr. (full name) (address)
	Both Spouses Have Honorific/Title: The Honorable (full name) and The Honorable (full name) (title) if currently in office (address)
Invitation, in envelope:	President* (surname)
Salutation:	Dear President* (surname):
Complimentary close:	Respectfully,
Place card:	President* (surname) (or full name) If more than one president with same surname, use full name
Introduction:	The Honorable (full name) *or* President* (full name), former President of the United States
Conversation:	President** (surname) or Mrs./Ms./Mr. (surname)

* Use this form unless a former president (or vice president) has another distinctive title (e.g., military) and prefers to be addressed by that title: General (full name), Retired (for envelope).
** It is now acceptable to use "President (surname)" for a former president. Never refer to a former president as "The President." The United States has only *one sitting* president, "The President."
+ Addressing spouse: See page 154

President-elect

Envelope:

	Official:	The Honorable
		(full name)
		President-elect
		(address)
	Social:+	The Honorable
		(full name)
		(address)
Invitation, in envelope:		Mr./Ms. (surname)
Salutation:		Dear Mr./Ms. (surname):
Complimentary close:		Respectfully,
Place card:		Mr./Ms. (surname)
Introduction:		The Honorable (full name),
		President-elect *or*
		Mr./Ms. (surname)
Conversation:		Mr./Ms. (surname)
+ Addressing spouse:		See page 154

Vice President

Envelope:

	Official:	The Vice President
		Eisenhower Executive Office Building
		Washington, DC 20501
	Social:+	The Vice President
		(address)
Invitation, in envelope:		The Vice President
Salutation:		Dear Mr. or Madam Vice President:
Complimentary close:		Respectfully,
Place card:		The Vice President *or*
		The Vice President of the United
		States of America (*use only when the*
		vice president is abroad)
Introduction:		The Vice President *or*
		The Vice President of the United
		States *or*

The Vice President of the United
States of America (*use only when the
vice president is abroad*)

Conversation:	Mr. or Madam Vice President
+ Addressing spouse:	See page 154

Vice President–elect

Envelope:

Official:	The Honorable
	(full name)
	Vice President–elect
	(address)
Social:+	The Honorable
	(full name)
	(address)
Invitation, in envelope:	Mr./Ms. (surname)
Salutation:	Dear Mr./Ms. (surname):
Complimentary close:	Respectfully,
Place card:	Mr./Ms. (surname)
Introduction:	The Honorable (full name), Vice President–elect
Conversation:	Mr./Ms. (surname)
+ Addressing spouse:	See page 154

Former Vice President

Envelope:

Official:	The Honorable
	(full name)
	(address)
Social:+	The Honorable
	(full name)
	(address)
Invitation, in envelope:	Mr./Ms. (surname)
Salutation:	Dear Mr./Ms. (surname):
Complimentary close:	Respectfully,
Place card:	Mr./Ms. (surname)

Introduction:	The Honorable (full name) *or* Mr./Ms. (surname)
Conversation:	Mr./Ms. (surname)
+ Addressing spouse:	See page 154

Cabinet Member

Envelope:

| | Official: | The Honorable (full name) Secretary of (department) (address) |
| | Social:+ | The Honorable (full name) Secretary of (department) (address) |

Invitation, in envelope:	The Secretary of (department)
Salutation:	Dear Mr./Madam Secretary:
Complimentary close:	Sincerely,
Place card:	The Secretary of (department)
Introduction:	The Honorable (full name), Secretary of (department)
Conversation:	Mr./Madam Secretary
+ Addressing spouse:	See page 154

Attorney General*

Envelope:

| | Official: | The Honorable (full name) Attorney General (address) |
| | Social:+ | The Honorable (full name) Attorney General (address) |

| Invitation, in envelope: | The Attorney General |

Salutation:	Dear Mr./Madam Attorney General:
Complimentary close:	Sincerely,
Place card:	The Attorney General
Introduction:	The Honorable (full name), Attorney General *or*
	Attorney General (surname)
Conversation:	Mr./Madam Attorney General *or*
	Mr./Ms. (surname)

* The heads of all cabinet agencies, except the attorney general, use the title "Secretary."

+ Addressing spouse:	See page 154

Acting Secretary

Examples:		Secretary-designate
		Secretary ad interim
		Acting Attorney General
		Attorney General General–designate
		Attorney General General ad interim
Envelope:		
	Official:*	(full name)
		(title)
		(address)
	Social:+	(full name)
		(address)
Invitation, in envelope:		The (title)
Salutation:		Dear Mr./Ms. (surname):
Complimentary close:		Sincerely,
Place card:		The (title)
Introduction:		(full name), (title) *or*
		(title), Mr./Ms. (surname)
Conversation:		Mr./Ms. (surname)

* "The Honorable" is used only for a previously held position; it does not come with an "acting" position.

+ Addressing spouse:	See page 154

Solicitor General

Envelope:

	Official:	The Honorable
		(full name)
		Solicitor General
		(address)
	Social:+	The Honorable
		(full name)
		(address)
Invitation, in envelope:		The Solicitor General
Salutation:		Dear Mr./Madam Solicitor General:
		Dear Mr./Ms.(surname):
Complimentary close:		Sincerely,
Place card:		The Solicitor General
Introduction:		The Honorable (full name), Solicitor General *or*
		The Solicitor General, Mr./Ms. (surname)
Conversation:		Mr./Madam Solicitor General *or*
		Mr./Ms. (surname)
+ Addressing spouse:		See page 154

Postmaster General

Envelope:

	Official:	The Honorable
		(full name)
		Postmaster General
		(address)
	Social:+	The Honorable
		(full name)
		(address)
Invitation, in envelope:		The Postmaster General
Salutation:		Dear Mr./Madam Postmaster General:
Complimentary close:		Sincerely,
Place card:		The Postmaster General
Introduction:		The Honorable (full name), Postmaster General *or*

	The Postmaster General, Mr./Ms. (surname)
Conversation:	Mr./Madam Postmaster General *or* Mr./Ms. (surname)
+ Addressing spouse:	See page 154

Surgeon General

The surgeon general will be a physician and have the rank of *Rear Admiral, Upper Half,* as commander of the officers of the U.S. Public Health Service.

Envelope:

	Official:	The Honorable (full name) Surgeon General (address)
	Social:+	The Honorable (full name) (address)
Invitation, in envelope:		Dr./Admiral (surname)
Salutation:		Dear Dr./Admiral (surname):
Complimentary close:		Sincerely,
Place card:		Dr./Admiral (surname)
Introduction:		The Honorable (full name), Surgeon General *or* The Surgeon General, Dr./Admiral (surname)
Conversation:		Dr./Admiral (surname)
+ Addressing spouse:		See page 154

Chief of Protocol

Envelope:

	Official:	The Honorable (full name) Chief of Protocol (address)

Social:+	The Honorable
	(full name)
	(address)
Invitation, in envelope:	The Chief of Protocol
Salutation:	Dear Ambassador (surname):
Complimentary close:	Sincerely,
Place card:	The Chief of Protocol
Introduction:	The Honorable (full name), Chief of
	Protocol *or*
	The Chief of Protocol, Ambassador
	(surname)
Conversation:	Ambassador (surname)
+ Addressing spouse:	See page 154

Commissioner of an Agency or Commission

Example:	Commissioner of Internal Revenue
Envelope:	
Official:	The Honorable
	(full name)
	Commissioner of (agency or name of
	commission)
	(address)
Social:+	The Honorable
	(full name)
	(address)
Invitation, in envelope:	Mr./Ms. (surname)
Salutation:	Dear Mr./Madam Commissioner:
Complimentary close:	Sincerely,
Place card:	Mr./Ms. (surname)
Introduction:	The Honorable (full name),
	Commissioner of (agency or name
	of commission) *or*
	The Commissioner of (agency or name
	of commission), Mr./Ms. (surname)
Conversation:	Mr./Ms. (surname)
+ Addressing spouse:	See page 154

Chairman of a Commission or Board

Envelope:

	Official:	The Honorable
		(full name)
		(full title of position held)
		(address)
	Social:+	The Honorable
		(full name)
		(address)
Invitation, in envelope:		Mr./Ms. (surname)
Salutation:		Dear Mr./Madam Chairman: *or*
		Dear Mr./Ms. (surname):
Complimentary close:		Sincerely,
Place card:		Mr./Ms. (surname)
Introduction:		The Honorable (full name), (full title of position held) *or*
		(full title of position held), Mr./Ms. (surname)
Conversation:		Mr./Ms. (surname)
+ Addressing spouse:		See page 154

Presidential Appointee Addressed as "The Honorable"

Examples:

Administrator of a federal council, commission, agency, board, or authority

Assistant secretary of an executive department or an armed force

Assistant to the president

Associate Attorney General

Associate deputy undersecretary of an executive department

Chairman of a federal council, commission, agency, board, or authority

Commissioner of a federal council, commission, agency, board, or authority

Comptroller General

Counselor to the president (or to another very high-ranking official)

Deputy assistant secretary of an executive department

Director of a federal council, commission, agency, board, or authority
Head of a federal agency, board, or authority
Legal advisor to a very high-ranking federal official
Librarian of Congress
Member of a federal council, commission, agency, board, or authority
President of a federal council, commission, agency, board, or authority
Public Printer of the United States
Special assistant to the president
Undersecretary or deputy of an executive department
U.S. Attorney

Envelope:

	Official:	The Honorable (full name) (full title of position held) (address)
	Social:+	The Honorable (full name) (address)
Invitation, in envelope:		Mr./Ms. (surname)
Salutation:		Dear Mr./Ms. (surname):
Complimentary close:		Sincerely,
Place card:		Mr./Ms. (surname)
Introduction:		The Honorable (full name), (full title of position held) *or* The (full title of position held), Mr./Ms. (surname)
Conversation:		Mr./Ms. (surname)
+ Addressing spouse:		See page 154

Presidential Appointee Not Addressed as "The Honorable"

Examples:

District Director (e.g., of the Internal Revenue Service)

Envelope:

	Official:	Mr./Ms. (full name) (title) (address)
	Social:+	Mr./Ms. (full name) (address)

Invitation, in envelope:	Mr./Ms. (surname)
Salutation:	Dear Mr./Ms. (surname):
Complimentary close:	Sincerely,
Place card:	Mr./Ms. (surname)
Introduction:	Mr./Ms. (full name), (title) *or* (title), Mr./Ms. (surname)
Conversation:	Mr./Ms. (surname)
+ Addressing spouse:	See page 154

Marshal for a Judicial District

Marshals are appointed by the president and approved by the Senate.
Envelope:

	Official:	The Honorable (full name) United States Marshal (judicial district) (address)
	Social:+	The Honorable (full name) (address)

Invitation, in envelope:	Mr./Ms. (surname)
Salutation:	Dear Marshal (surname):
Complimentary close:	Sincerely,
Place card:	Mr./Ms. (surname)
Introduction:	The Honorable (full name), United States Marshal of the (district)
Conversation:	Marshal (surname) *or* Mr./Ms. (surname)
+ Addressing spouse:	See page 154

Legislative Branch, Senate

Senator

Envelope:

Official:	The Honorable
	(full name)
	United States Senate
	(address)
Social:+	The Honorable
	(full name)
	(address)

Senator as President Pro Tempore of the Senate

The Honorable
(full name)
President Pro Tempore of the Senate
(address)

Senator as a Committee or Subcommittee Chairman

	The Honorable
	(full name)
	Chairman
	(committee or subcommittee)
	(address)
Invitation, in envelope:	Senator (surname)
Salutation:	Dear Senator (surname):
Complimentary close:	Sincerely,
Place card:	Senator (surname)
Introduction:	The Honorable (full name), United States Senator from (state)
	Introduction as President Pro Tempore of the Senate
	The Honorable (full name), President Pro Tempore of the Senate *or* The President Pro Tempore of the Senate, Senator (surname)

Conversation:		Senator (surname) *or*
		Senator
		Senate majority and minority leaders do not use additional titles.
+ Addressing spouse:		See page 154

Senator-elect

Envelope:		
	Official:	The Honorable
		(full name)
		United States Senator–elect
		(address)
	Social:+	(title)
		(full name)
		(address)
Invitation, in envelope:		Mr./Ms. (surname)
Salutation:		Dear Mr./Ms. (surname):
Complimentary close:		Sincerely,
Place card:		Mr./Ms. (surname)
Introduction:		The Honorable (full name), United States Senator–elect from (state) *or*
		The United States Senator–elect from (state) *or*
		Mr./Ms. (surname)
Conversation:		Mr./Ms. (surname)
+ Addressing spouse:		See page 154

Former Senator

Continued use of the honorific is standard, but a former senator may be addressed as Mr./Ms. (full name or surname) and identified as a former senator.

Envelope:		
	Official:	The Honorable
		(full name)
		(address)

Social:+	The Honorable (full name) (address)
Invitation, in envelope:	Senator (surname)
Salutation:	Dear Senator (surname):
Complimentary close:	Sincerely,
Place card:	Senator (surname)
Introduction:	The Honorable (full name), former United States Senator from (state) *or* The former United States Senator from (state), Senator (surname)
Conversation:	Senator (surname)
+ Addressing spouse:	See page 154

Secretary of the Senate

Envelope:

Official:	The Honorable (full name) Secretary of the Senate (address)
Social:+	The Honorable (full name) (address)
Invitation, in envelope:	Mr./Ms. (surname)
Salutation:	Dear Mr./Ms. (surname):
Complimentary close:	Sincerely,
Place card:	Mr./Ms. (surname)
Introduction:	The Honorable (full name), Secretary of the United States Senate *or* The Secretary of the United States Senate *or* Mr./Ms. (surname)
Conversation:	Mr./Ms. (surname)
+ Addressing spouse:	See page 154

Sergeant at Arms of the Senate

Envelope:

	Official:	The Honorable
		(full name)
		Sergeant at Arms
		(address)
	Social:+	The Honorable
		(full name)
		(address)
Invitation, in envelope:		Mr./Ms. (surname)
Salutation:		Dear Mr./Ms. (surname):
Complimentary close:		Sincerely,
Place card:		Mr./Ms. (surname)
Introduction:		The Honorable (full name), Sergeant at Arms of the United States Senate *or* The Sergeant at Arms of the United States Senate, *or* Mr./Ms. (surname)
Conversation:		Mr./Ms. (surname)
+ Addressing spouse:		See page 154

Chaplain of the Senate

Check for personal preference. If the chaplain has a PhD, Dr. is used; otherwise, use Reverend, Pastor, Father, or Rabbi.

Envelope:

	Official:	(title)
		(full name), (degrees held)
		Chaplain of the Senate
		(address)
	Social:+	(title)
		(full name)
		(address)
Invitation, in envelope:		(title) (surname)
Salutation:		Dear (title) (surname):
Complimentary close:		Sincerely,
Place card:		(title) (surname)

Introduction:	(title) (full name), Chaplain of the United States Senate *or* Chaplain of the United States Senate, (title) (surname)
Conversation:	(title) (surname)
+ Addressing spouse:	See page 154

Legislative Branch, House of Representatives

Speaker of the House of Representatives

Envelope:

	Official:	The Speaker of the House of Representatives United States Capitol Washington, DC 20515
	Social:+	The Speaker of the House of Representatives (address)
Invitation, in envelope:		The Speaker of the House of Representatives
Salutation:		Dear Mr./Madam Speaker:
Complimentary close:		Respectfully,
Place card:		The Speaker of the House
Introduction:		The Honorable (full name) The Speaker of the House of Representatives
Conversation:		Mr./Madam Speaker
+ Addressing spouse:		See page 154

Representative

Envelope:

| | Official: | The Honorable (full name) United States House of Representatives (address) |

Chairman of a Committee or
Subcommittee:

Envelope:

Official: The Honorable
(full name)
Chairman (committee or subcommittee
name)
(address)

Social:+ The Honorable
(full name)
(address)

Invitation, in envelope: Mr./Ms. (surname)
Salutation: Dear Mr./Ms. (surname):
Complimentary close: Sincerely,
Place card: Mr./Ms. (surname)
Introduction: The Honorable (full name),
Representative from (state) *or*
The Honorable (full name),
Representative from (district), (state) *or*
Representative from (state), Mr./Ms.
(surname) *or*
Representative from (district), (state),
Mr./Ms. (surname)
Conversation: Mr./Ms. (surname)

Non-traditional honorifics for members of the House of Representative are often, Congressman or Congresswoman (full name or surname). The representative's preference should be followed when possible.

+ Addressing spouse: See page 154

Resident Commissioner of Puerto Rico

Envelope:

Official: The Honorable
(full name)
United States House of Representatives
(address)

Social:+	The Honorable (full name) (address)
Invitation, in envelope:	Mr./Ms. (surname)
Salutation:	Dear Mr./Ms. (surname):
Complimentary close:	Sincerely,
Place card:	Mr./Ms. (surname)
Introduction:	The Honorable (full name), Resident Commissioner of Puerto Rico to the House of Representatives *or* The Resident Commissioner of Puerto Rico to the House of Representatives, Mr./Ms. (surname)
Conversation:	Mr./Madam Commissioner *or* Resident Commissioner *or* Mr./Ms. (surname)
+ Addressing spouse:	See page 154

Delegate to the House of Representatives

Envelope:

Official:	The Honorable (full name) Delegate of (jurisdiction) (address)
Social:+	The Honorable (full name) (address)
Invitation, in envelope:	Mr./Ms. (surname)
Salutation:	Dear Mr./Ms. (surname):
Complimentary close:	Sincerely,
Place card:	Mr./Ms. (surname)
Introduction:	The Honorable (full name), Delegate of (jurisdiction) the House of Representatives *or* The Delegate of (jurisdiction) to the House of Representatives, *or* Mr./Ms. (surname)

| Conversation: | Mr./Ms. (surname) |
| + Addressing spouse: | See page 154 |

Former Representative

Envelope:

	Official:	The Honorable
		(full name)
		(address)
	Social:+	The Honorable
		(full name)
		(address)
Invitation, in envelope:		Mr./Ms. (surname)
Salutation:		Dear Mr./Ms. (surname):
Complimentary close:		Sincerely,
Place card:		Mr./Ms. (surname)
Introduction:		The Honorable (full name), former Representative from (state) *or* The Honorable (full name), former Representative from (district) of (state) *or* The former Representative from (state), Mr./Ms (surname) *or* The former Representative from (district), (state), Mr./Ms. (surname)
Conversation:		Mr./Ms. (surname)
+ Addressing spouse:		See page 154

Clerk or Sergeant at Arms of the House of Representatives

Envelope:

	Official:	The Honorable
		(full name)
		(full title)
		(address)
	Social:+	The Honorable
		(full name)
		(address)

Invitation, in envelope: Mr./Ms. (surname)
Salutation: Dear Mr./Ms. (surname):
Complimentary close: Sincerely,
Place card: Mr./Ms. (surname)
Introduction: The Honorable (full name),
                              (full title) *or*
                              (full title), Mr./Ms. (surname)
Conversation: Mr./Ms. (surname)
+ Addressing spouse: See page 154

Chaplain of the House of Representatives

Check for personal preference. If the chaplain has a PhD, Dr. is
used; otherwise, use Reverend, Pastor, Father, or Rabbi.
Envelope:

                Official: (title)
                              (full name), (degrees held)
                              Chaplain of the House of
                              Representatives
                              (address)
                Social: (title)
                              (full name)
                              (address)
Invitation, in envelope: (title) (surname)
Salutation: Dear (title) (surname):
Complimentary close: Sincerely,
Place card: (title) (surname)
Introduction: (title) (full name), Chaplain of the
                              House of Representatives *or*
                              The Chaplain of the House of
                              Representatives, (title) (surname)
Conversation: (title) (surname)
+ Addressing spouse: See page 154

Judicial Branch

Chief Justice of the Supreme Court

The chief justice is not addressed as *The Honorable*.

Envelope:

Official:	The Chief Justice The Supreme Court of the United States One First Street, NE Washington, DC 20543
Social:+	The Chief Justice (address)

Invitation, in envelope:	The Chief Justice
Salutation:	Dear Chief Justice:
Complimentary close:	Sincerely,
Place card:	The Chief Justice
Introduction:	The Chief Justice of the Supreme Court of the United States
Conversation:	Chief Justice
+ Addressing spouse:	See page 154

Associate Justice of the Supreme Court

The given name of an associate justice is not used unless there are two justices with the same surname. Associate justices do not use *The Honorable*.

Envelope:

Official:	Justice (surname) The Supreme Court One First Street, NE Washington, DC 20543
Social:+	Justice (surname) (address)

Invitation, in envelope:	Justice (surname)
Salutation:	Dear Justice (surname):
Complimentary close:	Sincerely,
Place card:	Justice (surname)
Introduction:	Justice (surname) of the Supreme Court of the United States
Conversation:	Justice
+ Addressing spouse:	See page 154

Retired Chief Justice of the Supreme Court

Envelope:

	Official:	Chief Justice (surname)
		(address)
	Social:+	Chief Justice (surname)
		(address)
Invitation, in envelope:		Chief Justice (surname)
Salutation:		Dear Chief Justice (surname):
Complimentary close:		Sincerely,
Place card:		Chief Justice (surname)
Introduction:		The Honorable (full name), former Chief Justice of the Supreme Court of the United States *or* Former Chief Justice of the Supreme Court of the United States Chief Justice (surname)
Conversation:		Chief Justice
+ Addressing spouse:		See page 154

Retired Associate Justice of the Supreme Court

Envelope:

	Official:	The Honorable (full name) (address)
	Social:+	The Honorable (full name) (address)
Invitation, in envelope:		Justice (surname)
Salutation:		Dear Justice (surname):
Complimentary close:		Sincerely,
Place card:		Justice (surname)
Introduction:		Justice (full name), former Associate Justice of the Supreme Court of the United States *or* Former Associate Justice of the Supreme Court of the United States Justice (surname)

Conversation:	Justice (surname)
+ Addressing spouse:	See page 154

Chief Judge or Senior Judge of a Court

Envelope:

	Official:	The Honorable
		(full name)
		Chief Judge/Senior Judge
		(court)
		(address)
	Social:+	The Honorable
		(full name)
		(address)
Invitation, in envelope:		Judge (surname)
Salutation:		Dear Judge (surname):
Complimentary close:		Sincerely,
Place card:		Judge (surname)
Introduction:		The Honorable (full name), Chief Judge/Senior Judge, (court) *or* Chief Judge/Senior Judge, (court), Judge (surname)
Conversation:		Judge (surname)
+ Addressing spouse:		See page 154

Judge of a Court

Envelope:

	Official:	The Honorable
		(full name)
		(court)
		(address)
	Social:+	The Honorable
		(full name)
		(address)
Invitation, in envelope:		Judge (surname)
Salutation:		Dear Judge (surname):
Complimentary close:		Sincerely,

Place card:		Judge (surname)
Introduction:		The Honorable (full name), Judge of the (court) *or* Judge of the (court), Judge (surname)
Conversation:		Judge (surname)
+ Addressing spouse:		See page 154

Deputy or Chief Deputy Marshal or Inspector or Chief Inspector

The president appoints the U.S. marshal, who is approved by the Senate and addressed as *The Honorable*. (See the section in this chapter titled "Marshal for a Judicial District.")

Envelope:		
	Official:	Mr./Ms. (full name) (title) (judicial district) (address)
	Social:+	Mr./Ms. (full name) (address)
Invitation, in envelope:		Mr./Ms. (surname)
Salutation:		Dear (title) (surname):
Complimentary close:		Sincerely,
Place card:		Mr./Ms. (surname)
Introduction:		Mr./Ms. (full name), (title), (district) *or* (title), (district), Mr./Ms. (surname)
Conversation:		Mr./Ms. (surname)
+ Addressing spouse:		See page 154

Clerk of a Lower Court

Envelope:		
	Official:	Mr./Ms. (full name) Clerk of the (court) (address)
	Social:+	Mr./Ms. (full name) (address)
Invitation, in envelope:		Mr./Ms. (surname)
Salutation:		Dear Mr./Ms. (surname):

Complimentary close:	Sincerely,
Place card:	Mr./Ms. (surname)
Introduction:	Mr./Ms. (full name), Clerk of the (court) *or*
	Clerk of the (court), Mr./Ms. (surname)
Conversation:	Mr./Ms. (surname)
+ Addressing spouse:	See page 154

STATE GOVERNMENT OFFICIALS IN THE UNITED STATES

State Executive

Governor *

Envelope:		
	Official:	The Honorable (full name) Governor of (state) (address)
	Social:+	The Honorable (full name) Governor of (state) (address)
Invitation, in envelope:		The Governor of (state)
Salutation:		Dear Governor (surname):
Complimentary close:		Sincerely,
Place card:		The Governor *or* The Governor of (state) (*used when out of state*)
Introduction:		The Honorable (full name), Governor of (state)
Conversation:		Governor (surname) *or* Governor
+ Addressing spouse:		See page 154

* Note: The Massachusetts governor is officially addressed as Your/His/Her Excellency.

Acting Governor

Envelope:

	Official:	The Honorable (T. H. only if from another position) (full name) Acting Governor of (state) (address)
	Social:+	The Honorable (T. H. only if from another position) (full name) (address)

Invitation, in envelope:	The Acting Governor *or* The Acting Governor of (state)
Salutation:	Dear Mr./Ms. (surname):
Complimentary close:	Sincerely,
Place card:	The Acting Governor *or* The Acting Governor of (state)
Introduction:	The Honorable (full name), Acting Governor of (state) *or* The Acting Governor of (state), Mr./Ms. (surname)
Conversation:	Mr./Ms. (surname)
+ Addressing spouse:	See page 154

Governor-elect

Envelope:

	Official:	The Honorable (full name) Governor-elect of (state) (address)
	Social:+	The Honorable (full name) (address)

Invitation, in envelope:	Mr./Ms. (surname)
Salutation:	Dear Mr./Ms. (surname):
Complimentary close:	Sincerely,

Place card:	The Governor-elect *or*
	The Governor-elect of (state)
Introduction:	The Honorable (full name),
	Governor-elect of (state) *or*
	The Governor-elect of (state),
	Mr./Ms. (surname)
Conversation:	Mr./Ms. (surname)
+ Addressing spouse:	See page 154

Former Governor*

Envelope:

	Official:	The Honorable
		(full name)
		(address)
	Social:+	The Honorable
		(full name)
		(address)
Invitation, in envelope:		Governor (surname)
Salutation:		Dear Mr./Ms. (surname):
Complimentary close:		Sincerely,
Place card:		Governor (surname)
Introduction:		The Honorable (full name), former
		Governor of (state) *or*
		Former Governor of (state), Mr./Ms.
		(surname)
Conversation:		Mr./Ms. (surname) *or*
		Governor (surname)*

* As a courtesy, Governor may be used
+ Addressing spouse: See page 154

Lieutenant Governor

Envelope:

	Official:	The Honorable
		(full name)
		Lieutenant Governor of (state)
		(address)

Social:+	The Honorable	
	(full name)	
	Lieutenant Governor of (state)	
	(address)	
Invitation, in envelope:	Mr./Ms. (surname)	
Salutation:	Dear Mr./Ms. (surname):	
Complimentary close:	Sincerely,	
Place card:	The Lieutenant Governor	
	The Lieutenant Governor of (state)	
Introduction:	The Honorable (full name), Lieutenant Governor of (state) *or*	
	The Lieutenant Governor of (state), Mr./Ms. (surname)	
Conversation:	Mr./Ms. (surname)	
+ Addressing spouse:	See page 154	

Attorney General

Envelope:

	Official:	The Honorable
		(full name)
		Attorney General of (state)
		(address)
	Social:+	The Honorable
		(full name)
		Attorney General of (state)
		(address)
Invitation, in envelope:	The Attorney General	
Salutation:	Dear Mr./Madam Attorney General:	
Complimentary close:	Sincerely,	
Place card:	The Attorney General *or*	
	The Attorney General of (state)	
Introduction:	The Honorable (full name), Attorney General of the state of (state)	
Conversation:	Mr./Madam Attorney General	
+ Addressing spouse:	See page 154	

Secretary of State and Other Members of the Governor's Cabinet

Envelope:		
	Official:	The Honorable
		(full name)
		Secretary of (department) of (state)
		(address)
	Social:+	The Honorable
		(full name)
		Secretary of (department) of (state)
		(address)
Invitation, in envelope:		The Secretary of (department)
Salutation:		Dear Mr./Madam Secretary:
Complimentary close:		Sincerely,
Place card:		The Secretary of (department) of (state)
Introduction:		The Honorable (full name), Secretary of (department) of (state)
Conversation:		Mr./Madam Secretary
+ Addressing spouse:		See page 154

Legislative Branch

Senator

Envelope:		
	Official:	The Honorable
		(full name)
		Senate of (state) or (state) Senate
		(address)
	Social:+	The Honorable
		(full name)
		(address)
Invitation, in envelope:		Senator (surname) or
		Mr./Ms. (surname)
Salutation:		Dear Senator (surname): or
		Dear Mr./Ms. (surname):
Complimentary close:		Sincerely,

Place card:	Mr./Ms. (surname)* *or*
	Senator (surname)
Introduction:	The Honorable (full name), (name of
	state) State Senator *or*
	Senator (full name)
Conversation:	Senator *or* Mr./Ms. (surname)

* When in Washington, D.C., a state senator is referred to in correspondence as Mr. or Ms.

Senator is reserved for a federal officeholder; when privately entertained, a state senator may be referred to as *Senator*.

+ Addressing spouse:	See page 154

Representative or Delegate

Envelope:

Official:	The Honorable
	(full name)
	House of Representatives/State
	Assembly/House of Delegates of (state)
	(address)
Social:+	The Honorable
	(full name)
	(address)
Invitation, in envelope:	Mr./Ms. (surname)
Salutation:	Dear Mr./Ms. (surname):
Complimentary close:	Sincerely,
Place card:	Mr./Ms. (surname)
Introduction:	The Honorable (full name), (name of
	state) (title of elected position)
Conversation:	Mr./Ms. (surname)
+ Addressing spouse:	See page 154

Judicial Branch*

Chief Justice of a State Supreme Court

Envelope:

Official:	Chief Justice
	(full name)

	Supreme Court of (state)
	(address)
Social:+	Chief Justice
	(full name)
	(address)
Invitation, in envelope:	Chief Justice (surname)
Salutation:	Dear Chief Justice (surname):
Complimentary close:	Sincerely,
Place card:	Chief Justice (surname)
Introduction:	Chief Justice (full name), Supreme Court of (state)
Conversation:	Chief Justice (surname)

* Judges are addressed as *The Honorable*; the Chief Justice and Justices of a Supreme Court are not.
+ Addressing spouse: See page 154

Associate Justice of a State Supreme Court

Envelope:

Official:	Justice
	(full name)
	The Supreme Court of (state)
	(address)
Social:+	Justice
	(full name)
	(address)
Invitation, in envelope:	Justice (surname)
Salutation:	Dear Justice (surname):
Complimentary close:	Sincerely,
Place card:	Justice (surname)
Introduction:	Justice (full name), Supreme Court of (state)
Conversation:	Justice (surname)
+ Addressing spouse:	See page 154

Chief Judge of a State Court

Envelope:

	Official:	The Honorable (full name) Chief Judge of the (Court) (address)
	Social:+	The Honorable (full name) (address)

Invitation, in envelope:	Judge (surname)
Salutation:	Dear Judge (surname):
Complimentary close:	Sincerely,
Place card:	Justice (surname)
Introduction:	The Honorable (full name), Chief Judge, (court)
Conversation:	Judge (surname)
+ Addressing spouse:	See page 154

Judge of a State Court

Envelope:

	Official:	The Honorable (full name) (court) (address)
	Social:+	The Honorable (full name) (address)

Invitation, in envelope:	Judge (surname)
Salutation:	Dear Judge (surname):
Complimentary close:	Sincerely,
Place card:	Judge (surname)
Introduction:	The Honorable (full name), Judge of the (court)
Conversation:	Judge (surname)
+ Addressing spouse:	See page 154

MUNICIPAL GOVERNMENT OFFICIALS
IN THE UNITED STATES

Mayor

Envelope:

Official:	The Honorable
	(full name)
	Mayor of (municipality)
	(address)
Social:+	The Honorable
	(full name)
	(address)
Invitation, in envelope:	The Mayor of (municipality)
Salutation:	Dear Mayor (surname):
Complimentary close:	Sincerely,
Place card:	Mayor (surname)
Introduction:	The Honorable (full name), Mayor of (municipality) *or*
	The Mayor of (municipality) *or*
	Mayor (surname)
Conversation:	Mr./Ms. (surname) *or*
	Mayor (surname)
+ Addressing spouse:	See page 154

Former Mayor

Envelope:

Official:	The Honorable
	(full name)
	(address)
Social:+	The Honorable
	(full name)
	(address)
Invitation, in envelope:	Mr./Ms. (surname)
Salutation:	Dear Mr./Ms. (surname):
Complimentary close:	Sincerely,
Place card:	Mr./Ms. (surname)

Introduction: The Honorable (full name), former
                                 Mayor of (city) *or*
                                 The former Mayor of (city), Mr./Ms.
                                 (surname)
Conversation: Mr./Ms. (surname)
+ Addressing spouse: See page 154

Sheriff

Envelope:
                  Official: The Honorable
                                 (full name)
                                 Sheriff of (county/city)
                                 (address)
                  Social:+   The Honorable
                                 (full name)
                                 (address)
Invitation, in envelope: Mr./Ms. (surname)
Salutation: Dear Sheriff (surname):
Complimentary close: Sincerely,
Place card: Sheriff (surname) *or*
                                 Mr./Ms. (surname)
Introduction: The Honorable (full name), Sheriff of
                                 (county/city)
Conversation: Sheriff (surname)
+ Addressing spouse: See page 154

Chief of Police

Envelope:
                  Official: Mr./Ms. (full name)
                                 (full title of position) of (county/city)
                                 (address)
                  Social:+   Mr./Ms. (full name)
                                 (address)
Invitation, in envelope: Mr./Ms. (surname)
Salutation: Dear Chief (surname):
Complimentary close: Sincerely,

Place card:	Chief (surname) *or*
	Mr./Ms. (surname)
Introduction:	Mr./Ms. (full name), (full title of position) of (county/city)
Conversation:	Chief (surname)
+ Addressing spouse:	See page 154

City or County Judge

Envelope:

Official:	The Honorable
	(full name)
	Judge of (name of court)
	(city or county)
	(address)
Social:+	The Honorable
	(full name)
	(address)
Invitation, in envelope:	Judge (surname)
Salutation:	Dear Judge (surname):
Complimentary close:	Sincerely,
Place card:	Judge (surname)
Introduction:	The Honorable (full name), Judge of the (name of court) (city or county)
Conversation:	Judge (surname)
+ Addressing spouse:	See page 154

DIPLOMATS AND INTERNATIONAL REPRESENTATIVES OF THE UNITED STATES

Ambassador at Post outside the Western Hemisphere

Envelope:

Official:	The Honorable
	(full name)
	American Ambassador
	(address)

	Social:+	The Honorable
		(full name)
		American Ambassador
		(address)
Invitation, in envelope:		The American Ambassador
Salutation:		Dear Mr./Madam Ambassador:
Complimentary close:		Sincerely,
Place card:		The American Ambassador *or*
		The American Ambassador to
		(country) *or*
		Ambassador (surname)
Introduction:		The Honorable (full name), American Ambassador
Conversation:		Mr./Madam Ambassador
+ Addressing spouse:		See page 154

Ambassador at Post in the Western Hemisphere

Envelope:

	Official:	The Honorable
		(full name)
		Ambassador of the United States of America
		(address)
	Social:+	The Honorable
		(full name)
		Ambassador of the United States of America
		(address)
Invitation, in envelope:		The Ambassador of the United States of America
Salutation:		Dear Mr./Madam Ambassador:
Complimentary close:		Sincerely,
Place card:		The Ambassador of the United States *or*
		The Ambassador of the United States of America to (country) *or*
		Ambassador (surname)
Introduction:		The Honorable (full name), Ambassador of the United States of America

Conversation: Mr./Madam Ambassador
+ Addressing spouse: See page 154

Ambassador Away from Post*

Envelope:
                Official: The Honorable
                                 (full name)
                                 American Ambassador* to (country)
                Social:+   The Honorable
                                 (full name)
                                 American Ambassador*
                                 (address)
Invitation, in envelope: The American Ambassador*
Salutation: Dear Mr./Madam Ambassador:
Complimentary close: Sincerely,
Place card: The American Ambassador* or
                                 The American Ambassador* to
                                 (country) or
                                 Ambassador* (surname)
Introduction: The Honorable (full name), American
                                 Ambassador*
Conversation: Mr./Madam Ambassador
* In the Western Hemisphere, *Ambassador of the United States of America* is used; The *American Ambassador* is used elsewhere.
+ Addressing spouse: See page 154

Ambassador with a Military Rank*

Envelope:
                Official:

                At Post:

                                 (full rank) (full name)
                                 American Ambassador
                                 (address)

Away from Post:
              (full rank) (full name)
              American Ambassador to (country)
              (address)

    At Post in the Western Hemisphere:
              (full rank) (full name)
              Ambassador of the United States of
              America
              (address)
    Away from Post in the Western Hemisphere:
              (full rank) (full name)
              Ambassador of the United States of
              America to (country)
              (address)

Invitation, in envelope: Same as for other ambassadors
                            depending on hemisphere
Salutation: Dear (basic rank) (surname):
Complimentary close: Sincerely,
Place card: Same as for other ambassadors
                            depending on hemisphere
Introduction: (full rank) (full name), American
                            Ambassador *or*
                            (full rank) (full name), American
                            Ambassador to (country) *or*
                            (full rank) (full name), Ambassador of
                            the United States of America *or*
                            (full rank) (full name), Ambassador of
                            the United States of America to
                            (country)
Conversation: Mr./Madam Ambassador

* Section titled "Armed Services of the United States" contains information regarding titles and forms of address for each rank.
+ Addressing spouse: See page 154

Ambassador at Large

Use *Ambassador, American Ambassador*, or *Ambassador of the United
States of America* for clarity, as appropriate.

Envelope:

	Official:	The Honorable (full name) Ambassador at Large (address)
	Social:+	The Honorable (full name) (address)
Invitation, in envelope:		Ambassador (surname)
Salutation:		Dear Mr./Madam Ambassador:
Complimentary close:		Sincerely,
Place card:		Ambassador (surname)
Introduction:		The Honorable (full name), Ambassador at large *or* Ambassador at large, Ambassador (surname)
Conversation:		Mr./Madam Ambassador
+ Addressing spouse:		See page 154

Former Ambassador

Envelope:

	Official:	The Honorable* (full name) (address)
	Social:+	The Honorable (full name) (address)
Invitation, in envelope:		Ambassador (surname)
Salutation:		Dear Ambassador (surname):
Complimentary close:		Sincerely,
Place card:		Ambassador (surname)
Introduction:		The Honorable (full name), former Ambassador of the United States *or* Former Ambassador of the United States, Ambassador (surname)
Conversation:		Ambassador (surname)

* A former career diplomat or an individual confirmed by the Senate
with the rank of ambassador may use the honorific for life.
+ Addressing spouse: See page 154

Special Titled Positions

Envelope:

	Official:	The Honorable*
		(full name)
		(title)
		(country)
		(address)
	Social:+	The Honorable*
		(full name)
		(address)
Invitation, in envelope:		Mr./Ms. (surname)
Salutation:		Dear Mr./Ms. (surname):
Complimentary close:		Sincerely,
Place card:		Mr./Ms. (surname)
Introduction:		The Honorable* (full name), (title)
		(country) *or*
		(title)
		(country), Mr./Ms. (surname)
Conversation:		Mr./Ms. (surname)

* The Honorable is used when from a previously held position or a presidential appointment.

+ Addressing spouse: See page 154

Consul General

Envelope:

At Post:

Official: (full name)
American Consul General
(address)

Away from Post:

Official: (full name)
American Consul General for (place)
(address)

Social:+ Mr./Ms. (full name)
(address)

Invitation, in envelope:	Mr./Ms. (surname)
Salutation:	Dear Mr./Ms. (surname):
Complimentary close:	Sincerely,
Place card:	Mr./Ms. (surname)
Introduction:	Mr./Ms. (full name), American Consul General *or*
	The American Consul General, Mr./Ms. (surname)
Conversation:	Mr./Ms. (surname)

* In the Western Hemisphere, instead of *American Consul General*, use *Consul General of the United States of America* in all instances.

+ Addressing spouse: See page 154

Consul or Vice-Consul

Use the form for *Consul General* but identify as a *consul* or *vice-consul*.

Chargé d'Affaires:

A chargé is addressed by existing personal rank and identified as a chargé. A chargé with the rank of minister would be addressed as *The Honorable*.

Envelope:	Official:	Mr./Ms. (full name) Chargé d'affaires of the United States of America (address)
	Social:+	Mr./Ms. (full name) (address)
Invitation, in envelope:		Mr./Ms. (surname)
Salutation:		Sir/Madam: *or* Dear Mr./Ms. (surname):
Complimentary close:		Sincerely,
Place card:		Mr./Ms. (surname)
Introduction:		Mr./Ms. (full name), Chargé d'affaires of the United States of America *or* The Chargé d'affaires of the United States of America, Mr./Ms. (surname)
Conversation:		Mr./Ms. (surname)
+ Addressing spouse:		See page 154

Chargé d'Affaires Ad Interim

Use the form for *Chargés d'affaires* and identify as a *Chargé d'affaires ad interim*.

Deputy Chief of Mission

A Deputy Chief of Mission (DCM) is addressed by existing personal rank and identified as a deputy chief of mission.

A DCM with the rank of minister would be addressed as *The Honorable*.

Envelope:		
	Official:	Mr./Ms. (full name)
		Deputy Chief of Mission of the
		(embassy of country)
		(address)
	Social:+	Mr./Ms. (surname)
		(address)
Invitation, in envelope:		Mr./Ms. (surname)
Salutation:		Dear Mr./Ms. (surname): *or*
		Sir: or Madam:
Complimentary close:		Sincerely,
Place card:		Mr./Ms. (surname)
Introduction:		Mr./Ms. (full name), Deputy Chief of Mission *or*
		The Deputy Chief of Mission of the (embassy of country), Mr./Ms. (surname)
Conversation:		Mr./Ms. (surname)
+ Addressing spouse:		See page 154

Personal or Special Representative of the President

Special Assistant or Advisor to the President

Envelope:

In the United States:

	Official:	The Honorable
		(full name)
		(specific title) to the President
		(address)

When Abroad:

	Official:	The Honorable
		(full name)
		(specific title) to the President of the
		United States of America
		(address)
	Social:+	The Honorable
		(full name)
		(address)
Invitation, in envelope:		Mr./Ms. (surname)
Salutation:		Dear Mr./Ms. (surname):
Complimentary close:		Sincerely,
Place card:		Mr./Ms. (surname)
Introduction:		The Honorable (full name), (specific title) *or*
		The (specific title), Mr./Ms. (surname)
Conversation:		Mr./Ms. (surname)
+ Addressing spouse:		See page 154

AMERICAN REPRESENTATIVES TO INTERNATIONAL ORGANIZATIONS

Representative to an International Organization with the Rank of Ambassador

Envelope:

	Official:	The Honorable
		(full name)
		United States Ambassador to
		(organization)
		(address)
	Social:+	The Honorable
		(full name)
		(address)
Invitation, in envelope:		Ambassador (surname)
Salutation:		Dear Mr./Madam Ambassador:

Complimentary close: Sincerely,
Place card: Ambassador (surname)
Introduction: The Honorable (full name), United
                          States representative to (organization)
Conversation: Mr./Madam Ambassador
+ Addressing spouse: See page 154

Representative to an International Organization

Envelope:

              Official: The Honorable
                          (full name)
                          United States Representative to
                          (organization)
                          (address)
              Social:+   The Honorable
                          (full name)
                          (address)
Invitation, in envelope: Mr./Ms. (surname)
Salutation: Dear Mr./Ms. (surname):
Complimentary close: Sincerely,
Place card: Mr./Ms. (surname)
Introduction: Mr./Ms. (full name), United States
                          Representative to (organization)
Conversation: Mr./Ms. (surname)
+ Addressing spouse: See page 154

Representative to an International Organization with a Military Rank

Envelope:

              Official: (rank) (full name) USA/USN/USAF/
                          USMC/USCG
                          (position and organization)
                          (address)
              Social:+   (rank) (full name)
                          (address)

Invitation, in envelope:	(rank) (surname)
Salutation:	Dear (rank) (surname):
Complimentary close:	Sincerely,
Place card:	(rank) (surname)
Introduction:	(rank) (full name), (position and title) to (organization)
Conversation:	(rank) (surname)
+ Addressing spouse:	See page 154

MEMBERS OF THE ARMED SERVICES OF THE UNITED STATES

Military Abbreviations for Branches of Service

Branches of service are abbreviated by the Department of Defense without periods. Ranks can be abbreviated to save space on place cards or for simplicity.

U.S. ARMY

U.S. Army	USA
U.S. Army Reserve	USAR
U.S. Army, Retired	USA, Retired/USA Ret.

U.S. MARINE CORPS

U.S. Marine Corps	USMC
U.S. Marine Corps Reserve	USMCR
U.S. Marine Corps, Retired	USMC, Retired/USMC Ret.

U.S. NAVY

U.S. Navy	USN
U.S. Navy Reserve	USNR
U.S. Navy, Retired	USN, Retired/USN Ret.

U.S. AIR FORCE

U.S. Air Force	USAF
U.S. Air Force Reserve	USAFR
U.S. Air Force, Retired	USAF, Retired/USAF Ret.

U.S. COAST GUARD

U.S. Coast Guard	USCG
U.S. Coast Guard Reserve	USCGR
U.S. Coast Guard, Retired	USCG, Retired/USCG Ret.

U.S. ARMY

COMMISSIONED PERSONNEL

General of the Army	(reserved for wartime)	
General		O-10
Lieutenant General	LTG	O-9
Major General	MG	O-8
Brigadier General	BG	O-7
Colonel	COL	O-6
Lieutenant Colonel	LTC	O-5
Major	MAJ	O-4
Captain	CPT	O-3
First Lieutenant	1LT	O-2
Second Lieutenant	2LT	O-1

WARRANT OFFICERS

Master Warrant Officer 5	CW5	W-5
Chief Warrant Officer 4	CW4	W-4
Chief Warrant Officer 3	CW3	W-3
Chief Warrant Officer 2	CW2	W-2
Warrant Officer	WO1	W-1

ENLISTED PERSONNEL

Sergeant Major of the Army	SMA	E-9
Command Sergeant Major	CSM	E-9
Sergeant Major	SGM	E-9
First Sergeant	1SG	E-8
Master Sergeant	MSG	E-8
Sergeant First Class	SFC	E-7
Staff Sergeant	SSG	E-6
Sergeant	SGT	E-5

Corporal	CPL	E-4
Specialist	SPC	E-4
Private First Class	PFC	E-3
Private, E-2	PV2	E-2
Private, E-1	PV	E-1

U.S. MARINE CORPS

COMMISSIONED PERSONNEL

General	Gen	O-10
Lieutenant General	LtGen	O-9
Major General	MajGen	O-8
Brigadier General	BrigGen	O-7
Colonel	Col	O-6
Lieutenant Colonel	LtCol	O-5
Major	Maj	O-4
Captain	Capt	O-3
First Lieutenant	1st Lt	O-2
Second Lieutenant	2nd Lt	O-1

WARRANT OFFICERS

Chief Warrant Officer 5	CWO5	W-5
Chief Warrant Officer 4	CWO4	W-4
Chief Warrant Officer 3	CWO3	W-3
Chief Warrant Officer 2	CWO2	W-2
Warrant Officer 1	WO1	W-1

ENLISTED PERSONNEL

Sergeant Major of the Marine Corps	SgtMaj MC	E-9
Sergeant Major	SgtMaj	E-9
Master Gunnery Sergeant	MGySgt	E-9
First Sergeant	1st Sgt	E-8
Master Sergeant	MSgt	E-8
Gunnery Sergeant	GySgt	E-7
Staff Sergeant	SSgt	E-6
Sergeant	Sgt	E-5
Corporal	Cpl	E-4

Lance Corporal	LCpl	E-3
Private First Class	PFC	E-2
Private	Pvt	E-1

U.S. NAVY

COMMISSIONED PERSONNEL

Fleet Admiral	FADM	O-11
Admiral	ADM	O-10
Vice Admiral	VADM	O-9
Rear Admiral (Upper Half)	RADM	O-8
Rear Admiral (Lower Half)	RDML	O-7
Captain	CAPT	O-6
Commander	CDR	O-5
Lieutenant Commander	LCDR	O-4
Lieutenant	LT	O-3
Lieutenant, junior grade	LTJG	O-2
Ensign	ENS	O-1

WARRANT OFFICERS

USN Chief Warrant Officer	CWO5	W-5
USN Chief Warrant Officer 4	CWO4	W-4
USN Chief Warrant Officer 3	CWO3	W-3
USN Chief Warrant Officer 2	CWO2	W-2
USN Warrant Officer 1	WO1	W-1

ENLISTED PERSONNEL

Master Chief Petty Officer of the Navy	MCPON	E-9
Master Chief Petty Officer	MCPO	E-9
Senior Chief Petty Officer	SCPO	E-8
Chief Petty Officer	CPO	E-7
Petty Officer First Class	PO1	E-6
Petty Officer Second Class	PO2	E-5
Petty Officer Third Class	PO3	E-4
Seaman	SN	E-3
Seaman Apprentice	SA	E-2
Seaman Recruit	SR	E-1

U.S. AIR FORCE

COMMISSIONED PERSONNEL

General of the Air Force	(reserved for wartime)	
General	Gen	O-10
Lieutenant General	LtGen	O-9
Major General	MajGen	O-8
Brigadier General	BrigGen	O-7
Colonel	Col	O-6
Lieutenant Colonel	LtCol	O-5
Major	Maj	O-4
Captain	Capt	O-3
First Lieutenant	1st Lt	O-2
Second Lieutenant	2nd Lt	O-1

WARRANT OFFICERS

There are no warrant officers.

ENLISTED PERSONNEL

Chief Master Sergeant of the Air Force	CMSAF	E-9
Command Chief Master Sergeant	CCMSgt	E-9
First Sergeant, E-9	1st Sgt	E-9
Chief Master Sergeant	CMSgt	E-9
First Sergeant, E-8	1st Sgt	E-8
Senior Master Sergeant	SMSgt	E-8
First Sergeant, E-7	1st Sgt	E-7
Master Sergeant	MSgt	E-7
Technical Sergeant	TSgt	E-6
Staff Sergeant	SSgt	E-5
Senior Airman	SrA	E-4
Airman First Class	A1C	E-3
Airman	Amn	E-2
Airman Basic	AB	E-1

U.S. COAST GUARD

COMMISSIONED PERSONNEL

Admiral	ADM	O-10
Vice Admiral	VADM	O-9
Rear Admiral (Upper Half)	RADM (UH)	O-8

Rear Admiral (Lower Half)	RADM (LH)	O-8
Captain	CAPT	O-6
Commander	CDR	O-5
Lieutenant Commander	LCDR	O-4
Lieutenant	LT	O-3
Lieutenant, junior grade	LTJG	O-2
Ensign	ENS	O-1

WARRANT OFFICERS

Chief Warrant Officer 4	CWO4	W-4
Chief Warrant Officer 3	CWO3	W-3
Chief Warrant Officer 2	CWO2	W-2

ENLISTED PERSONNEL

Master Chief Petty Officer of the Coast Guard	MCPO-CG	E-9
Command Master Chief Petty Officer	MCPOC	E-9
Master Chief Petty Officer	MCPO	E-9
Senior Chief Petty Officer	SCPO	E-8
Chief Petty Officer	CPO	E-7
Petty Officer First Class	PO1	E-6
Petty Officer Second Class	PO2	E-5
Petty Officer Third Class	PO3	E-4
Seaman	SN	E-3
Seaman Apprentice	SA	E-2
Seaman Recruit	SR	E-1

Secretary of Defense or a Secretary of an Armed Service

Envelope:

Official:
> The Honorable
> (full name)
> Secretary of Defense/Secretary of
> (armed service)
> (address)

Social:+
> The Honorable
> (full name)
> Secretary of Defense/Secretary of
> (armed service)
> (address)

Invitation, in envelope:	The Secretary of Defense/The Secretary of (armed service)
Salutation:	Dear Mr./Madam Secretary:
Complimentary close:	Sincerely,
Place card:	The Secretary of Defense/Secretary of (armed service)
Introduction:	The Honorable (full name), Secretary of Defense/ Secretary of (armed service)
Conversation:	Mr./Madam Secretary
+ Addressing spouse:	See page 154

Under Secretary of an Armed Service

Envelope:

	Official:	The Honorable (full name) (full title of position held) (address)
	Social:+	The Honorable (full name) (address)
Invitation, in envelope:		Mr./Ms. (surname)
Salutation:		Dear Mr./Ms. (surname):
Complimentary close:		Sincerely,
Place card:		Mr./Ms. (surname)
Introduction:		The Honorable (full name), (full title of position) or The (full title of position held), Mr./ Ms. (surname)
Conversation:		Mr./Ms. (surname)
+ Addressing spouse:		See page 154

Chairman, Joint Chiefs of Staff

Addressed by rank. Identify as *chairman.*
Envelope:

| | Official: | (full rank) (full name), (post nominal for branch of service) |

		Chairman of the Joint Chiefs of Staff (address)
	Social:+	(full rank) (full name) (address)
Invitation, in envelope:		(basic rank) (surname)
Salutation:		Dear (basic rank) (surname):
Complimentary close:		Sincerely,
Place card:		(basic rank)/(service-specific abbreviated rank) (surname)
Introduction:		(full rank) (full name), Chairman of the Joint Chiefs of Staff *or* Chairman of the Joint Chiefs of Staff, (basic rank) (surname)
Conversation:		(basic rank) (surname)
+ Addressing spouse:		See page 154

Chaplain in the Armed Services

Envelope:		
	Official:	Chaplain (full name) (full rank) (post nominal for branch of service) (address)
	Social:+	Chaplain (full name) (address)
Invitation, in envelope:		Chaplain (surname)
Salutation:		Dear Chaplain (surname):
Complimentary close:		Sincerely,
Place card:		Chaplain (surname)
Introduction:		Chaplain (full name), (full rank), (branch of service), (current assignment and location)
Conversation:		Chaplain (surname)
+ Addressing spouse:		See page 154

Army (USA), Air Force (USAF), and Marine Corps (USMC)

Chief of Staff of the Army

Addressed by rank. Identify as *chief of staff*.
Envelope:

Official:	(full rank) (full name) Chief of Staff of the Army (address)
Social:+	(full rank) (full name) (address)
Invitation, in envelope:	(basic rank) (surname)
Salutation:	Dear (basic rank) (surname):
Complimentary close:	Sincerely,
Place card:	(basic rank)/(service-specific abbreviated rank) (surname)
Introduction:	(full rank) (full name), Chief of Staff of the Army *or* The Chief of Staff of the Army, (basic rank) (surname)
Conversation:	(basic rank) (surname)
+ Addressing spouse:	See page 154

Chief of Staff of the Air Force

Addressed by rank. Identify as *chief of staff*.
Envelope:

Official:	(full rank) (full name) Chief of Staff of the Air Force (address)
Social:+	(full rank) (full name) (address)
Invitation, in envelope:	(basic rank) (surname)
Salutation:	Dear (basic rank) (surname):
Complimentary close:	Sincerely,
Place card:	(basic rank)/(service-specific abbreviated rank) (surname)
Introduction:	(full rank) (full name), Chief of Staff of the Air Force *or*

	The Chief of Staff of the Air Force,
	(basic rank) (surname)
Conversation:	(basic rank) (surname)
+ Addressing spouse:	See page 154

Commandant of the Marine Corps

Address by rank. Identify as *commandant*.
Envelope:

	Official:	(full rank) (full name)
		Commandant of the Marine Corps
		(address)
	Social:+	(full rank) (full name)
		(address)
Invitation, in envelope:		(basic rank) (surname)
Salutation:		Dear (basic rank) (surname):
Complimentary close:		Sincerely,
Place card:		(base rank)/(service-specific abbreviated rank) (surname)
Introduction:		(full rank) (full name), Commandant of the Marine Corps *or*
		The Commandant of the Marine Corps, (basic rank) (surname)
Conversation:		(basic rank) (surname)
+ Addressing spouse:		See page 154

General, Lieutenant General, Major General, or Brigadier General

Envelope:

	Official:	(full rank) (full name), USA/USAF/USMC
		(title/position)
		(address)
	Social:+	(full rank) (full name)
		(address)
Invitation, in envelope:		General (surname)
Salutation:		Dear General (surname):
Complimentary close:		Sincerely,

Place card:	General/(service-specific abbreviated rank) (surname)
Introduction:	(full rank) (full name), (position/command/name of base/service) *or* (position/command/name of base), General (surname)
Conversation:	General (surname)
+ Addressing spouse:	See page 154

Colonel

Envelope:

	Official:	Colonel (full name), USA/USAF/USMC (address)
	Social:+	Colonel (full name) (address)
Invitation, in envelope:		Colonel (surname)
Salutation:		Dear Colonel (surname):
Complimentary close:		Sincerely,
Place card:		Colonel/(service-specific abbreviated rank) (surname)
Introduction:		Colonel (full name), (position/command/name of base/service) *or* (position/command/name of base), Colonel (surname)
Conversation:		Colonel (surname)
+ Addressing spouse:		See page 154

Lieutenant Colonel

Envelope:

	Official:	Lieutenant Colonel (full name), USA/USAF/USMC (address)
	Social:+	Lieutenant Colonel (full name) (address)
Invitation, in envelope:		Colonel (surname)

Salutation: Dear Colonel (surname):
Complimentary close: Sincerely,
Place card: Colonel/(service-specific abbreviated
                                rank) (surname)
Introduction: Lieutenant Colonel (full name),
                                (position/command/name of
                                base/service) *or*
                                (position/command/name of base),
                                Colonel (surname)
Conversation: Colonel (surname)
+ Addressing spouse: See page 154

Major or Captain

Envelope:
            Official: (rank) (full name), USA/USAF/USMC
                                (address)
            Social:+   (rank) (full name)
                                (address)
Invitation, in envelope: (rank) (surname)
Salutation: Dear (rank) (surname):
Complimentary close: Sincerely,
Place card: (rank)/(service-specific abbreviated
                                rank) (surname)
Introduction: (rank) (full name), (position/command/
                                name of base/service) *or*
                                (position/command/name of base)
                                (rank) (surname)
Conversation: (rank) (surname)
+ Addressing spouse: See page 154

First Lieutenant or Second Lieutenant

Envelope:
            Official: Lieutenant (full name), USA/USAF/
                                USMC
                                (address)
            Social:+   Lieutenant (full name)
                                (address)

Invitation, in envelope:	Lieutenant (surname)
Salutation:	Dear Lieutenant (surname):
Complimentary close:	Sincerely,
Place card:	Lieutenant/(service-specific abbreviated rank) (surname)
Introduction:	Lieutenant (full name), (position/command/name of base/service) *or* (position/command/name of base), Lieutenant (surname)
Conversation:	Lieutenant (surname)
+ Addressing spouse:	See page 154

Retired Officer, USA, USAF, or USMC

Envelope:		
	Official:	(full rank) (full name), USA/USAF/USMC, Retired (address)
	Social:+	(full rank) (full name) (address)
Invitation, in envelope:		(basic rank) (surname)
Salutation:		Dear (basic rank) (surname):
Complimentary close:		Sincerely,
Place card:		(basic rank)/(service-specific abbreviated rank) (surname)
Introduction:		(full rank) (full name), United States Army/Air Force/Marine Corps, Retired
Conversation:		(basic rank) (surname)
+ Addressing spouse:		See page 154

Cadet, United States Military Academy

Envelope:		
	Official:	Cadet (full name), USA Company (____), Corps of Cadets United States Military Academy West Point, NY 10996
Invitation, in envelope:		Cadet (surname)
Salutation:		Dear Cadet (surname):

Complimentary close:	Sincerely,
Place card:	Cadet (surname)
Introduction:	Cadet (full name), United States Military Academy
Conversation:	Cadet (surname)

Cadet, United States Air Force Academy

Cadet First Class is abbreviated as C1C. Cadet Second Class is abbreviated as C2C.

Envelope:

	Official:	Cadet (full name), USAF
		Room (___), (___) Hall
		United States Air Force Academy
		Colorado Springs, CO 80840
Invitation, in envelope:		Cadet (surname)
Salutation:		Dear Cadet (surname):
Complimentary close:		Sincerely,
Place card:		Cadet (surname) or
		C1C/C2C (surname)
Introduction:		Cadet (full name), United States Air Force Academy
Conversation:		Cadet (surname)

Chief Warrant Officer or Warrant Officer, USA/USMC

Envelope:

	Official:	Chief Warrant Officer/Warrant Officer (full name), USA/USMC (position/command/name of base) (address)
	Social:+	Chief Warrant Officer/Warrant Officer (full name) (address)
Invitation, in envelope:		Chief Warrant Officer/Warrant Officer (surname)
Salutation:		Dear Chief Warrant Officer/ Warrant Officer (surname):

Complimentary close:		Sincerely,
Place card:		(rank)/(service-specific abbreviated rank) Mr./Ms. (surname)
Introduction:		(full rank), (full name), (position/command/name of base/service) *or* (position/command/name of base), Chief Warrant Officer/Warrant Officer *or* Warrant Officer (surname)
Conversation:		Chief Warrant Officer/Warrant Officer (surname)
+ Addressing spouse:		See page 154

Sergeant Major of the Army, Command Sergeant Major, or Sergeant Major, USA

Envelope:		
	Official:	(full rank) (full name), USA (address)
	Social:+	Sergeant Major (full name) (address)
Invitation, in envelope:		Sergeant Major (surname)
Salutation:		Dear Sergeant Major (surname):
Complimentary close:		Sincerely,
Place card:		Sergeant Major (surname) *or* SMA/CSM/SGM (surname)
Introduction:		Sergeant Major (full name), (position/command/name of base/USA) *or* (position/command/name of base), Sergeant Major (surname)
Conversation:		Sergeant Major (surname)
+ Addressing spouse:		See page 154

First Sergeant and Master Sergeant, USA

Envelope:		
	Official:	(full rating) (full name), USA (address)
	Social:+	(full rating) (full name) (address)

Invitation, in envelope:	(full rating) (surname)
Salutation:	Dear (full rating) (surname):
Complimentary close:	Sincerely,
Place card:	(full rating) (surname) *or* ISG/MSG(surname)
Introduction:	(full rating) (full name), position/command/name of base/USA) *or* (position/command/name of base), (full rating) (surname)
Conversation:	(full rating) (surname)
+ Addressing spouse:	See page 154

Platoon Sergeant, Sergeant First Class, Staff Sergeant, or Sergeant, USA

Envelope:

	Official:	(full rating) (full name), USA (address)
	Social:+	(full rating) (full name) (address)
Invitation, in envelope:		Sergeant (surname)
Salutation:		Dear Sergeant (surname):
Complimentary close:		Sincerely,
Place card:		Sergeant (surname) *or* PSG/SFC/SSG/SGT (surname)
Introduction:		(full rating) (full name), (position/command/name of base/USA) *or* (position/command/name of base), Sergeant (surname)
Conversation:		Sergeant (surname)
+ Addressing spouse:		See page 154

Corporal, Specialist, or Private, USA

Envelope:

	Official:	(rank) (full name), USA (address)
	Social:+	(rank) (full name) (address)

Invitation, in envelope:	(rank) (surname)
Salutation:	Dear (rank) (surname):
Complimentary close:	Sincerely,
Place card:	(rank) (surname) *or*
	CPL/SPC/PV2/PV1 (surname)
Introduction:	(rank) (full name), (position/command/ name of base/USA) *or* (position/command/name of base, (rank) (surname)
Conversation:	(rank) (surname)
+ Addressing spouse:	See page 154

Private First Class, USA

Envelope:

	Official:	Private First Class (full name), USA (address)
	Social:+	Private (full name) (address)
Invitation, in envelope:		Private (surname)
Salutation:		Dear Private (surname):
Complimentary close:		Sincerely,
Place card:		Private (surname) *or* PFC (surname)
Introduction:		Private (full name), (position/ command/name of base/USA) *or* (position/command/name of base), Private (surname)
Conversation:		Private (surname)
+ Addressing spouse:		See page 154

Chief Master Sergeant, Command Chief Master Sergeant, or Chief Master Sergeant, USAF

Envelope:

	Official:	(full rating) (full name), USAF (address)
	Social:+	(full rating) (full name) (address)
Invitation, in envelope:		Chief (surname)

Salutation: Dear Chief (surname):
Complimentary close: Sincerely,
Place card: Chief (surname) *or*
                         (service-specific abbreviated rank)
                         (surname)
Introduction: (full rating) (full name), (position/
                         command/name of base/USAF) *or*
                         (position/command/name of base), (full
                         rating) (surname)
Conversation: Chief (surname)
+ Addressing spouse: See page 154

Senior Master Sergeant, First Sergeant, Master Sergeant, Technical Sergeant, or Staff Sergeant, USAF

Envelope:
                Official: (full rating) (full name), USAF
                             (address)
                 Social:+   (full rating) (full name)
                             (address)
Invitation, in envelope: Sergeant (surname)
Salutation: Dear Sergeant (surname):
Complimentary close: Sincerely,
Place card: Sergeant (surname) *or*
                         (service-specific abbreviated rank)
                         (surname)
Introduction: (full rating) (full name), (position/
                         command/name of base/USAF) *or*
                         (position/command/name of base),
                         (full rating) (surname)
Conversation: Sergeant (surname)
+ Addressing spouse: See page 154

Senior Airman, Airman First Class, Airman, or Airman Basic, USAF

Envelope:
                Official: (full rating) (full name), USAF
                             (address)

	Social:+	(full rating) (full name) (address)
Invitation, in envelope:		Airman (surname)
Salutation:		Dear Airman (surname):
Complimentary close:		Sincerely,
Place card:		Airman (surname) *or* SrA/AIC/Amn/AB (surname)
Introduction:		(full rating) (full name), (position/ command/name of base/USAF) *or* (position/command/name of base), (full rating) (surname)
Conversation:		Airman (surname)
+ Addressing spouse:		See page 154

Sergeant Major of the Marine Corps or Sergeant Major, USMC

Envelope:		
	Official:	(full rank) (full name), USMC (address)
	Social:+	(full rank) (full name) (address)
Invitation, in envelope:		Sergeant Major (surname)
Salutation:		Dear Sergeant Major (surname):
Complimentary close:		Sincerely,
Place card:		Sergeant Major (surname) *or* SgtMaj (surname)
Introduction:		(full rank) (full name), (position/ command/name of base/USMC) *or* (position/command/name of base), (full rating) (surname)
Conversation:		Sergeant Major (surname)
+ Addressing spouse:		See page 154

First Sergeant, Master Sergeant, Gunnery Sergeant, Staff Sergeant, Sergeant, Private First Class, or Private, USMC

Envelope:		
	Official:	(full rank) (full name), USMC (address)

Social:+	(full rank) (full name) (address)
Invitation, in envelope:	(full rating) (surname)
Salutation:	Dear (full rank) (surname):
Complimentary close:	Sincerely,
Place card:	(full rank)/(service-specific abbreviated rating) (surname)
Introduction:	(full rank) (full name), (position/command/name of base/service) *or* (position/command/name of base), (full rank) (surname)
Conversation:	(full rank) (surname)
+ Addressing spouse:	See page 154

Corporal or Lance Corporal, USMC

Envelope:

Official:	(full rank) (full name), USMC (address)
Social:+	(full rank) (full name) (address)
Invitation, in envelope:	Corporal (surname)
Salutation:	Dear Corporal (surname):
Complimentary close:	Sincerely,
Place card:	Corporal (surname) *or* Cpl/LCpl (surname)
Introduction:	(full rank) (full name), (position/command/name of base/USMC) *or* (position/command/name of base), Corporal (surname)
Conversation:	Corporal (surname)
+ Addressing spouse:	See page 154

Navy, USN; Coast Guard, USCG

Chief of Naval Operations

Addressed by rank. Identify as *Chief of Naval Operations.*

Envelope:

Official:	(full rank) (full name)
	Chief of Naval Operations
	(address)
Social:+	(full rank) (full name)
	(address)
Invitation, in envelope:	(basic rank) (surname)
Salutation:	Dear (basic rank) (surname):
Complimentary close:	Sincerely,
Place card:	(basic rank)/(service-specific
	abbreviated rank) (surname)
Introduction:	(full rank) (full name), Chief of Naval
	Operations *or*
	The Chief of Naval Operations, (basic
	rank) (surname)
Conversation:	(basic rank) (surname)
+ Addressing spouse:	See page 154

Commandant of the Coast Guard

Address by rank. Identify as *The Commandant.*

Envelope:

Official:	(full rank) (full name)
	Commandant of the Coast Guard
	(address)
Social:+	(full rank) (full name)
	(address)
Invitation, in envelope:	(basic rank) (surname)
Salutation:	Dear (basic rank) (surname):
Complimentary close:	Sincerely,
Place card:	(basic rank)/(service-specific
	abbreviated rank) (surname)
Introduction:	(full rank) (full name), Commandant of
	the Coast Guard *or*
	The Commandant of the Coast Guard,
	(basic rank) (surname)
Conversation:	(basic rank) (surname)
+ Addressing spouse:	See page 154

Admiral, Vice Admiral, or Rear Admiral

Envelope:

	Official:	(full rank) (full name), USN/USCG (title/position) (address)
	Social:+	(full rank) (full name) (address)
Invitation, in envelope:		Admiral, Vice Admiral/Rear Admiral (surname)
Salutation:		Dear Admiral (surname):
Complimentary close:		Sincerely,
Place card:		Admiral, Vice Admiral/Rear Admiral/ (service-specific abbreviated rank) (surname)
Introduction:		(full rank) (full name), (position/ command/name of base/service) *or* (position/command/name of base), Admiral , Vice Admiral/Rear Admiral (surname)
Conversation:		Admiral , Vice Admiral/Rear Admiral (surname)
+ Addressing spouse:		See page 154

Captain or Commander

Envelope:

	Official:	(rank) (full name), USN/USCG (address)
	Social:+	(rank) (full name) (address)
Invitation, in envelope:		(rank) (surname)
Salutation:		Dear (rank) (surname):
Complimentary close:		Sincerely,
Place Card:		Captain/CAPT or Commander/CDR (surname)
Introduction:		(rank) (full name), (position/command/ name of base/service) *or* (position/command/name of base), (rank) (surname)

Conversation:	(rank) (surname)
+ Addressing spouse:	See page 154

Lieutenant Commander

Envelope:

	Official:	Lieutenant Commander (full name), USN/USCG (address)
	Social:+	Lieutenant Commander (full name) (address)
Invitation, in envelope:		Commander (surname)
Salutation:		Dear Commander (surname):
Complimentary close:		Sincerely,
Place card:		Commander (surname) *or* LCDR (surname)
Introduction:		Lieutenant Commander (full name), (position/command/name of base) *or* (position/command/name of base), Commander (surname)
Conversation:		Commander (surname)
+ Addressing spouse:		See page 154

Lieutenant or Lieutenant, junior grade

Addressing a lieutenant as Mr./Ms. (surname) is an internal practice of the navy used aboard ship, but in other circumstances, military personnel should be addressed by rank.
Envelope:

	Official:	Lieutenant/Lieutenant, junior grade (full name), USN/USCG (address)
	Social:+	Lieutenant/Lieutenant, junior grade (address)
Invitation, in envelope:		Lieutenant (surname)
Salutation:		Dear Lieutenant (surname):
Complimentary close:		Sincerely,
Place card:		Lieutenant (surname) *or* LT/LTJG (surname)

Introduction:	Lieutenant/Lieutenant, junior grade (full name), (position/command/name of base/service) (position/command/name of base), Lieutenant (surname)
Conversation:	Lieutenant (surname)
+ Addressing spouse:	See page 154

Ensign

Envelope:

	Official:	Ensign (full name), USN/USCG (address)
	Social:+	Ensign (full name) (address)
Invitation, in envelope:		Ensign (surname)
Salutation:		Dear Ensign (surname):
Complimentary close:		Sincerely,
Place card:		Ensign/ENS (surname)
Introduction:		Ensign (full name), (position/command/ name of base/service) *or* (position/command/name of base), Ensign (surname)
Conversation:		Ensign (surname)
+ Addressing spouse:		See page 154

Retired Officer, USN or USCG

Envelope:

	Official:	(full rank) (full name), USN/USCG, Retired (address)
	Social:+	(full rank) (full name) (address)
Invitation, in envelope:		(basic rank) (surname)
Salutation:		Dear (basic rank) (surname):
Complimentary close:		Sincerely,
Place card:		(basic rank)/(service-specific abbreviated rank) (surname)

Introduction:	(full rank) (full name), United States Navy/Coast Guard, Retired
Conversation:	(basic rank) (surname)
+ Addressing spouse:	See page 154

Cadet, United States Naval Academy

Envelope:

Official:	Midshipman (full name), USN Room (___), (___) Hall United States Naval Academy Annapolis, MD 21402
Invitation, in envelope:	Midshipman (surname)
Salutation:	Dear Midshipman (surname):
Complimentary close:	Sincerely,
Place card:	Midshipman (surname)
Introduction:	Midshipman (full name), United States Naval Academy
Conversation:	Midshipman (surname)

Cadet, United States Coast Guard Academy

Envelope:

Official:	Cadet (full name), USCG United States Coast Guard Academy New London, CT 06320
Invitation, in envelope:	Cadet (surname)
Salutation:	Dear Cadet (surname):
Complimentary close:	Sincerely,
Place card:	Cadet (surname)
Introduction:	Cadet (full name), United States Coast Guard Academy
Conversation:	Cadet (surname)

Chief Warrant Officer or Warrant Officer, USN/USCG

Envelope:

Official:	Chief Warrant Officer (full name), USN/USCG (address)

	Social:+	Chief Warrant Officer (full name) (address)
Invitation, in envelope:		Mr./Ms. (full name)
Salutation:		Dear Mr./Ms. (surname):
Complimentary close:		Sincerely,
Place card:		Chief Warrant Officer (surname) *or* CWO2, 3, 4, or 5 (surname) *or* Warrant Officer (surname) or WO1 (surname)
Introduction:		(full rank) (full name), (position/ command, name of base/service) *or* (position/command/name of base), (full rank) (surname) *or* (position/command/name of base), Mr./Ms. (surname)
Conversation:		(Chief) Warrant Officer (surname) Mr./Ms. (surname)
+ Addressing spouse:		See page 154

Master Chief Petty Officer of the Navy

Master Chief Petty Officer of the Coast Guard

Fleet/Command Master Chief Petty Officer, USN/USCG

Master Chief Petty Officer, USN/USCG

Envelope:		
	Official:	(full rating) (full name), USN/USCG (address)
	Social:+	(full rating) (full name) (address)
Invitation, in envelope:		Master Chief (surname)
Salutation:		Dear Master Chief (surname):
Complimentary close:		Sincerely,
Place card:		Master Chief (surname) *or* (service-specific abbreviated rank) (surname)

Introduction:	(full rating) (full name), (position/command/name of base) *or* (position/command/name of base), (full rating) (surname)
Conversation:	Master Chief (surname)
+ Addressing spouse:	See page 154

Senior Chief Petty Officer

Envelope:

	Official:	Senior Chief Petty Officer (full name), USN/USCG (address)
	Social:+	Senior Chief Petty Officer (full name) (address)
Invitation, in envelope:		Senior Chief (surname)
Salutation:		Dear Senior Chief (surname):
Complimentary close:		Sincerely,
Place card:		Senior Chief (surname) SCPO (surname)
Introduction:		Senior Chief Petty Officer (full name), (position/command/name of base/etc.) *or* (position/command/name of base), Senior Chief Petty Officer (surname)
Conversation:		Senior Chief (surname)
+ Addressing spouse:		See page 154

Chief Petty Officer

Envelope:

	Official:	Chief Petty Officer (full name), USN/USCG (address)
	Social:+	Chief Petty Officer (full name) (address)
Invitation, in envelope:		Chief (surname)
Salutation:		Dear Chief (surname):
Complimentary close:		Sincerely,

Place card:		Chief (surname)
		CPO (surname)
Introduction:		Chief Petty Officer (full name) (position/command/name of base) *or* (position/command/name of base), Chief Petty Officer (surname)
Conversation:		Chief (surname)
+ Addressing spouse:		See page 154

Petty Officer First Class, Second Class, or Third Class

Envelope:		
	Official:	(full rating) (full name), USN/USCG (address)
	Social:+	(full rating) (full name) (address)
Invitation, in envelope:		Petty Officer (surname)
Salutation:		Dear Petty Officer (surname):
Complimentary close:		Sincerely,
Place card:		Petty Officer (surname) (service-specific abbreviated rank) (surname)
Introduction:		(full rating) (full name), (position/command/name of base) *or* (position/command/name of base), (full rating) (surname)
Conversation:		Petty Officer (surname)
+ Addressing spouse:		See page 154

Seaman, Seaman Apprentice, or Seaman Recruit

Envelope:		
	Official:	(full rating) (full name), USN/USCG (address)
	Social:+	(full rating) (full name) (address)
Invitation, in envelope:		Seaman (surname)
Salutation:		Dear Seaman (surname):

Complimentary close:	Sincerely,
Place card:	Seaman (surname)
	SN/SA/SR (surname)
Introduction:	(full rating) (full name), (position/command/name of base) *or* (position, command/name of base), (full rating) (surname)
Conversation:	Seaman (surname)
+ Addressing spouse:	See page 154

INTERNATIONAL OFFICIALS

Chief of State or Head of Government

President

Always check for personal preference.
Addressed as His/Her Excellency.
Envelope:

Official:	His/Her Excellency (personal honorific if presented) (full name), (post nominal as presented) President of (full name of country) (address)
Social:+	His/Her Excellency (personal honorific if presented) (full name) (post nominal as presented) President of (full name of country) (address)

Invitation, in envelope:	The President of (full name of country)
Salutation:	Your Excellency:
Complimentary close:	Respectfully,
Place card:	The President of (full name of country)
Introduction:	His/Her Excellency (personal honorific if presented) (full name), (full name of country) *or* The President of (full name of country)

Conversation: Your Excellency
+ Addressing spouse: See page 154

**Chairman of the Council of Ministers, of the Presidency
(Bosnia and Herzegovina)**

Chancellor (Austria, Germany)

Executive President (Zimbabwe)

Premier (China) Supreme Leader (Iran)

Always check for personal preference. Addressed as *His/Her Excellency*.
Envelope:

	Official:	His/Her Excellency
		(personal honorific if presented)
		(full name)
		(title of office)
		of (full name of country)
		(address)
	Social:+	His/Her Excellency
		(personal honorific if presented
		(full name)
		(title of office)
		of (full name of country)
		(address)

Invitation, in envelope: The (title of office) of (full name of
                             country)
Salutation: Your Excellency:
Complimentary close: Respectfully,
Place card: The (title of office) of (full name of
                             country)
Introduction: His/Her Excellency (personal honorific
                             if presented) (full name), (title of
                             office), (full name of country)
Conversation: Your Excellency
+ Addressing spouse: See page 154

Prime Minister

Always check for personal preference. Depending on the country, prime ministers may be addressed as *His/Her Excellency, The Honorable*, or *The Right Honourable* or without any courtesy title. Check traditional practice.

When addressed as *His/Her Excellency*:

Envelope:

	Official:	His/Her Excellency (personal honorific if presented) (full name), (post nominal as presented) Prime Minister of (full name of country) (address)
	Social:+	His/Her Excellency (personal honorific if presented) (full name) (post nominal as presented) Prime Minister of (full name of country) (address)
Invitation, in envelope:		The Prime Minister of (full name of country)
Salutation:		Your Excellency:
Complimentary close:		Respectfully,
Place card:		The Prime Minister of (full name of country)
Introduction:		His/Her Excellency (full name), Prime Minister of (full name of country) *or* The Prime Minister of (full name of country) *or* His/Her Excellency (full name)
Conversation:		Your Excellency Mr./Madam Prime Minister
+ Addressing spouse:		See page 154

Departments, Ministries, and Secretariats

Cabinet Minister and Secretaries

Although *His/Her Excellency* is most often used to address a member of a foreign cabinet, *The Honourable* or *The Right Honourable* may also be used, depending on the country. When in the United States, *The Honorable* is often used. As with all foreign dignitaries, always check for preference.

Addressed as *His/Her Excellency*

Envelope:		
	Official:	His/Her Excellency
		(personal honorific if presented)
		(full name), (post nominal)
		(title of office) of (full name of country)
		(address)
	Social:+	His/Her Excellency
		(personal honorific if presented
		(full name), (post nominal)
		(title of office) of (full name of country)
		(address)
Invitation, in envelope:		The (title of office)
Salutation:		Your Excellency:
Complimentary close:		Sincerely,
Place card:		The (title of office) *or*
		His/Her Excellency (personal honorific if presented) (full name)
Introduction:		His/Her Excellency (full name), (title of office) of (full name of country) *or* (title of office) of (full name of country), His/Her Excellency (full name)
Conversation:		Your Excellency
+ Addressing spouse:		See page 154

Deputy Minister or Under Secretary

In the United States, these officials are often addressed as *The Honorable*. Check tradition for usage.

Envelope:

	Official:	Mr./Ms. (full name)
		(title) of (full name of country)
		(address)
	Social:+	Mr./Ms. (full name)
		(title) of (full name of country)
		(address)
Invitation, in envelope:		The (title of office)
Salutation:		Dear (title of office):
		Dear Mr./Ms. (surname):
Complimentary close:		Sincerely,
Place card:		The (title of office) *or*
		Mr. (surname)/Ms. (surname)
Introduction:		Mr./Ms. (full name), (title) of (full name of country)
Conversation:		Mr./Ms. (surname)
+ Addressing spouse:		See page 154

Ruling Family Member: Chief of State or Head of Government

Correspondence with a Member of a Ruling Family

Correspondence is not directly addressed to a member of a ruling family unless it is from someone personally acquainted with that member. Otherwise, correspondence should be addressed to a specified court official.

Always check for the official name and title of the chief of state or head of government.

Envelope examples include

The Private Secretary to
His/Her Majesty the King/Queen
(address)

His/Her Excellency
The Chief of the Royal Protocol
(address)

Salutation: Dear Sir/Madam: *or*
                                Dear Mr./Ms. (surname):

Emperor or Empress

Envelope: His/Her Imperial Majesty
                                Emperor/Empress of (country)
                                (address)
Invitation, in envelope: His/Her Imperial Majesty
                                The Emperor/Empress of (country)
Salutation: Your Imperial Majesty:
Complimentary close: Most Respectfully,
                                Salutation By Subjects:
                                I remain Your Imperial Majesty's
                                faithful and devoted servant,
Place card: His/Her Imperial Majesty (or H.I.M.)
                                The Emperor or Empress of (country)
Introduction: His/Her Imperial Majesty Emperor/
                                Empress of (country)
Conversation: Your Imperial Majesty

King or Queen

Envelope: His/Her Majesty
                                The King/Queen of (country)
                                (address) *or*
                                Their Majesties
                                The King and Queen of (country/people)
                                (address)
Invitation, in envelope: His/Her Majesty
                                The King/Queen of (country/people) *or*
                                Their Majesties
                                The King and Queen of (country/
                                people)
Salutation: Your Majesty:
Complimentary close: Most Respectfully, *or*
                                By Subjects:
                                I remain Your Majesty's faithful and
                                devoted servant, *or*

	I have the honor to remain Your Majesty's obedient servant,
Place card:	His/Her Majesty (or H.M.) The King/Queen of (country/people)
Introduction:	His/Her Majesty King/Queen of (country/people) *or* Their Majesties King and Queen of (country/people)
Conversation:	Your Majesty

Other Official Royalty

Crown Prince or Princess of a Royal Family

For the crown prince and princess of the Japanese imperial throne, use *His/Her Imperial Highness* in place of *His/Her Royal Highness*.

Check the proper form of address for each country.

Envelope:	His/Her Royal Highness (title) (name) *or* Crown Prince/Princess of (country) (address)
Invitation, in envelope:	His/Her Royal Highness (title) (name)
Salutation:	Your Royal Highness:
Complimentary close:	Respectfully,
Place card:	His/Her Royal Highness (title) (name)
Introduction:	His/Her Royal Highness (title) (name), Crown Prince/Princess of (country) *or* The Crown Prince/Princess of (country), His/Her Royal Highness (title) (name)
Conversation:	Your Royal Highness

Prince or Princess of a Royal Family

Check the proper form of address for each country.

| Envelope: | His/Her Royal Highness Prince/Princess (name) (address) |

Invitation, in envelope:	His/Her Royal Highness Prince/Princess (name)
Salutation:	Your Royal Highness:
Complimentary close:	Respectfully,
Place card:	His/Her Royal Highness Prince/ Princess (name)
Introduction:	His/Her Royal Highness Prince/ Princess (name)
Conversation:	Your Royal Highness

Foreign Diplomats

Ambassador, Extraordinary and Plenipotentiary

Envelope:		
	Official:	His/Her Excellency (personal honorific if presented) (full name), (post nominal) Ambassador of (full name of country)* (address)
	Social:+	His/Her Excellency (personal honorific if presented) (full name), (post nominal) Ambassador of (full name of country)* (address)
Invitation, in envelope:		The Ambassador of (full name of country)*
Salutation:		Your Excellency: Dear Mr./Madam Ambassador:
Complimentary close:		Sincerely,
Place card:		The Ambassador of (full name of country)*
Introduction:		His/Her Excellency (personal honorific if presented) (full name), Ambassador of (full name of country)* *or* Ambassador of (full name of country), Ambassador (surname)*
Conversation:		Your Excellency Mr./Madam Ambassador

* Brazil and Great Britain address their ambassadors as The Brazilian Ambassador and The British Ambassador
+ Addressing spouse: See page 154

Ambassador with a Personal Title

Envelope:

	Official:	His/Her Excellency (appropriate form for title) (full name) Ambassador of (full name of country) (address)
	Social:+	His/Her Excellency (appropriate form for title) (full name) Ambassador of (full name of country) (address)
Invitation, in envelope:		The Ambassador of (full name of country)
Salutation:		Your Excellency: Dear Mr./Madam Ambassador:
Complimentary close:		Sincerely,
Place card:		The Ambassador of (full name of country)
Introduction:		His/Her Excellency (appropriate form for their title) (full name), Ambassador of (full name of country) *or* Ambassador of (full name of country), Ambassador (surname)
Conversation:		Your Excellency Mr./Madam Ambassador
+ Addressing spouse:		See page 154

Appointed Ambassador

Envelope:

	Official:	His/Her Excellency (full name) Appointed Ambassador of (full name of country) (address)

Social:+	His/Her Excellency (full name) (address)
Invitation, in envelope:	The Appointed Ambassador of (full name of country)
Salutation:	Your Excellency: Dear Mr./Madam Ambassador:
Complimentary close:	Sincerely,
Place card:	The Appointed Ambassador of (full name of country)
Introduction:	His/Her Excellency (full name), Appointed Ambassador of (full name of country)
Conversation:	Your Excellency Mr./Madam Ambassador
+ Addressing spouse:	See page 154

Minister Plenipotentiary

His/Her Excellency is reserved for an accredited minister.
Envelope:

Official:	The Honorable (full name) Embassy of (full name of country) (address)
Social:+	The Honorable (full name) (address)
Invitation, in envelope:	The Honorable (full name)
Salutation:	Dear Minister (surname):
Complimentary close:	Sincerely,
Place card:	The Honorable (full name)
Introduction:	The Honorable (full name), Minister of (full name of country)
Conversation:	Minister (surname)
+ Addressing spouse:	See page 154

Minister-Counselor

Always check for preference and tradition. His/Her Excellency is normally not used for a minister-counselor. If His/Her Excellency is appropriate, interchange this honorific with the form for minister and identify the subject as Minister-Counselor of (country). If no courtesy title is accorded, address as Mr./Ms. (name).

Chargé d'Affaires, Chargé d'Affaires Ad Interim, Chargé d'Affaires Ad Hoc, and Chargé d'Affaires Pro Tempore

Always check for preference and tradition. Address holders of these positions as His/Her Excellency only if they carry the rank of minister. If no courtesy title is used, then identify by title or office and address as Mr./Ms. (name).

Counselor; Attaché or Assistant Attaché; First, Second, or Third Secretary; General Consul, Consul, or Vice-consul

Always check for preference and tradition. Addressed as The Honorable if title is from another previously held position. If no courtesy title is used, then identify by title or office and address as Mr./Ms. (name).

International Organizations

Secretary General of the United Nations

Envelope:

Official: His/Her Excellency
(personal honorific if presented)
(full name)
Secretary General of the United Nations
(address)

Social:+ His/Her Excellency
(personal honorific if presented)
(full name)
Secretary General of the United Nations
(address)

Invitation, in envelope:	The Secretary General of the United Nations
Salutation:	Your Excellency: *or*
	Dear Mr./Madam Secretary General: *or*
	Dear (personal honorific if presented) (surname):
Complimentary close:	Sincerely,
Place card:	The Secretary General of the United Nations *or*
	His/Her Excellency (H. E.) (personal honorific, if presented) (full name)
Introduction:	His/Her Excellency Secretary General of the United Nations *or*
	The Secretary General of the United Nations, Mr./Ms./Dr. (surname)
Conversation:	Your Excellency *or*
	Mr./Madam Secretary General *or*
	(personal honorific if presented) (surname)
+ Addressing spouse:	See page 154

Secretary General of the Organization of American States

Envelope:

	Official:	His/Her Excellency (personal honorific if presented) (full name) Secretary General of the Organization of American States (address)
	Social:+	His/Her Excellency (personal honorific if presented (full name) Secretary General of the Organization of American States (address)
Invitation, in envelope:		The Secretary General of the Organization of American States

Salutation: Your Excellency
                          Dear Mr./Madam Secretary General:
Complimentary close: Sincerely,
Place card: The Secretary General of the
                          Organization of American States *or*
                          His/Her Excellency (H. E.) (full name)
Introduction: His/Her Excellency (full name),
                          Secretary General of the Organization
                          of American States
Conversation: Your Excellency
                          Mr./Madam Secretary General
+ Addressing spouse: See page 154

Ambassador to an International Organization

Envelope:
        Official: His/Her Excellency
                          (full name)
                          (position and organization)
                          (address)
        Social:+   His/Her Excellency
                          (full name)
                          (address)
Invitation, in envelope: The (position and organization)
Salutation: Your Excellency: *or*
                          Dear Mr./Madam Ambassador:
Complimentary close: Sincerely,
Place card: The (position and organization) *or*
                          His/Her Excellency/(H. E.) (full name)
Introduction: His/Her Excellency (full name),
                          representative of (country) to
                          (organization) *or*
                          The Representative of (country) to
                          (organization), Ambassador (surname)
Conversation: Mr./Madam Ambassador
                          Ambassador (surname)
+ Addressing spouse: See page 154

Religious Officials

Anglican

Archbishop of Canterbury (Church of England)

Envelope:

Official:	The Most Reverend and Right Honourable
	(full name)
	Archbishop of Canterbury
	(address)
	London SE1 7JU
Social:	The Most Reverend (full name)
	(address)
Invitation, in envelope:	Archbishop (surname)
Salutation:	Dear Archbishop (surname):
Complimentary close:	Sincerely,
Place card:	Archbishop (surname)
Introduction:	The Most Reverend (full name),
	Archbishop of Canterbury
Conversation:	Archbishop (surname)
	Your Grace
+ Addressing spouse:	See page 154

Buddhist

Dalai Lama

Envelope:	His Holiness
	The Dalai Lama
	(address)
Invitation, in envelope:	His Holiness
	The Dalai Lama
Salutation:	Your Holiness:
Complimentary close:	Respectfully,
Place card:	His Holiness (H. H.) The Dalai Lama *or*
	The Dalai Lama
Introduction:	His Holiness the Dalai Lama
Conversation:	Your Holiness

Christian Orthodox

Ecumenical Patriarch, Patriarch, or Patriarch of Constantinople

Envelope:	His All Holiness The Ecumenical Patriarch (address)
Invitation, in envelope:	His All Holiness The Ecumenical Patriarch
Salutation:	Your All Holiness:
Complimentary close:	Respectfully,
Place card:	His All Holiness The Ecumenical Patriarch *or* The Ecumenical Patriarch
Introduction:	His All Holiness the Ecumenical Patriarch
Conversation:	Your All Holiness

Patriarch

Addressed as "His Beatitude"*

Envelope:	His Beatitude Patriarch of (place) (address)
Invitation, in envelope:	His Beatitude Patriarch (name and number)
Salutation:	Your Beatitude:
Complimentary close:	Respectfully,
Place card:	His Beatitude (H. B.) Patriarch (name and number) *or* Patriarch (name and number)
Introduction:	His Beatitude Patriarch (name and number) of (place)
Conversation:	Your Beatitude (*formal*) Papa (*informal*)
*Addressed as His Beatitude:	(name), Patriarch of Antioch and All the East

(name), Pope and Patriarch of
Alexandria and All Africa
(name), Patriarch of the Holy City of
Jerusalem and All Palestine

Patriarch with "His Holiness"*

Addressed as "His Holiness"*

Envelope:	His Holiness
	Patriarch (name and number) of (place)
	(address)
Invitation, in envelope:	His Holiness or The Most Holy
	Patriarch (name and number) of (place)
Salutation:	Your All Holiness:
Complimentary close:	Respectfully,
Place card:	His Holiness Patriarch (name and
	number)
Introduction:	His Holiness Patriarch (name and
	number) of (place)
Conversation:	Your Holiness

* Addressed as His Holiness or The Most Holy
(name), Patriarch of Moscow
(name), Patriarch of Bulgaria
(name), The Patriarchs of Georgia,
Serbia, and Romania

Archbishop

Addressed as "His Eminence"*

Envelope:	His Eminence or The Most Reverend
	Archbishop (name) of (place)
	(position)
	(address)
Invitation, in envelope:	Archbishop (name)
Salutation:	Your Eminence:
Complimentary close:	Sincerely,
Place card:	His Eminence (H. E.) Archbishop
	(name) or
	Archbishop (name)

| Introduction: | His Eminence Archbishop (name) of (place) |
| Conversation: | Your Eminence or Archbishop (name) |

* Addressed as His Eminence or His Excellence

(name), Archbishop of Chicago and Detroit Diocese (name), Archbishop of Sydney,
Australia, and New Zealand Diocese (name), Archbishop of Crete

Archbishop

Addressed as "His Beatitude"*

Envelope:	His Beatitude Archbishop (name and number) (address)
Invitation, in envelope:	Archbishop (name and number)
Salutation:	Your Beatitude:
Complimentary close:	Sincerely,
Place card:	His Beatitude (H. B.) Archbishop (name and number) *or* Archbishop (name and number)
Introduction:	His Beatitude Archbishop (name and number) of (place)
Conversation:	Your Beatitude or Archbishop (name)

*Addressed as His Beatitude

(name), Archbishop of Washington and New York,
Metropolitan of All America and Canada
(name), Archbishop of Tirana and All Albania
(name), Archbishop of Athens and All Greece
(name), Archbishop of New Justiniana and All Cyprus

Christian Science*

Christian Science is commonly called the Church of Christ, Scientist.

Practitioner*

Envelope:	(full name), C. S.+
	(address)
Invitation, in envelope:	Mr./Ms. (surname)
Salutation:	Dear Mr./Ms. (surname):
Complimentary close:	Sincerely,
Place card:	Mr./Ms. (surname)
Introduction:	Mr./Ms. (full name), Christian Science
	Practitioner *or*
	Mr./Ms. (surname)
Conversation:	Mr./Ms. (surname)
	Elder
+Addressing spouse:	See page 154

*There are no ordained clergy in Christian Science.

The church comprises the First Church of Christ, Scientist, in Boston, Massachusetts. It is also known as the Mother Church and has branches, each of which begins with a number.

Example: Fifth Church of Christ, Scientist, Los Angeles

The Church of Jesus Christ of Latter-day Saints

Commonly called the Mormon Church.

President

Envelope:	President (full name)+
	The Church of Jesus Christ of
	Latter-day Saints
	(address)
Invitation, in envelope:	
Only president:	President (full name)
With spouse:	President and Sister (president's full
	name)

Salutation:	Dear President (surname):
Complimentary close:	Sincerely,
Place card:	President (full name)
	Sister (president's full name)
Introduction:	(full name) President of the Church of Jesus Christ of Latter-day Saints *or* President (surname)
Conversation:	President (surname)
+ Addressing spouse:	See page 154

Episcopal

Presiding Bishop

Envelope:		
	Official:	The Most Reverend (full name), (post nominal as appropriate) Presiding Bishop of the Episcopal Church (address)
	Social:+	The Most Reverend (full name) (address)
Invitation, in envelope:		Bishop (surname)
Salutation:		Dear Bishop (surname):
Complimentary close:		Sincerely,
Place card:		Bishop (surname)
Introduction:		The Most Reverend (full name) Presiding Bishop of the Episcopal Church *or* Bishop (surname) (*informal*)
Conversation:		Bishop (surname) Your Grace
+Addressing spouse:		See page 154

Bishop

Envelope:

	Official:	The Right Reverend (full name), (post nominal as appropriate) Bishop of (diocese) (address)
	Social:+	The Right Reverend (full name) (address)

Invitation, in envelope:	Bishop (surname)
Salutation:	Dear Bishop (surname):
Complimentary close:	Sincerely,
Place card:	Bishop (surname)
Introduction:	The Right Reverend (full name), Bishop of (area) *or* Bishop (surname)
Conversation:	Bishop (surname) Your Grace
+Addressing spouse:	See page 154

Archdeacon, Dean, or Deacon

In each of the following instances, use the correct honorific and title:

Title	*Honorific*
Archdeacon	The Venerable
Dean	The Very Reverend
Deacon	The Reverend

Envelope:

	Official:	(honorific) (full name), (post nominal as appropriate) (title) of (where the individual presides: diocese, cathedral, church) (address)

	Social:+	(honorific) (full name) (address)
Invitation, in envelope:		(title) (surname)
Salutation:		Dear (title):
Complimentary close:		Sincerely,
Place card:		(title) (surname)
Introduction:		(honorific) (full name), (title) of (place) *or* (title) (surname) (*informal*)
Conversation:		(title) (surname)
+Addressing spouse:		See page 154

Canon

Envelope:

	Official:	The Reverend Canon (full name), (degrees held) (title) of (church) (address)
	Social:+	The Reverend Canon (full name) (address)
Invitation, in envelope:		Canon (surname)
Salutation:		Dear Canon (surname):
Complimentary close:		Sincerely,
Place card:		Canon (surname)
Introduction:		The Reverend Canon (full name), (church) in (location) *or* Canon (surname)
Conversation:		Canon (surname) Canon
+Addressing spouse:		See page 154

Canon (Lay; Senior Members of a Diocesan or Cathedral's Staff)

Envelope:

| | Official: | Canon (full name), (degrees held)
(title) of (church)
(address) |

Social:+	Canon (full name) (address)
Invitation, in envelope:	Canon (surname)
Salutation:	Dear Canon (surname):
Complimentary close:	Sincerely,
Place card:	Canon (surname)
Introduction:	Canon (full name), (church) in (location) *or* Canon (surname) (*informal*)
Conversation:	Canon (surname) Canon
+Addressing spouse:	See page 154

Vicar, Rector, or Priest

Envelope:		
	Official:	The Reverend (full name), (degree held) (title) of (church) (address)
	Social:+	The Reverend (full name) (address)
Invitation, in envelope:		Dr. or Reverend (surname)
Salutation:		Dear Dr. or Reverend (surname):
Complimentary close:		Sincerely,
Place card:		Dr. or Reverend (surname)
Introduction:		The Reverend (full name), (title) of (church) in (location) *or* Dr. or Reverend (surname) (*informal*
Conversation:		Dr. or Reverend (surname)
+Addressing spouse:		See page 154

Hindu

Chief Priest or Priest

Envelope:	Pandit* Sri (name) ji (temple) (address)

Invitation, in envelope:	Pandit Sri (name) ji**
Salutation:	Respected Pandit (name) ji:
Complimentary close:	Sincerely,
Place card:	Pandit Sri (name) ji
Introduction:	Pandit Sri (name) ji, (temple) in (location) *or*
	Pandit Sri (name) ji
Conversation:	Sri (name) ji
	Pandit-ji

* Pandit is a courtesy title used to address a learned man. It is accepted everywhere.

** The Sanskrit honorific *Sri* is used as Mr. is used in English.

In the north of India, *Maharaja* is often used.

In both the north and south of India, *Swami* is used.

The word *ji* is added to the name in lowercase letters without a hyphen.

Jehovah's Witness

Elder*

Envelope:	Elder (full name)+
	(Kingdom Hall) (location)
	(address)
Invitation, in envelope:	Elder (surname)
Salutation:	Dear Elder (surname):
Complimentary close:	Sincerely,
Place card:	Elder (surname)
Introduction:	Elder (full name), (position) (Kingdom Hall) in (location)
Conversation:	Elder (surname)
	Mr. (surname)
*Note:	Elders are always men.
+Addressing spouse:	See page 154

Jewish

*Rabbi**

Envelope:

	Official:	Rabbi (full name)
		(congregation)
		(address)
	Social:+	Rabbi (full name)
		(address)
Invitation, in envelope:		Rabbi (surname)
Salutation:		Dear Rabbi (surname):
Complimentary close:		Sincerely,
Place card:		Rabbi (surname)
Introduction:		Rabbi (full name), (congregation) in (location)
Conversation:		Rabbi (surname)

*Rabbi Dr. is sometimes used by personal preference or in academia. Consult for preference.

+Addressing spouse: See page 154

Cantor

Envelope:

	Official:	Cantor (full name)
		(congregation)
		(address)
	Social:+	Cantor (full name)
		(address)
Invitation, in envelope:		Cantor (surname)
Salutation:		Dear Cantor (surname):
Complimentary close:		Sincerely,
Place card:		Cantor (surname)
Introduction:		Cantor (full name), (congregation) in (location)
Conversation:		Cantor (surname)
+Addressing spouse:		See page 154

Muslim, Shia Islam*

Grand Ayatollah or Ayatollah

Envelope:

	Official:	His Eminence Grand Ayatollah (or Ayatollah) (full name) (mosque or other official address) (address)
	Social:	His Eminence Grand Ayatollah (or Ayatollah) (full name) (address)

Invitation, in envelope: His Eminence (H. E.)
Grand Ayatollah (or Ayatollah)
(surname)

Salutation: Your Eminence:

Complimentary close: Respectfully,

Place card: His Eminence (H. E.) Grand Ayatollah
(or Ayatollah) (surname)

Introduction: His Eminence Grand Ayatollah (or
Ayatollah) (full name), (mosque/
institution) in (location)
or one person to another:
His Eminence Grand Ayatollah
(Ayatollah) (full name)

Conversation: Sayyid (surname)

*Shia Islam, the second-largest branch of Islam, regards Ali (brother and cousin of the Prophet Mohammed) as its head.

Sayyid and sayida, meaning "leader," are the masculine and feminine honorifics for descendents of the Prophet.

Sayida can be used for the wife of a Shiite cleric in the place of Mrs. Check for preference.

Imam*

Envelope:

	Official:	Sayyid/Sheikh** (full name)
		(mosque)
		(address)
	Social:	Sayyid/Sheikh (full name)
		(address)

Invitation, in envelope: Sayyid/Sheikh (surname)

Salutation: Dear Iman (surname):

Complimentary close: Sincerely,

Place card: Sayyid/Sheikh (surname)

Introduction: Sayyid/Sheikh (full name), Imam
(mosque) in (location) *or*
Sayyid/Sheikh (full name) (*informal*)

Conversation: Sayyid/Sheikh (surname)
Sayyid/Sheikh (*informal*)

*Imam is not used as an honorific for Shiite clerics.

**Sayyid is an honorific for a descendant of the Prophet.

"Sheikh" is an honorific for a man who is not a descendent of the Prophet.

Muslim, Sunni Islam

Grand Sheikh or Grand Imam

Envelope:

	Official:	
	and Social:	His Eminence
		(honorific if presented) (full name)
		(title)
		(address)

Invitation, in envelope: His Eminence

Salutation: Your Eminence:

Complimentary close: Respectfully,

Place card: His Eminence (H. E.) The (title) *or*
The (title)

Introduction: His Eminence (honorific) (name),
(title)

Conversation: Your Eminence
Sayyida or *sayida* in the Sunni tradition is the honorific for all women.
Check personal preference for a woman's name on social invitations.

Grand Mufti

Envelope:

	Official	
	and Social:	His Eminence
		(honorific if presented) (full name)
		(address)

Invitation, in envelope: His Eminence
                            The Grand Mufti of (place)
Salutation: Your Eminence:
Complimentary close: Respectfully,
Place card: His Eminence (H. E.) The Grand
                            Mufti of (place)
Introduction: His Eminence (full name), Grand
                            Mufti of (place)
Conversation: Your Eminence

Imam*

Envelope:

	Official:	Imam (full name)
		(mosque)
		(address)
	Social:	Imam (full name)
		(address)

Invitation, in envelope: Imam (surname)
Salutation: Dear Imam (surname):
Complimentary close: Sincerely,
Place card: Imam (surname)
Introduction: Imam (full name), (mosque) in
                            (location)
                            Imam (full name) (*informal*)
Conversation: Imam (surname)
*For a Sunni cleric, *Imam* is used as an honorific. Consult for preference.

Other Denominations*

The following are examples of some existing denominations and their titles used in greeting:

Denomination	Title(s) used in greeting
African American Baptist	Minister (surname)
African American Episcopal	Minister or Pastor
Baptist	Reverend or Pastor
Church of Christ	Pastor or no special title
Fellowship Church	Pastor
Lutheran	Pastor
Methodist	Reverend, Bishop, or Pastor
Presbyterian	Reverend or Pastor
Seventh-Day Adventist	Elder or Pastor
Scientology	Minister or Chaplain
(a religion that holds in common many of the beliefs of other religions and philosophies)	
Society of Friends (commonly called Quakers)	No ordained clergy
Unitarian	Reverend
United Church of Christ	Pastor, Mr. or Ms.

Form of Address for Other Denominations

Envelope:

	Official:	(honorific or title) (full name), (degrees held) (name of institution) (address)
	Social:+	(title) (full name) (address)
Invitation, in envelope:		(title) (surname)
Salutation:		Dear (title) (surname):
Complimentary close:		Sincerely,
Place card:		(title) (surname)
Introduction:		(title) (full name), (church), (location—if appropriate)

Conversation:	(title) (surname)
+Addressing spouse:	See page 154

Roman Catholic Church

The Pope

Envelope:	His Holiness
	The Pope*
	The Apostolic Palace
	00120 Vatican City State, Europe
Invitation, in envelope:	His Holiness The Pope*
Salutation:	Your Holiness: *or*
	Most Holy Father:*
Complimentary close:	Most respectfully, *or*
	Your most humble servant,
Place card:	His Holiness The Pope*
Introduction:	His Holiness The Pope*
Conversation:	Your Holiness *or*
	Most Holy Father*

*The Pope's proper name should never be used.

Cardinal

Envelope:	His Eminence
	(given name) Cardinal (surname)
	Archbishop of (place)
	(address) *or*
	His Eminence
	Cardinal (given name) (surname)
	Archbishop of (place)
	(address)
Invitation, in envelope:	His Eminence
	Cardinal (surname)
Salutation:	Your Eminence: (*formal*)
	Dear Cardinal: (*informal*)
Complimentary close:	Respectfully,
Place card:	His Eminence Cardinal (surname)

Introduction:	His Eminence Cardinal (surname)
	(*formal*)
Conversation:	Eminence *or*
	Your Eminence
	Cardinal (surname)

Apostolic Delegate

Papal Nuncio, Pro-Nuncio, Nuncio

The Apostolic Delegate to the United States, Washington, D.C.

Envelope:	The Most Reverend
	(full name), (post nominal as
	appropriate)
	Titular Archbishop/Bishop of (place)
	The Apostolic Nuncio to the United
	States
	(address)
Invitation, in envelope:	His Excellency
	The Apostolic Nuncio
Salutation:	Most Reverend Sir: (for an archbishop)
	Your Excellency: (for an ambassador)
Complimentary close:	Respectfully,
Place card:	His Excellency (H. E.) The Apostolic
	Nuncio
Introduction:	The Most Reverend (full name), Titular
	Archbishop/Bishop of (place)
	The Apostolic Nuncio to (place)
Conversation:	Your Excellency

*A papal representative to the United States will hold the diplomatic rank of ambassador and the hierarchical rank of cardinal, archbishop, or bishop. He may have the title "Titular Archbishop/Bishop of (place)" since he will not have an archdiocese or diocese to supervise. He is addressed by hierarchical rank, as "Titular Archbishop/Bishop," and identified as a diplomat with the title "Ambassador."

Archbishop

Envelope:	The Most Reverend (full name) Archbishop of (diocese) (address)
Invitation, in envelope:	The Most Reverend Archbishop (surname)
Salutation:	Dear Archbishop (surname): Your Excellency:
Complimentary close:	Respectfully,
Place card:	Archbishop (surname)
Introduction:	The Most Reverend (full name) of (place)
Conversation:	Archbishop (surname) *or* Your Grace

Bishop

Envelope:	The Most Reverend (full name) Bishop of (place) (address)
Invitation, in envelope:	The Most Reverend Bishop (surname)
Salutation:	Dear Bishop (surname):
Complimentary close:	Respectfully,
Place card:	Bishop (surname)
Introduction:	The Most Reverend (full name), Bishop (place)
Conversation:	Bishop (surname) Your Excellency

Monsignor

Envelope:	The Reverend Monsignor (full name), (post nominal as appropriate) (address)
Invitation, in envelope:	Monsignor (surname)
Salutation:	Dear Monsignor (surname):

Complimentary close:	Sincerely,
Place card:	Monsignor (or Msgr.) (surname)
Introduction:	The Reverend Monsignor of (full name), (church) in (location)
Conversation:	Monsignor (surname)

Priest

Envelope:	The Reverend (full name), (initials of order when necessary) (church) (address)
Invitation, in envelope:	Father (surname)
Salutation:	Dear Father (surname):
Complimentary close:	Sincerely,
Place card:	Father (surname)
Introduction:	The Reverend (full name), (order), (church) (location)
Conversation:	Father (surname) *or* Reverend (surname) *or* Father (*informal*)

Brother or Friar

Envelope:	Brother/Friar (full name) (institution/monastery) (address)
Invitation, in envelope:	Brother/Friar (given name)
Salutation:	Dear Bother/Friar (given name):
Complimentary close:	Sincerely,
Place card:	Brother/Friar (surname)
Introduction:	Brother/Friar (full name), of the (order), of the (monastery/institution) in (location)
Conversation:	Brother/Friar (given name)

Mother Superior

If using the Mother Superior's given or family name, replace (full name) with (given name). Some orders use *Sister Servant*, which would replace *Mother*.

Envelope:	Mother (full name), (initials of order) Superior (convent/institution) (address)
Invitation, in envelope:	Mother (full name)
Salutation:	Dear Mother:
	Dear Mother (full name):
Complimentary close:	Sincerely,
Place card:	Mother (full name)
Introduction:	Mother (full name), of the (order), of the (convent/institution) in (location)
Conversation:	Mother (full name)

Nun

If using the nun's given or family name, replace (full name) with (given name).

Envelope:	Sister (full name), (initials of order) (convent/institution) (address)
Invitation, in envelope:	Sister (full name)
Salutation:	Dear Sister:
	Dear Sister (full name):
Complimentary close:	Sincerely,
Place card:	Sister (full name)
Introduction:	Sister (full name), of the (order), of the (convent/institution)in (location)
Conversation:	Sister (full name)

Private U.S. Citizens

Academics

Chancellor or President

Envelope:

Official:	Chancellor/President (full name) (name of university) (address)
Social:+	Dr./Chancellor/President (full name) (address)

Invitation, in envelope:	Dr./Chancellor/President (surname)
Salutation:	Dear Dr./Chancellor/President (surname):
Complimentary close:	Sincerely,
Place card:	Dr./Chancellor/President (surname)
Introduction:	Dr./Chancellor/President (full name), (title) of (institution)
Conversation:	Dr./Chancellor/President (surname)
+Addressing spouse:	See page 154

Professionals

Physician

Envelope:

Official:	(full name), (appropriate acronym) (name of hospital, clinic) (office address)
Social:+	Dr. (full name) (address)

Invitation, in envelope:	Dr. (surname)
Salutation:	Dear Dr. (surname):
Complimentary close:	Sincerely,
Place card:	Dr. (surname)
Introduction:	Dr. (full name)
Conversation:	Dr. (surname)

Abbreviations: Medicine (MD), Dental (DDS), and
                                  Veterinary (DVM)
+Addressing spouse: See page 154

Doctor (PhD or MD)

When both spouses are doctors, their names may appear on correspondence as:

The Doctors Smith (omit given first names)

Attorney at Law

Envelope:
                Official: Mr./Ms. (full name)
                                  Attorney at Law
                                  (name of firm)
                                  (office address) *or*
                                  (full name), Esq.*
                                  (name of firm)
                                  (office address)
                Social:+   Mr./Ms. (full name)
                                  (home address)
Invitation, in envelope: Mr./Ms. (surname)
Salutation: Dear Mr./Ms. (surname):
Complimentary close: Sincerely,
Place card: Mr./Ms. (surname)
Introduction: Mr./Ms. (full name), Attorney at Law,
                                  (firm name)
Conversation: Mr./Ms. (surname)
+Addressing spouse: See page 154
*Used less today than in the past, Esq. stands for esquire and is used
mostly between attorneys.

Businesspeople

Corporate President, Chief Executive, or Executive

Envelope:

	Official:	Mr./Ms. (full name)
		(title/position)
		(name of company)
		(address)
	Social:+	Mr./Ms. (full name)
		(address)
Invitation, in envelope:		Mr./Ms. (surname)
Salutation:		Dear Mr./Ms. (surname):
Complimentary close:		Sincerely,
Place card:		Mr./Ms. (surname)
Introduction:		Mr./Ms. (full name), (title/position), (name of company)
Conversation:		Mr./Ms. (surname)
+Addressing spouse:		See page 154

Man or Woman in Business

A woman may be referred to in business as Ms. regardless of her marital status.

Envelope:

	Official:	Mr./Ms. (full name)
		(name of business)
		(address)
	Social:+	Mr./Ms. (full name)
		(address)
Invitation, in envelope:		Mr./Ms. (surname)
Salutation:		Dear Mr./Ms. (surname):
Complimentary close:		Sincerely,
Place card:		Mr./Ms. (surname)
Introduction:		Mr./Ms. (full name)
Conversation:		Mr./Ms. surname)
+Addressing spouse:		See page 154

Private Citizens

Women

- Single woman: Eighteen years old or younger is known as Miss.
- Married woman: Married women make distinctions concerning their names.
- Women: A woman may be referred to as Ms. regardless of marital or business status. However, many unmarried women prefer and continue to use the title Miss, which is also correct.

Consult for the woman's preference.

Girl: Eighteen Years Old or Younger

Envelope:	Miss (full name)
	(address)
Invitation, in envelope:	Miss (surname)
Salutation:	Dear Miss (surname):
Complimentary close:	Sincerely,
Place card:	Miss (surname)
Introduction:	Miss (full name or surname)
Conversation:	(given name)

Married Woman

Sara Jones married Henry Roberts (*shared surname*). She can choose any of the following names:

Mrs. Henry Roberts
Mrs. Sara Roberts
Ms. Sara Roberts

or she can use her surname with her husband's:

Sara Jones Roberts
Sara J. Roberts

Married Woman Who Has Taken Her Husband's Surname+

This is the modern form.

Envelope:	(preferred name: woman's name can be any from "Married Woman") (address)
Invitation, in envelope:	Mrs./Ms. (full name or surname)
Salutation:	Dear Mrs./Ms. (surname): *or* Dear (given name),
Complimentary close:	Sincerely,
Place card:	Mrs./Ms. (surname)
Introduction:	(any of the preferred names)
Conversation:	(any of the preferred names)
+Addressing spouse:	See page 154

Married Couple (Woman Has Taken Her Husband's Surname)+

This is the traditional form.

Envelope:	Mr. and Mrs. Henry Jones (address)
Invitation, in envelope:	Mr. and Mrs. Jones
Salutation:	Dear Mr. and Mrs. Jones:
Complimentary close:	Sincerely,
Place card:	Mr./Mrs. Jones
Introduction:	Mr./Mrs. Henry Jones
Conversation:	Mr./Mrs. Jones
+Addressing spouse:	See page 154

Married Woman Who Has Kept Her Own Surname+

Many women prefer to keep their own surnames instead of taking their husband's.

A woman was Sara Jones before her marriage, afterward she is known as Ms. Sara Jones

She is married to Henry Roberts:

The couple is known as Mr. Henry Roberts *and* Ms. Sara Jones. The "and" indicates the distinction of marriage.

Envelope:	Mr. Henry Roberts and Ms. Sara Jones (address)

Invitation, in envelope:	Mr. Roberts and Ms. Jones
Salutation:	Dear Mr. Roberts and Ms. Jones:
Complimentary close:	Sincerely,
Place card:	Mr. Roberts/Ms. Jones
Introduction:	Mr. Henry Roberts/Ms. Sara Jones
Conversation:	Mr. Roberts/Ms. Jones
+Addressing spouse:	See page 154

Wife Who Outranks Husband in Professional or Educational Degree

The wife's name may appear first on correspondence, especially if she is the primary person to whom correspondence is addressed.

Dr. Sara Jones and Mr. Henry Jones

Couple Living Together but Not Married

One name below the other without "and" indicates the couple is not married. The first name listed on an envelope is traditionally that of a male or that of the person to whom the invitation is sent. Otherwise, when both addressees are male or female, names may be listed alphabetically.

COUPLE OF DIFFERENT SEXES

Envelope:	Mr. Henry Roberts
	Ms. Sara Jones
	(address)

COUPLE OF THE SAME SEX

Envelope:	Mr. Tom Judd
	Mr. John Smith
	(address)
Invitation, in envelope:	Mr. Roberts and Ms. Jones
	Mr. Judd and Mr. Smith
Salutation:	Dear Mr. Roberts and Ms. Jones:
	Dear Mr. Judd and Mr. Smith:
Complimentary close:	Sincerely,
Place card:	Mr. Roberts/Ms. Jones
	Mr. Judd/Mr. Smith

Introduction:	Mr. Henry Roberts/Ms. Sara Jones
	Mr. Tom Judd/Mr. John Smith
Conversation:	Mr. Roberts/Ms. Jones
	Mr. Judd/Mr. Smith

Widow

Envelope:	Mrs. Henry Roberts (*husband's name used*)
	Mrs. Sara Roberts (*given name*)
	(address)
Invitation, in envelope:	Mrs. Roberts
Salutation:	Dear Mrs. Roberts:
Complimentary close:	Sincerely,
Place card:	Mrs. Roberts
Introduction:	Mrs. (preferred full name)
Conversation:	Mrs. Roberts

Divorcee

A divorcee can keep her former husband's last name but not his given name. When children are involved, many women keep their former husband's surname. Others opt for the courtesy title Ms.

Still others return to their maiden name. In today's world, it has become common for a woman *not* to use her maiden name with her former husband's surname: Mrs. Jones Roberts. When there are multiple divorces, a woman usually takes back her maiden name.

Sara Jones was married to Henry Roberts.

Envelope:	Mrs. Sara Roberts
	Ms. Sara Roberts
	Ms. Sara Jones (*maiden name used*)
	(address)
Invitation, in envelope:	Mrs./Ms. (correct surname)
Salutation:	Dear Mrs. Roberts:
	Dear Ms. Roberts:
	Dear Ms. Jones: (*maiden name used*)
Complimentary close:	Sincerely,
Place card:	Mrs./Ms. (preferred surname)

| Introduction: | Mrs./Ms. (preferred full name) |
| Conversation: | Mrs./Ms. (preferred surname) |

Boy: Fourteen Years Old or Younger

Master is used as a title in a very formal way (e.g., for weddings or on invitations); it is abbreviated Mstr.

Envelope:	Master (full name)
	(address)
Invitation, in envelope:	Master (surname)
Salutation:	Dear Master (surname):
Complimentary close:	Sincerely,
Place card:	Master (surname)
Introduction:	Master (full name or surname)
Conversation:	(given name)

Men's Names and Titles

MAN NAMED AFTER HIS FATHER

A man named after his father, John March, is known as John March Jr. as long as his father is alive. He may drop the suffix (an affix added to the end of a word) or continue to use it after his father's death depending on his preference. If the man has used this suffix for many years, he may continue to keep that name for the future. Keeping this name also differentiates between his wife and his mother when his mother is living.

When a man is named after his father, John March Jr., he is called "the third": John March III.

MAN NAMED AFTER HIS GRANDFATHER, UNCLE, OR COUSIN

A man named after his grandfather, uncle, or cousin uses the suffix "II."

When the grandfather, uncle, or cousin is Henry March, the boy named for this person is Henry March II.

SPOUSE'S TITLE

The wife of each man uses the same suffix as her husband after her name (e.g., Mrs. John March Jr.).

When a name has a numeral suffix, John March III, no punctuation is necessary, though it is not incorrect to insert punctuation.

Junior, when spelled out, is spelled in lower case: junior.

Names for News Releases

General information to rely upon for official occasions:
The Honorable or His/Her Excellency is not required for news releases.
The Honorable abbreviated: T. H.
His/Her Excellency abbreviated: H. E.
When using The Honorable:
Correct example: The Honorable John Jones, secretary of state
    The Honorable Sam Smith, mayor of Miami
    The Honorable Mary Brown, U.S. senator (R/Utah)
    His Excellency Jose Garcia, minister of defense (country)
Incorrect example: The Honorable Mr. John Jones, secretary of state
    The Honorable Mayor Sam Smith, mayor of Miami
    The Honorable Sen. Mary Brown, U.S. senator
    His Excellency, Mr. Jose Garcia, minister of defense
The name of the guest, followed by profession, is adequate:
John Jones, Secretary of Labor
Sam Smith, mayor of Miami
Mary Brown, United States senator (R-UT.)
Jose Garcia, minister of defense, (country)
The U.S. president and spouse for a state dinner may or may not be listed, but when listed they should be listed by their official titles.
    The President and Mrs. (surname)
    The President and Ms. (full name)—surname is different
    The President and Mr. (full name)—the president is a woman
Listing foreign chief of state or head of government and spouse:
His Excellency (name), (title) of (country) and Mrs. (surname)—same surname
His Excellency (name), (title) of (country) and Ms. (full name)—surname is different
Her Excellency (name), (title) of (country) and Mr. (full name)—same or different surname

Royalty: His/Her Majesty (title) (name) of (country) and (title) (name)
    or (name) (title)
Example: His Majesty King Juan Carlos I of Spain and Queen Sofia
    Her Majesty Queen Elizabeth II of (country) and His Royal Highness
The Prince Philip, Duke of Edinburgh
(see chapter 5, Titles and Forms of Address)

Listing married and unmarried couples:
"and" between a couple's name indicates that they are married.
 If "not married," list the names one below the other without "and" or
    say "guest."
For a printed dinner list, it is also appropriate to list each name, one
below the other, with or without "and" "guest," or a title description
beside each name, be consistant.

Married Couples with Same Last Name

George Wells, editor, Simon & Shuster
and Sara Wells (professional title if applicable)

Married Couples with Different Last Names

Henry Roberts, President, Hart Inc.
and Sara Jones, Director, Berry and Co.

The "and" indicates that the couple is married.

Guest

George Winston, Attorney, Littlefield and Light
Helen West, guest, writer

or

Tom Jones, Watkins & Holt News
John Smith, pianist

One name under the other without "and" can show that one person is
a guest or that the couple is not married regardless of relationship.

ADDRESSING SPOUSES OF PRINCIPAL OFFICIALS

Social invitation salutations have a comma (,) following the surname.

The Honorable is used only in connection with those who are entitled to use it; for those not so entitled, omit The Honorable and use the preferred title of office or military rank. Honorifics are Mr. and Ms. in text; use accordingly.

The Honorable is rarely used with a title. It is one or the other.

For a foreign official, use "His/Her Excellency" or "The Honourable" as appropriate with correct spelling.

Wife as Spouse

Couple Shares a Surname

Envelope: Social: Mrs. (husband's full name)
                             (address)

Couple Shares a Surname and Husband Has the Title

In only one instance are an honorific and a title used together: when the couple shares a surname on a social invitation. The full name of the principal, at cabinet level, (husband) is not used, and in this case, "the" precedes the husband's title of office.
Envelope:
                Social: The Honorable
                             The Secretary of Commerce
                             and Mrs. (husband's surname)
                             (address)

Addressed after Cabinet Level

Envelope:
                Social: The Honorable (when entitled to use)
                             (full name)
                             and Mrs. (or title)/(rank) (surname)/
                             Ms. (full name)
                             (address)

Military

Envelope: (rank) (full name)
                                       and Mrs. (full name)
                                       (address)

Wife Has Different Surname

Envelope: Ms. (full name)
                                       (address)

Couple Does Not Share Surname

This form can be used when a couple does share a surname by writing
Mrs. (surname).

Envelope: The Honorable
                                       (full name of principal)
                                       Secretary of (department)
                                       and Ms. (full name)
                                       (address)

Both Spouses Are Entitled to an Honorific

The first name listed is the principal addressee.

Envelope: The Honorable
                                       (full name of principal)
                                       (title/office)
                                       and The Honorable
                                       (full name of spouse)
                                       (title/office)
                                       (address)

Both Spouses Have a Title, Wife Not Entitled to "The Honorable"

The first name listed on correspondence should be the person to
whom the correspondence is directed, and that person's address
should be used.

Envelope: The Honorable (*use only when addressee
                                       is entitled*)

	(full name of principal)
	(title/office)
	and
	(title) (full name)
	(address)
Invitation, in envelope:	Mrs./Ms. (surname)
	or with spouse
	Mr. (or title/rank) and Mrs. (or title/rank) (surname) *or*
	Mr. (surname) and Ms. (surname)
Salutation:	Dear Mrs./Ms. (or title/rank) (surname):
	Dear Mr. (or title/rank) and Mrs. (or title/rank) (surname):
	Dear Mr. (surname) and Ms. (surname):
Complimentary close:	Sincerely,
Place card:	Mrs./Ms. (or title/rank) (surname)
Introduction:	Mrs./Ms. (or title/rank) (full name)
Conversation:	Mrs./Ms. (or title/rank) (surname)

Husband as Spouse

A man's full name is always used.

Couple Shares a Surname

Envelope:	Social:	Mr. (full name)
		(address)

Couple Shares a Surname and Wife Has the Title

In only one instance are an honorific and a title used together: when a couple shares a surname on a social invitation. The full name of the principal (wife), at cabinet level, is not used, and in this case "the" precedes the wife's title of office.

Envelope:

Social: The Honorable
The Secretary of Transportation
and Mr. (full name)
(address)

Addressed after Cabinet Level

Envelope: The Honorable (when entitled to use)
(full name)
and Mr. (or title/rank) (full name)
(address)

Military

Envelope: (rank) (full name)
and Mr. (full name)
(address)

Husband Has Different Surname

Envelope: Mr. (full name)
(address)

Couple Does Not Share a Surname

Envelope: The Honorable
(full name of principal)
Secretary of (department)
and Mr. (full name)
(address)

Both Spouses Are Entitled to an Honorific

The first name listed is principal addressee.

Envelope: The Honorable
                             (full name of principal)
                             (title/office)
                             and The Honorable
                             (full name of spouse)
                             (title/office)
                             (address)

Both Spouses Have a Title, Husband Not Entitled to "The Honorable"

The first name listed on correspondence should be the person to whom the correspondence is directed, and that person's address should be used.

Envelope: The Honorable (*use only when entitled*)
                             (full name of principal)
                             (title/office)
                             and
                             (title/office) (full name)
                             (address)
Invitation, in envelope: Mr./ (title/rank) (surname) *or*
                             (title/rank) (surname) and Mr.
                             (surname) *or*
                             Ms. (surname) and Mr. (surname)
Salutation: Dear Mr./ (title/rank) (surname): *or*
                             Dear (title/rank)
                             (surname) and Mr. (title/rank)
                             (surname): *or*
                             Dear Ms. (surname) and Mr.
                             (surname):
Complimentary close: Sincerely,
Place card: Mr. (or title/rank) (surname)
Introduction: Mr. (or title/rank) (full name)
Conversation: Mr. (or title/rank) (surname)

Wife with Highest-Ranking Title: Example with Familiar Names

When a letter is sent to a specific addressee, the addressee is listed first, and his or her office address is used. If there is no specific addressee, the highest ranking in the Order of Precedence is listed first, and his or her office address is used.

Envelope:

Official:	The Honorable
	Elizabeth Dole
	Secretary of Labor
	and
	The Honorable
	Bob Dole
	United States Senator (when *current*
	Senate member)
	(secretary's office address)

Couple Has Same Surname

Envelope:

Social:	The Honorable
	The Secretary of Labor
	and
	The Honorable
	Bob Dole (no title used, *retired from*
	Senate)
	(secretary's address)
Invitation, in envelope:	The Secretary of Labor and
	Senator Dole
Salutation:	Dear Madam Secretary and
	Senator Dole:
Complimentary close:	Sincerely,
Place card:	The Secretary of Labor
	Senator Dole
Introduction:	The Honorable Elizabeth Dole
	Secretary of Labor
	The Honorable Bob Dole, United
	States Senator from (state) *or*
	Former United States Senator if retired

Conversation: Madam Secretary
                                 Senator Dole

Husband with Highest-Ranking Title: Example with Familiar Names

When a letter is sent to a specific addressee, that addressee is listed first, and his or her office address is used. If there is no specific addressee, the highest ranking in the Order of Precedence is listed first, and his or her office address is used.

Envelope:
                    Official and
                    Social: The Honorable
                                   William Jefferson Clinton
                                   and
                                   The Honorable
                                   Hillary Rodham Clinton
                                   Secretary of State
                                   (office address of former president)

Couple Has Same Surname, Addressed to First Addressee

Envelope
                                   The Honorable
                                   The Secretary of State
                                   and
                                   The Honorable
                                   William J. Clinton
                                   (office address of the secretary of state)
Invitation, in envelope: President Clinton and
                                   The Secretary of State
                                   (office address of the former president)
                                   or
                                   The Secretary of State and
                                   President Clinton
                                   (office address of the secretary of state)

Salutation:	Dear President Clinton and Madam Secretary: *or*
	Dear Mr. Clinton and Madam Secretary: *or*
	Dear Madam Secretary and President Clinton: *or*
	Dear Madame Secretary and Mr. Clinton:
Complimentary close:	Sincerely,
Place card:	President Clinton or Mr. Clinton
	The Secretary of State
Introduction:	The Honorable William J. Clinton, former president *or*
	Former president William J. Clinton
	The Honorable Hillary Rodham Clinton, secretary of state
Conversation:	President Clinton
	Mr. Clinton
	Madam Secretary

Chapter 6

Official Visits with the President

The President welcomes His Excellency Atal Bihari Vajpayee of The Republic of India to the White House South Lawn Ceremony for an Official Visit, September 2000. Courtesy William J. Clinton Presidential Library.

163

FOREIGN DIGNITARIES AND DIPLOMATS visit the United States for many reasons: upon official invitation by the U.S. president, the vice president, cabinet secretaries, business dignitaries, and groups, and often in a personal capacity to enjoy the country, to meet friends, or for medical appointments. These visits are an opportunity for the president and fellow Americans to welcome visitors by showcasing the best of the country, its citizens, and its hospitality.

When a foreign chief of state or head of government is invited for a visit by the U.S. president, it is usually for a state, official, or working visit. When the president is the host, the place of honor is to the president's right.

Components of these categories of visits may change with each administration.

TYPES OF VISITS

State Visits

An invitation for a state visit is issued by the U.S. president to a chief of state (reigning monarch, ruler, or president of a country). The invitation typically offers Blair House, located across the street from the White House, as the dignitary's residence during the visit. Red carpet, national anthems, military honor cordon, and colors are extended to visitors upon their arrival at Andrews Air Force Base. If they arrive at a commercial airport, a modified arrival ceremony is performed on the street outside Blair House.

A state visit consists of a South Lawn full-honors arrival ceremony, including a twenty-one-gun salute, a meeting with the president, a state luncheon at the State Department, and a state dinner at the White House. When a spouse accompanies the visiting dignitary, the spouse is included in the ceremony, dinner, and lunch but not the meeting with the president. The spouse of the U.S. president usually hosts a tea or coffee for the visiting spouse after the arrival ceremony while the meeting with the president is taking place.

Official Visits

An official visit is extended by the U.S. president to a head of government (usually a prime minister or chancellor of a foreign country). Official visits include a nineteen-gun salute. The dinner associated with an official visit is called a state dinner and a luncheon is held at the State Department.

Official Working Visits or Working Visits

The U.S. president may extend an invitation to a chief of state or head of government for an official working visit or a working visit. This invitation is usually for substantive talks. Elements of these visits are considered on a visit-by-visit basis.

While in Washington, the dignitary and part of the delegation may be invited to stay at Blair House. The length of stay, decided on a case-by-case basis, varies from one to two days. The visit will include a working meeting (possibly a working lunch or dinner), and sometimes media availability is offered.

Private Visits

A private visit occurs when a chief of state or head of government arrives in the United States without an invitation from the president. A private visit does not include a visit to the White House or a stay at Blair House. A meeting requested by the visiting dignitary or U.S. president would require approval, and arrangements would be made without involving ceremonies.

PLANNING FOR VISITS

The National Security Council recommends to the U.S. president a certain visit category with a foreign dignitary. Upon the president's approval, the arrangements are made to ensure the visit's success. Invitations are issued and dates are set. The chief of protocol hosts a meeting with the foreign ambassador to discuss the forthcoming visit. The chief of protocol and the foreign ambassador may then review any information that remains unclear.

A protocol visits officer will be assigned to formulate the itinerary and to coordinate logistics, ensuring that all details are implemented in the scenario program. This is a highly specialized and important job; the protocol officer will maintain and revise the visiting dignitary's minute-by-minute schedule.

Blair House Meeting

Outlining Visit Parameters

The U.S. Protocol Office arranges a meeting at Blair House to outline the parameters of the visit and to specify the responsibilities of the U.S. and visiting government. This meeting will ensure that every effort is being made for a successful visit. The chief of protocol calls the meeting with representatives from the following offices in attendance: the National Security Council, the State Department (country director or country desk officer), the Press Office, Blair House (general manager), the White House Social Office, the State Department Language Services, the U.S. Secret Service, and the Bureau of Diplomatic Security. It is extremely important for Secret Service and Diplomatic Security to be informed immediately when a visit is scheduled so they may make arrangements for the foreign leader's security. Foreign embassy officials and the foreign advance team are also in attendance. Present from the Protocol Office will be the assistant chief for visits, the visits protocol officer (who coordinates the visit), a ceremonials officer, the press officer, the officer handling spousal arrangements, the gifts officer, and any other protocol officer involved in the visit.

During the meeting, day-to-day events will be coordinated, security arrangements discussed, the process to ensure correct spelling and pronunciation of foreign names decided, site walk-throughs arranged, the customs and border-protection process discussed, the arrival at Andrews Air Force Base or a commercial airport detailed, and a clear understanding reached by all participants of the accommodations at Blair House.

Customs and Border Protection

In order to ensure the courteous and expeditious arrival of high-ranking foreign visitors at U.S. ports of entry, the Office of Protocol works in collaboration with Customs and Border Protection (Office of Homeland Security, Immigration and Customs Enforcement), the U.S. Secret Service, and the Bureau of Diplomatic Security. Together, they have established a set of formal procedures.

The following are among those eligible for courtesies of the port:

- Chiefs of state
- Heads of government
- Foreign ministers or other cabinet-level dignitaries
- Newly accredited foreign ambassadors
- Immediate family members of the ambassador
- Royal family members

To arrange for these courtesies of the port, it is incumbent upon foreign embassies to formally notify the Office of Protocol at least twenty-four (24) hours in advance. Such requests are forwarded to the agencies involved with port entry, enabling them to make necessary arrangements as outlined by the Office of Protocol.

Protocol Officer for Visits

This is an important and detail-oriented job, to say the least. The protocol visits officer is responsible for the day-to-day liaison with the foreign embassy and for drafting all the minute-by-minute schedules throughout the visit. The protocol officer will accompany the visiting dignitary throughout the visit and must coordinate all its phases, including the arrival at Andrews Air Force Base or a commercial airport, the daily events, and the dignitary's departure from Washington, D.C. On very special visits, when the dignitary's itinerary includes travel within the United States on official business, a protocol officer may be assigned to travel with the dignitary throughout the official trip.

ARRIVAL

Arrival at Andrews Air Force Base

On the arrival day or evening, for a state or official visit, the visiting chief of state or head of government normally arrives at Andrews Air Force Base, Maryland. The dignified arrival ceremony includes a red carpet and a military honor cordon with colors. The foreign and U.S. anthems are played. The chief of protocol greets the dignitary and traveling party along with the American ambassador to the visiting country, State Department officers, the foreign ambassador to the United States, members of the diplomatic corps, and foreign embassy officers. The dignitary may either motorcade or helicopter into Washington. When the dignitary arrives by helicopter, the view of Washington is spectacular; the Potomac River, the Washington Monument, Jefferson's and Lincoln's memorials, the U.S. Capitol, and the White House are in view.

When not arriving for a state or official visit, the dignitary is greeted at arrival by the chief of protocol or deputy chief of protocol and a welcoming committee. The dignitary will then motorcade into Washington.

Blair House Arrival

The general manager of Blair House stands at the house's front entrance to greet the arriving dignitary and party who will reside there during the visit. The beautifully appointed rooms and gracious Blair House staff warmly welcome the visitors to their home away from home. Every effort is made to accommodate the wishes of the visiting dignitary, the traveling party, and those invited to Blair House by the dignitary for visits and meetings during the stay. It is not mandatory that the dignitary accept the invitation to reside at Blair House, but most find this accommodation to be an excellent choice from the standpoint of security, privacy, and geography. (See chapter 12, "Blair House.")

Gift Exchange

Usually, the evening before or the morning of the visit, a gift exchange takes place between the U.S. and foreign protocol gift officers. A White House press release describes the gift or gifts given by the U.S. president. (See chapter 13, "Official Gift Giving.")

WHITE HOUSE EVENTS

State or Official Arrival Ceremonies on the South Lawn

A South Lawn arrival ceremony is given only for a state visit by a chief of state or an official visit by a head of government. The formal welcoming ceremony, which marks the beginning of a state or official visit, is arranged by the Military District of Washington, the Protocol

Office, and the White House Social Office. C-SPAN often provides live coverage of this impressive ceremony; therefore, the general public becomes part of the honored audience.

The morning begins early on the day of the formal state or official arrival welcoming ceremony, located on the South Lawn of the White House. The foreign dignitary and spouse have spent the night at Blair House and are preparing for a timely departure from the house in limousines, which will arrive at the South Lawn at the appointed hour for the welcoming ceremony.

The stately scene on the lawn is resplendent, showcasing American history and military ceremony, with the south side of the White House visible in the background. The other side of the lawn provides a view of the Washington Monument and the Jefferson Memorial. Invited guests (both American and foreign), members of Congress, and the media make up the audience. They arrive at their appointed times through the gates indicated on their invitations and stand in roped sections for their groups. Guests are given small flags of both the United States and the country being honored and a program listing the morning's events embossed with the presidential seal.

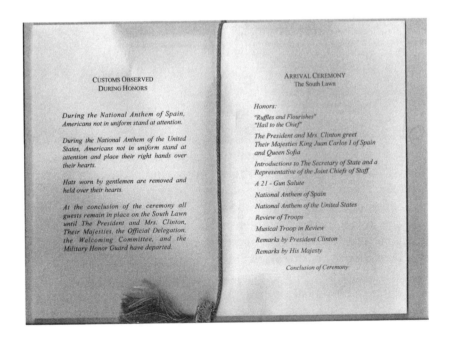

CUSTOMS OBSERVED
DURING HONORS

During the National Anthem of Spain, Americans not in uniform stand at attention.

During the National Anthem of the United States, Americans not in uniform stand at attention and place their right hands over their hearts.

Hats worn by gentlemen are removed and held over their hearts.

At the conclusion of the ceremony all guests remain in place on the South Lawn until The President and Mrs. Clinton, Their Majesties, the Official Delegation, the Welcoming Committee, and the Military Honor Guard have departed.

ARRIVAL CEREMONY
The South Lawn

Honors:
"Ruffles and Flourishes"
"Hail to the Chief"

The President and Mrs. Clinton greet Their Majesties King Juan Carlos I of Spain and Queen Sofia

Introductions to The Secretary of State and a Representative of the Joint Chiefs of Staff

A 21 - Gun Salute

National Anthem of Spain

National Anthem of the United States

Review of Troops

Musical Troop in Review

Remarks by President Clinton

Remarks by His Majesty

Conclusion of Ceremony

The welcoming committee consists of members of the U.S. official delegation who arrive and take their appointed places. Members of the foreign country's official delegation, including the dean of the diplomatic corps, arrive and are escorted to their places on the lawn. The Military District of Washington directs the army, marine, navy, air force, and coast guard ceremonial units of the armed forces lined in military position facing the reviewing stand and the White House; the pageantry is impressive. The Army Herald Trumpets located on the balcony of the South Portico sound a trumpet volley.

At the appointed time, the chief of protocol takes his or her place outside and to the left of the Diplomatic Room entrance door. The announcement, "Ladies and gentleman, the President of the United States, accompanied by Mrs./Mr./Ms. (preferred name of spouse)," is made.

The herald trumpets perform four ruffles and flourishes; the ruffles are played on drums, and the flourishes are played on bugles. The White House doors from the Diplomatic Room are opened by military aides, and the president and spouse walk out as "Hail to the Chief" is played. The president and spouse walk down the red carpet to greet the visiting chief of state or head of government, who arrives with his or her spouse in a black limousine.

A fanfare sounds, and military aides open the car doors. The couple steps forward to be welcomed by the U.S. president and spouse. The limousine moves forward, and the couples proceed to the welcoming committee, where they are introduced; the committee consists of the vice president and spouse, the secretary of state, a representative of the Joint Chiefs of Staff, and other top government officials.

The spouses walk to their places on the lawn and to the right front of the reviewing stand, and the dignitaries move to the reviewing stand. The chiefs of protocol from both countries take their places located on the lawn to the left rear of the platform; security agents are positioned in the area with protocol.

The foreign national anthem is played first, as a courtesy to the foreign leader's country, followed by the U.S. national anthem.

The following customs are observed during honors:

- During the national anthem of the visiting country, Americans stand at attention and face the the visiting country's flag.

- During the U.S. national anthem, "The Star Spangled Banner," Americans face the U.S. flag and place their right hands over their hearts.
- During the U.S. national anthem, civilian men wearing hats remove them, hold them at their left shoulder with their right hand, putting the right hand over their hearts. Women wearing caps or casual hats should do likewise, but do not have to remove formal hats.
- During the U.S. national anthem, military personnel salute but do not remove hats.
- During the anthems, a twenty-one-gun salute is fired for a chief of state.
- Following the anthems, there should be no clapping.
- During an official visit by a head of government, a nineteen-gun salute is fired.
- Cannons are located on the public lawn called the Ellipse.

GUN SALUTES AND VOLLEYS

Gun salutes are the firing of cannons or arms as a military or naval honor. In naval tradition, this custom began when a warship would fire its cannon harmlessly out to sea to show it was disarmed and not hostile. Today, a twenty-one-gun volley is the salute for a chief of state, decreasing with the rank of the recipient of the honor to a nineteen-gun volley for a head of government.

The president and visiting chief of state or head of government now review the troops. The president tips his or her head while passing the U.S. flag. The foreign leader may choose to stop and face the flags, salute, or tip his or her head, according to his or her normal custom. As the leaders approach the reviewing stand, they pass invited guests and have the option of shaking a few hands or continuing to walk and nod to guests.

The Old Guard Fife and Drum Corps, using instruments and wearing uniforms patterned after those worn by Continental army musicians during the American Revolution, parade past the reviewing stand. The only one of its kind in the armed forces, this unit is part of the Third United States Infantry. "Yankee Doodle," a song from colonial times, is played at all South Lawn state and official arrival ceremonies with the exception of a visit involving a dignitary from the United Kingdom, when it is not played.

The drum major of the unit is very distinguished. The drum major wears the light infantry cap, and the espontoon carried looks like a spear. The espontoon is a weapon that officers carried during the eighteenth century. Today, the drum major uses the weapon to issue silent commands while performing. The drum major is authorized to salute with the left hand, since the right hand is engaged with the espontoon. The drum major is the only person in the U.S. Army so authorized.

The president and the foreign dignitary make welcoming remarks, after which the commander of troops indicates that the arrival ceremony has concluded. The leaders exit the reviewing stand, are joined by their spouses, and walk to the entrance of the diplomatic reception room. They are followed by the chiefs of protocol and members of the official welcoming committee.

Receiving Line

The invited guests depart the lawn ceremony through the assigned gates. Normally at this time, a receiving line is formed in the White House Entrance Hall for the welcoming committee and foreign dignitaries to meet the U.S. president and the visiting chief of state or head of government.

Meetings

After the receiving line, the president escorts the foreign dignitary to the West Wing Oval Office for a meeting, often with government officials in attendance. Simultaneously, the other officials from both countries may have a separate meeting in the Roosevelt Room, or the foreign officials may depart for other meetings. A joint media appearance may or may not be available.

The spouses retire to the White House Yellow Oval Room on the second floor or another reception room in the White House for tea or coffee and conversation.

When the meetings conclude, the foreign leader usually departs from the West Wing, and his or her spouse from the diplomatic reception room, to continue their days as planned.

Media Affairs

Every attempt should be made to accommodate both foreign and national media at official venues. Planning must be done in advance for U.S. media and visiting media to know which events are open or closed to media coverage. Specific times for media arrival, departure, and setup, along with plans for transportation, are of extreme importance. Once the visit has been announced, the protocol press officer contacts the foreign embassy's Public Affairs

---

THE TALKING HAT

During a visit, when media availability is extended, the visiting dignitary speaks from the president's lectern or from another lectern nearby. Occasionally, the dignitary will not be the same height as the U.S. president, as was the case in 1991 when Queen Elizabeth II spoke at the White House.

That day, the lectern was adjusted to the president's height—approximately 6'2". The queen, however, stands only about 5'4". From the media's viewpoint, the queen was reduced to a hat bobbing up and down as she gave her address behind a towering lectern. The line in the paper the next day read: "The Talking Hat."

Ideally, it will never again appear that "the hat" is doing the talking. The Queen graciously remarked to the U.S. Congress in a later address that she hoped they could "see" her. Such an example proves once again that when it comes to protocol, the devil is in the details.

Office to work out details. There will be a confirmation list of the number of media personnel who may attend an event and have been given clearance to access an event. Dress code for the media is business attire.

Adequate time should be allocated for security clearance of media equipment. The official photographer should know the instructions for his or her participation in each event.

State Dinners

State dinners are held on the evening of the state or official arrival. For additional information, see chapter 7, "Official Entertaining."

ARLINGTON NATIONAL CEMETERY

When the foreign dignitary wishes to lay a wreath at Arlington National Cemetery at the Tomb of the Unknowns (also known as the Tomb of the Unknown Soldier), the protocol visits officer makes arrangements for the visit to Arlington, and the protocol press officer arranges media coverage of the event.

As the dignitary's motorcade approaches on Roosevelt Drive, an appropriate cannon salute is fired while the party is en route. The chief of protocol or deputy chief greets the dignitary at the East Entrance and introduces him or her to the host. The host is usually the commanding general of the Military District of Washington. The Military District of Washington ceremonies officer will then brief the dignitary concerning the ceremony.

The entire party will be escorted opposite the colors of the dignitary's country. The party will halt. The color guard will then come to "present arms," and all members of the official party will salute the colors. The troops will be brought to present arms, and the band will then sound four "ruffles and flourishes," followed by the national anthem of the dignitary's country, then the U.S. national anthem, during which the official party and all spectators will salute (which means standing at attention or with hand over heart, whichever is appropriate).

Following honors, the guard will "order arms." The dignitary will be escorted up the stairway and halt in front of the tomb, at which point the troops will be brought to present arms. The colors and the official party will follow, halting on the steps. At this point, the wreath bearer and the bugler will move forward. Assisted by the wreath bearer, the dignitary will place the wreath on a stand located in front of the dignitary. As this is occurring, the bugler will move forward. When the dignitary has placed his or her hands upon the wreath, the honor guard will come to present arms. The dignitary will move forward, hands on the wreath as the wreath bearer backs toward the tomb and places the wreath in position. The dignitary will then return to his or her position beside the host and assume a proper position to salute (standing at attention or with hand over heart, whichever is appropriate). The drummer will sound four muffled ruffles, at which time the official party will render the appropriate salute, and the bugler will sound taps.

Following taps, the honor guard will be brought to order arms. The host will escort the dignitary to the right of the tomb, where the dignitary may read the inscription. The color guard with the colors of the dignitary's country will follow the same route into the plaza and continue through the colonnade to the Amphitheater West Entrance to await the dignitary's departure. The party will then pass into the Display Room, where the superintendent of Arlington National Cemetery will escort the dignitary on a tour of the Display Room. After farewell remarks have been exchanged, the dignitary and official party depart from the Amphitheater West Entrance and leave Arlington National Cemetery through the Memorial Gate.

The public is often touring at the Tomb of the Unknowns while this ceremony is taking place. The general public may stay and observe the ceremony.

JOINT MEETING OF CONGRESS

The embassy for the visiting foreign dignitary makes arrangements for visits with certain senators or members of the House of Representatives at the U.S. Capitol upon the request of the foreign dignitary.

When a foreign dignitary addresses a joint meeting of Congress, a detailed scenario of the event will be organized by the protocol visits officer and the Ceremonials Division of the Office of Protocol. The address will take place in the House of Representatives Chamber at the U.S. Capitol. Respective sergeants at arms serve as protocol officers for the House of Representatives and the Senate.

DEPARTURE FROM ANDREWS AIR FORCE BASE

When a state or official visit is concluded, the chief of protocol or deputy chief of protocol will bid farewell, usually along with the same individuals who formed the Andrews Air Force Base welcoming committee. The departure ceremony is appointed with a red carpet and includes the appropriate nineteen- or twenty-one-gun salute, the Army Herald Trumpets, and a military honor cordon through which the dignitary passes on his or her way to the departing aircraft for the farewell.

At the conclusion of a working or an official working visit, the chief or deputy chief of protocol and the departure committee bid farewell. No other ceremony is included at Andrews Air Force Base or another departure airport in the area.

U.S. PROTECTIVE DIVISIONS

U.S. Secret Service

The U.S. Secret Service is a division of the Department of Homeland Security. The Special Agents and Uniformed divisions make up the service's sworn members.

The U.S. Secret Service is the federal governmental law-enforcement agency that protects, through its Special Agents Division, the U.S. president, former presidents, vice presidents, presidential and vice presidential candidates, and their families. The Secret Service also provides protection for foreign chiefs of state and heads of government when these dignitaries are visiting the United States. Protection is provided for chiefs of state and heads of government from their entry into until their departure from the United States.

The Secret Service has two distinct areas of responsibility: protection (ensuring the safety of important government officials) and treasury services (the prevention and investigation of counterfeiting of U.S. currency and bond notes and of major fraud).

From the viewpoint of the Office of Protocol, the Secret Service Presidential Protective Division, with which the Office of Protocol works daily, deserves the respect of every citizen for the tireless and dedicated services its agents perform for the nation. The Secret Service is one of the most elite law-enforcement organizations in the world.

Bureau of Diplomatic Security

The security and law-enforcement agency of the U.S. Department of State, the Bureau of Diplomatic Security, protects the secretary of state. This bureau also provides security for foreign ministers and other foreign high-ranking officials, including high-ranking royalty (other than chiefs of state and heads of government) from their arrival in until their departure from the United States.

Diplomatic Security has become a world leader in the protection of people, property, and information. In the areas of international investigation (threat analysis, cybersecurity, counterterrorism, and security technology), Diplomatic Security operates globally. Diplomatic Security also investigates passport and visa fraud and conducts personnel security investigations.

U.S. diplomatic missions around the world operate under a security program designed by Diplomatic Security, which plays a role in protecting U.S. embassies and personnel overseas, thereby helping to ensure that the United States can conduct diplomatic relations safely and securely.

Personnel in the Office of Protocol work daily with, and have great respect for, the agents of the Bureau of Diplomatic Security. The agents and agency are to be commended for their work in providing a safe and secure environment within which to accomplish the goals of foreign policy.

Telephone Numbers for Offices Related to National and International Security

United States Secret Service:	(202) 406-5708
Bureau of Diplomatic Security:	(571) 345-2502
Department of Homeland Security:	(202) 282-8000
Central Intelligence Agency:	(703) 482-0623
Federal Bureau of Investigation:	(202) 324-3000

Chapter 7

Official Entertaining

Madeleine K. Albright, Secretary of State, hosts the Diplomatic Corps and spouses for dinner, Benjamin Franklin Room, State Department. Author's collection.

FORMAL DINNER AT THE WHITE HOUSE

WASHINGTON, D.C., IS THE NATION'S CAPITAL and, to many, the capital of entertaining.

The president's residence, the White House, is the ultimate backdrop for dinners at which the president honors chiefs of state, heads of government, and other distinguished guests.

Red Carpet Rolls Out

An invitation to a state dinner at the White House (for a chief of state or head of government) is highly coveted; any dinner at the White House is certain to set the standard for excellence in entertaining for a formal event. A view of what those on the guest list can expect follows.

Invitation Is Extended

Events at the White House are sometimes planned with a short amount of turnaround time. Guests are often notified first by telephone or e-mail so that they can plan for the event and make reservations. A formal invitation will follow by mail.

An invitation to dinner at the White House will be embossed with the gold presidential seal at the top. It will read,

> The President and Mrs. (surname)
> or
> The President and Ms. (full name)
> or
> The President and Mr. (full name)
> request the pleasure of the company of
> (guest's name or title)
> at a dinner to be held at
> The White House
> on day, month, and year
> at (time in text) o'clock.

The invitation will usually include two enclosure cards. The first card reads,

On the occasion of the visit of
(the appropriate title and name of the honored guest or guests)

On the occasion of the visit of
Their Majesties
King Juan Carlos I
of Spain
and Queen Sofia

The second card reads,

Please respond to
The Social Secretary
The White House
at your earliest convenience
giving name, date of birth and social security number of your guest.

The appropriate medium for response will be noted in the lower left corner. Response should be immediate (within twenty-four hours).

Please respond to
The Social Secretary
The White House
at your earliest convenience
giving name, date of birth
and social security number of your guest
(202) 456-2510

At the entrance gate, invited guests will be required to present photo and other required identification

An invitation to the White House, extended by the president, cannot be declined except under the most desperate situations; it takes precedence over all other invitations. There are only four acceptable reasons for declining the honor of such an invitation:

- A recent death in the family
- Serious illness
- Unavoidable absence far from Washington
- A family wedding

In the note of regret, the reason should be stated.

Responding

An acceptance or regret should be conveyed to the White House social secretary in the manner it was received or by express mail within twenty-four hours of receipt.

Evening Attire

Dress will be specified on the invitation. In most cases, it will be black-tie. Women may wear a long floor-length gown or short, dressy cocktail dress; it is also acceptable to wear dressy, long pants with an elegant top. Men wear formal black tie, which may be rented if not owned. It is always in good taste to follow conservative dress standards.

PEDAL PUSHERS PUSH THE BOUNDARIES

At one state dinner, a traditional black tie occasion, White House guests looked on in disbelief; they could practically hear fashion police sirens echoing from the dining room walls. A celebrity and icon of American domesticity had worn silk pedal pushers to the dinner. This "statement" (seemingly broadcasting a message of nonconformity) reminded all that celebrity status isn't necessarily indicative of one's grasp of etiquette or of some celebrities' willingness to comply with expectations regarding attire.

Occasionally, the invitation will say white tie. A white-tie occasion is usually reserved for royalty. Gloves are normally worn to a white-tie event.

When and How to Arrive

Never arrive late; instead, be a few minutes early. Guests usually enter through the East Entrance. It is most convenient to engage a driver who can drop off and pick up guests at this entrance.

The White House Social Office staff will greet and confirm names on the guest list. Guests must pass through a magnetometer and then proceed along the East Colonnade, where a coat check is provided, when needed.

The media are stationed in the East Portico, where pictures are snapped and celebrity comments are occasionally solicited.

Cell phones must be turned off or left in automobiles.

There is no smoking in the White House.

When you arrive in the lower Cross Hall, the Vermeil (pronounced "ver-MAY") Room is located on the left. Paintings of former first ladies are on display there. (The only ladies' powder room for White House guests is located there as well.)

The Library is on the right, with a fireplace area occasionally used for television interviews. Historical books and significant paintings are kept in this room. (The only gentlemen's room for White House guests is also located there.)

Before ascending the stairway, guests will be given a table seating card bearing the guest's name on its outer envelope; a military aide will also use it to announce the guest's entrance into the East Room and then to the president for the receiving line.

Being Announced into the East Room

White House social aides (young men and women from all branches of the U.S. military services) will escort guests to the East Room. Guests will present their table seating/announcement cards and be formally announced into the room. Guests should retain their seating/announcement cards for the receiving-line announcement.

Guests should introduce themselves, converse, and enjoy available refreshments. Many guests may be famous, and it is acceptable to introduce oneself to a guest if he or she is not engaged in conversation; however, it is not acceptable to ask for an autograph or photograph.

PROTOCOL FROM TWO PERSPECTIVES

At a White House dinner during my time as chief of protocol, I introduced myself to Goldie Hawn, telling her how much I had enjoyed her hilarious film *Protocol*. She flattered me, telling me that I was the "real thing" and we stepped to the side of the room to swap our two very different versions of protocol stories.

During this time, the president and spouse are greeting the honored guest and spouse at the North Portico.

The president, spouse, and honored guests will then go to the Yellow Oval Room on the second floor for greetings, then return via the grand stairway to the Entrance Hall, during which time the U.S. Marine Band will play "Hail to the Chief."

The music can be heard in the East Room, and guests sometimes think that the president is entering in the room, but that is not the case. The president, spouse, and honored guests are arriving at the Entrance Hall for official pictures and forming the receiving line in the Cross Hall.

Arriving in the East Room

Of special interest in the East Room is the famous portrait of George Washington on the east wall. This portrait is actually a copy made by Gilbert Stuart which he painted from his original painting, *Lansdowne*, which hangs in the National Portrait Gallery of the Smithsonian Institution. Dolley Madison had the replica *Lansdowne* cut from its frame to be saved before the British torched the White House during the War of 1812. This portrait is the only object that has remained in the White House since it was first occupied, around 1800.

On that same wall, to the left, hangs the posthumous portrait of Martha Washington, painted by Eliphalet Frazer Andrews in 1878.

Martha Washington died in 1802 after George Washington's death in December 1799.

In 1938, the Steinway & Son piano company gave the White House an elegant grand piano. It is supported by gilt legs, formed as American eagles, designed by Eric Gugler, and decorated with gilt stenciling by Dunbar Beck. This national treasure is sometimes moved to the Entrance Hall.

It Happened in the East Room

Abigail Adams hung the presidential laundry in the unfinished East Room in 1801 because no convenient place was available outside.

During the Civil War, Union troops occupied the room. After his assassination, President Abraham Lincoln lay in repose on a black-draped catafalque in this room. Seven of the eight presidents who died in office, including Lincoln and John F. Kennedy, lay in repose in the East Room prior to burial.

Theodore Roosevelt's children were known to have roller-skated in the East Room.

Receiving Line

Guests will be asked to have their seating/announcement cards ready to hand to a military aide, who will announce them to the president, the honored guest, the president's spouse, and the honored guest's spouse.

Guests proceed through the receiving line following the Order of Precedence, meaning that on diplomatic occasions, a man often precedes his spouse or guest.

Members of the media, gathered behind ropes, take photos and record names. The White House photographer takes a photo of each guest greeting the president, which will be mailed at a later date.

Forms of Address

President:	Mr. President (when male)
	Madam President (when female)
The president's spouse:	Mrs., Ms., Mr. (surname)

Honored guests: (titles as they appear on the first
                                   enclosure of the event invitation)

Receiving Line Etiquette

- Dispose of a drink or anything in hand before entering the receiving line.
- Remove gloves to shake hands.
- Do not engage the president, spouse, or visiting chief of state or head of government or spouse in conversation. "Good evening, Mr. or Madam President" or "How do you do?" is sufficient. Many guests must pass through the line in a limited time.
- At this time, do not ask for an autograph or make any special requests.

State Dining Room

The State Dining Room seats approximately 140 guests. Above the mantel hangs the portrait of Abraham Lincoln, painted in 1869, by George P. A. Healy. Of special interest in the State Dining Room is "The White House Prayer," which is carved into the fireplace mantel. The prayer was written in a letter from John Adams to his wife, Abigail.

> I Pray Heaven to Bestow
> The Best of Blessings on
> THIS HOUSE
> and on All that shall hereafter
> Inhabit it. May none but Honest
> and Wise Men ever rule under This Roof

Entering the State Dining Room

A social aide will direct guests to the State Dining Room. Guests will present their seating cards and be directed to their tables.

Husbands and wives are not seated at the same table.

FOLLOW THE LEADER

A traditional tale that circulates around the White House illustrates that it is not always in guests' best interest to do as their host or hostess does.

A group of White House guests with table manner trepidations were eager to conduct themselves appropriately while being hosted by President Calvin Coolidge. Thus, when the president removed his coffee cup from its saucer and poured coffee into it, the guests did the same. He added cream, they followed, and when he added sugar, they added sugar. They were quite embarrassed, however, when he lowered the saucer to the floor to be lapped by the cat.

An appointed government official, cabinet member, chief of protocol, or the like, will be the table's host or hostess.

It is polite for guests to introduce themselves to their table host or hostess and to other guests before being seated. The correct way to take a seat at, and rise to depart from, a chair at the table is to sit and rise from the chair's left (The chair's left is determined when standing behind the chair.) It is acceptable not to do this, but it is easier when everyone knows this approach.

President, Spouse, Honored Guest, and Spouse Enter

"Hail to the Chief" is played by the U.S. Marine Band, The Presidents' Own. The president, spouse, and honored guest(s) are announced. Guests should stand and remain standing until the president is seated.

White House Butlers

Many of the White House butlers have been part of the White House professional staff for years. Their skills and courteous manners are a delight to observe as they move flawlessly around the room.

President's Toast and Return Toast

When the president and all guests are seated, the media enter the State Dining Room to report on the traditional president's toast.

The president toasts the visiting chief of state or head of government, who returns the toast.

Guests remain seated, lifting their glasses after each toast.

The media depart, and dinner is served.

Dinner Is Served

Each place will be preset with four glasses: two for white wine, one for red wine, and one for water.

Silverware is appropriate to the meal. A good rule to remember is that utensils are always used from the outside in. The dessert spoon and fork are placed at the top of the dinner plate to be used when dessert is served.

A service plate, linen napkin, place card, table number card, and menu card will be on the table.

The china used at dinner is from the White House china collection. The top of the menu card will be embossed with the gold presidential seal. A guest should place the napkin in his or her lap and, after reading the menu card, place the card just above the plate.

Dinner service may be French (the server holds the platter to the left of the guest and serves the food onto the plate) or American (the server holds the platter to the guest's left, and the guest serves the food onto his or her plate using utensils on the platter). Dishes will be removed from the right.

There are two different styles for holding utensils: American (holding the fork tines up and keeping the fork in the right hand) and European or Continental (holding the fork tines down and keeping the fork in the left hand and the knife in the right throughout the meal). Either is correct.

Guests should wait until their host or hostess lifts his or her fork before eating.

Finger bowls may or may not be used. While they always add nostalgia to the meal, many question what to do when the bowl is set before them. At the White House, finger bowls (filled with water, a flower petal floating on top) are brought to each place on a dessert plate lined with a doily. After dipping his or her fingertips in the bowl, one hand at a time, then drying them with the napkin, the guest should set the bowl and doily aside at the top left of the serving plate. The dessert will then be served on the remaining dessert plate that accompanied the finger bowl.

When dinner is over, the napkin should be placed, lightly folded, on the table where the plate was, if it has been removed, or to its left if the plate is still on the table.

Guests may take the menu and place cards upon their departure.

Conversation

It is difficult to talk across a table of ten, so it is not necessary to try. It is important to talk to the person to one's right and left and not to leave anyone in close proximity out of the conversation. The old rule of speaking first to the person on one's right and then to the person on one's left is no longer used in the United States, except when a guest of honor is sitting to one's right.

Leaving the Table

A guest should not leave the table except for the most urgent reason; a social aide will immediately assist a guest who departs in the middle of the dinner. If an unexpected departure from the table occurs during the meal, but the guest is returning, the napkin should be placed, lightly folded, in the guest's chair.

Strolling Strings

When the president has finished dinner and dessert has been served, the Army or Air Force Strolling Strings enter the State Dining Room. These musicians walk through the room playing a series of songs performed exclusively from memory and without a conductor. The president stands, thanks them, and invites the guests to join him or her in the East Room for entertainment.

Guests stand as the president, spouse, chief of state or head of government, and spouse leave the room. Guests then follow to be seated in the East Room. The Strolling Strings line either side of the Cross Hall playing music, and butlers offer trays of demitasse and after-dinner drinks along the Cross Hall.

After-Dinner Entertainment

Programs for after-dinner entertainment are placed on the guests' seats prior to their arrival. After-dinner entertainment may occasionally take place in the State Dining Room. Entertainment may range from jazz to opera and will last approximately twenty minutes. At its conclusion, the president and spouse take the stage and thank the performers.

PLÁCIDO DOMINGO

Plácido Domingo has been called a "Renaissance Man of Music" because of his important activities in singing, conducting and administration. His singing career takes him to the major opera stages of the world in a repertory of one hundred sixteen different roles, more than any other singer in history. He conducts not only opera with the major companies in the United States and abroad, but also purely symphonic concerts with some of the foremost orchestras. Mr. Domingo is the Artistic Director of the Washington Opera and the Artistic Director designate of the Los Angeles Opera. He has made more than one hundred recordings for which he has won eight Grammy Awards.

Born in Madrid, Mr. Domingo moved to Mexico at the age of eight with his parents, who formed their own zarzuela company and traveled across the country performing the popular Spanish genre. It was the lively zarzuelas—which originated in 17th century Spain and masterfully combine musical ensembles, arias, dialogue, popular songs and comedy—that gave him his first love of music. In his teens he studied piano, conducting and voice at the Mexico City Conservatory. His operatic singing debut was in Monterrey as Alfredo in *La Traviata*. After two and a half years with the Israel National Opera he joined the New York City Opera, where he created the title role of Ginastera's *Don Rodrigo* in its United States premiere. He gave his Metropolitan Opera debut in 1968 as Maurizio in *Adriana Lecouvreur* and has since performed there on more than four hundred occasions. When he sang *I Pagliacci* last fall, it was his eighteenth opening night of a Met season, thus surpassing the record set by Caruso at the beginning of the last century.

The President and Mrs. Clinton welcome Plácido Domingo with great pleasure, as his friendship with the leaders of both countries serves as a testament to the musical bond between two cultures. Tonight Mr. Domingo celebrates the visit of Their Majesties King Juan Carlos I of Spain and Queen Sofia with a performance that features some of the most beloved zarzuelas of the 20th century.

PROGRAM

Selections by
Plácido Domingo
Tenor
Ana Maria Martinez
Soprano
Eugene Kohn
Piano

"No puede ser!"   *Pablo Sorozábal*
LA TABERNERA DEL PUERTO   (1897-1988)

"D'España vengo"   *Pablo Luna*
EL NIÑO JUDIO   (1879-1942)

"Madrileña bonita"   *Pablo Sorozábal*
LA DEL MANOJO DE ROSAS   (1897-1988)

"En mi tierra extremeña"   *F. Moreno Torroba*
LUISA FERNANDA   (1891-1982)

"Tonight"   *Leonard Bernstein*
WEST SIDE STORY   (1918-1990)

Dancing

The guests are next invited to the Entrance Hall for dancing. There they enjoy champagne as the president and spouse escort the chief of state or head of government to the North Portico to bid them farewell. The president and spouse dance the first dance, after which guests may join in. The president and spouse will be the first to retire to their private residence; guests depart shortly thereafter.

Departing

Social and military aides will direct guests back to the East Entrance for departure. Cars will be called by aides according to the numbers associated with guests' names upon their arrival.

Helpful Information for This Occasion

Occasionally, dinner may be held in either the East Room or a beautifully appointed tent on the lawn rather than in the State Dining Room.

Gifts are not to be brought to any formal occasion. If giving a gift is appropriate, it should be sent before or after the event to the White House Social Office. An invitation to the White House in and of itself does not necessitate a gift.

A thank-you note may be written if desired, but it is not inappropriate not to do so.

STATE LUNCHEON AT THE STATE DEPARTMENT

Often the location for official luncheons and dinners, the State Department is therefore visited by many diplomats and officials (both foreign and domestic). It is the cabinet-level foreign affairs agency of the U.S. government, and its primary focus is U.S. foreign policy. The State Department is administered by the secretary of state.

The secretary of state and/or the vice president hosts a luncheon in the Benjamin Franklin State Dining Room at the State Department following a state or official arrival ceremony on the South Lawn at the

White House. Business attire should be worn. A receiving line will precede or follow the luncheon. During the luncheon, the secretary of state and/or the vice president and the visiting foreign official will make remarks.

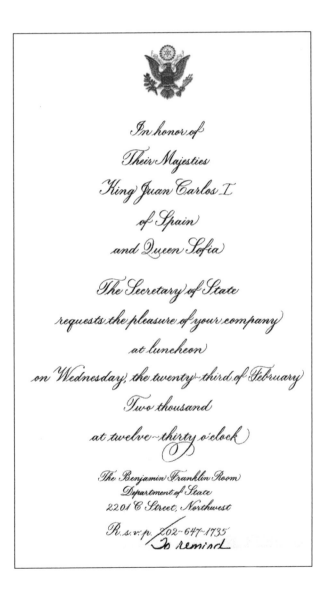

In honor of

Their Majesties

King Juan Carlos I

of Spain

and Queen Sofia

The Secretary of State

requests the pleasure of your company

at luncheon

on Wednesday, the twenty-third of February

Two thousand

at twelve-thirty o'clock

The Benjamin Franklin Room
Department of State
2201 C Street, Northwest

R.s.v.p. 202-647-1735
To remind

FORMAL DINNER AT THE STATE DEPARTMENT

Diplomatic Reception Rooms

The Diplomatic Reception Rooms on the eighth floor of the State Department are quite handsome. Used for official entertaining, these rooms house a collection of museum-caliber American furnishings. (These American furnishings date from 1750 through 1825 and comprise one of the finest collections in the United States.) The collection was assembled under the direction of the former chairman of the Fine Arts Committee, Clement E. Conger. Conger assisted in the architectural transformation of the Diplomatic Reception Rooms from ordinary spaces into the stately areas used today. The funds to purchase these fabulous antiques were all donated; no tax dollars were used to acquire the collection.

After stepping from the elevator, one arrives in the Edward Vason Jones Memorial Hall. The first room in the hall is modeled after the drawing room at Marmion, an eighteenth-century house in King George County, Virginia. The architect whose name now is associated with the room was the architect who transformed the main reception rooms into visions of splendor.

Entrance Hall

The design of the Entrance Hall leading to the other rooms is also based on plantation houses on the James River in Virginia: Carter's Grove and Westover. The hall boasts thirteen-foot ceilings, and a Tabriz rug tops its mahogany floor. Adorning this hall is a cut-glass chandelier of English origin dating from the 1800s and a bombé desk from Boston (circa 1755–1770). Above the desk hangs a New York Looking Glass (circa 1765). One of the collection's masterpieces, a secretary desk (circa 1753) by Benjamin Frothingham Jr., graces the wall to the left.

Gallery

Palladian windows (tripart windows with a larger and typically arched center panel) inspired by Jefferson-era Philadelphia homes bookend the room. Portraits, landscape paintings, and American Queen Anne and Chippendale furniture complete the visual panorama as guests make their way to the luncheon or dinner they have been invited to attend.

John Quincy Adams State Drawing Room

It is here that the secretary of state or vice president receives guests at state or official luncheons and dinners. The furniture comprises masterpieces of eighteenth-century cabinetmakers. Portraits displayed on the raised-panel walls with hand-carved architectural details include those of John Quincy Adams and his wife, Louisa Catherine, one of John Jay, one of Andrew Jackson, and another of Henry Clay. For those who find history intriguing, not much can parallel the thrill of seeing silver pieces crafted by Paul Revere, Chinese export porcelain that once belonged to George Washington, and the desk on which the Treaty of Paris was signed in 1783, ending the American Revolution.

"ONE DESK I DON'T NEED TO SEE"

During a visit to the State Department, former prime minister of Great Britain Lady Thatcher was asked if she would like to view the desk on which the Treaty of Paris was signed. The signing of this treaty, by U.S. and British representatives in 1783, ended the war of the American Revolution. Lady Thatcher refused, remarking, "That is one desk I don't need to see."

Thomas Jefferson State Reception Room

As they proceed to the monumental State Dining Room through the Jefferson Reception Room, guests view a masterpiece of neoclassical design with perfect proportions, Doric entablatures (moldings and bands lying horizontally above a column, resting on its capital), pedimented glass doors, triple-sash windows, and an eighteenth-century Cararra marble mantle.

Benjamin Franklin State Dining Room

The largest of the Diplomatic Reception Rooms was named after Benjamin Franklin, who is known as the "Father of the American Foreign Service." This room was completed in 1985 after an architectural redesign by John Blatteau.

    A portrait of Benjamin Franklin, painted by David Martin in London in 1767, hangs at the far end of the room. The room's long walls are lined with full-standing scagliola (colored and polished plaster) Corinthian columns; engaged columns (columns embedded in a wall and projecting from its surface) adorn the short walls. The decorative plaster ornament of the entablature and the coffered (decorative sunken panels) cove above the entablature are gilded to enhance the appearance of the room. The Great Seal of the United States, formed in plaster and coated in gilt, decorates the center of the ceiling. Eight

Adam-style cut-glass chandeliers shine brilliantly to illuminate the room's features.

The floor is covered with a Savonnerie-style carpet designed especially for the room. The carpet's design elements include the Great Seal of the United States, symbols of the four important crops of the early republic, the four seasons, and in the field, fifty stars representing the states of the Union. Both foreign and American guests are entertained in the impressive State Dining Room.

TRUMAN DINNER IN THE BENJAMIN FRANKLIN ROOM

On the evening of Thursday, September 21, 2000, at seven o'clock, Secretary of State Madeleine K. Albright hosted a dinner in honor of the dedication of the State Department building as the Harry S. Truman Building. As an honor to Harry S. Truman, former U.S. president (April 12, 1945–January 20, 1953), the menu for the dinner was the same as that served at the White House on October 11, 1949, at a dinner President Truman held in honor of His Excellency Jawaharlal Nehru, prime minister of India. The menu and the invitation are reproduced here to provide a glimpse of Truman-era cuisine, which made for a delightful evening of reminiscence for guests fifty-one years later.

ANECDOTES ATTRIBUTED TO
PRESIDENT HARRY S. TRUMAN

Truman described his affinity for the Missouri mule: "My favorite animal is the mule. He has more horse sense than a horse. He knows when to stop eating and he knows when to stop working."

Truman remarked of Princess Elizabeth during her first visit to Washington in November, 1951: "When I was a little boy I read about a fairy princess. And there she is."

Following Truman's nomination to the vice presidency in 1944, his cousin, Gen. Ralph E. Truman, told Truman's mother that she must be proud of her son. She responded with a smile, "Oh, well, I liked him just as well before."

---

*On the occasion of the
Dedication of the Harry S Truman Building
The Secretary of State
requests the pleasure of your company
at dinner
on Thursday, the twenty-first of September
Two thousand
at seven o'clock*

R.s.v.p.
202-647-1735
Business Attire

The Benjamin Franklin Room
Department of State
2201 C Street, Northwest

Menu

Soup Julienne
Bread Sticks
Assorted Olives   Celery Hearts

Panned Fillet of Sole
Tyrolienne Sauce   Sliced Cucumbers
Brown and White Sandwiches

Roasted Turkey
Oyster Dressing
Brown Gravy   Cranberry Sauce

French String Beans
Buttered Beets   Casserole of Squash

Gingerale and Peach Salad
Shredded Lettuce   French Dressing
Toasted Triscuits

Vanilla Ice Cream
and Orange Ice Molds
Angel Food Cake

Nuts   Candy   Demitasse   Liqueurs

ENTERTAINING BY GOVERNMENT
OFFICIALS AND PRIVATE CITIZENS

The designation "official entertaining" in Washington, D.C., or anywhere in the United States simply means that official guests of the United States are present. The president, the first family, and administration officials, senior members of executive agencies, members of Congress, members of the diplomatic corps, and private individuals all entertain officially.

Customs for entertaining, including those traditions employed for functions at the White House, may vary with each incoming administration. The following will provide a broad outline of what can be expected and will illustrate those practices that have become standard procedure for diplomatic entertaining over the years. Washington is a city of government diplomatic entertaining; consequently, it serves as an example for diplomatic entertaining around the United States, both officially and privately.

Official entertaining is usually intended to develop relationships between people that will strengthen bonds within and between the government, foreign nations, the diplomatic corps, the media, and business and social communities. This type of entertaining helps achieve U.S. objectives, both domestically and abroad.

Dinners and Luncheons Hosted by Government Officials or Private Citizens

Time

- Dinners are usually held close to 8:00 p.m. and luncheons close to 12:30 p.m.
- In the United States, guests are expected to arrive on time. This is not always the case in a foreign country.

Guest of Honor

The dinner or luncheon may be in honor of the following:

- A chief of state or head of government
- Foreign cabinet members or foreign ambassadors
- Other top-ranking foreign government officials
- American top-ranking government officials

When and Where Events Will Take Place

The guest of honor will be notified about the invitation and given several dates and times for the event (his or her schedule may be consulted for convenience).

If the event is held somewhere other than the host's residence or an official place of entertainment, the guest should be informed and the venue scheduled as early as possible as many establishments are booked months in advance.

Guest List

A great deal of thought always goes into the guest list.

- The list should include both American and foreign guests and the honoree's friends.
- The honoree should be consulted about whom he or she would like included.
- If the guest of honor is staying in a private residence, it is in good taste to invite his or her host to the event.
- The Americans invited should typically have an interest in the country or in the individual being honored. Consideration should be given to government officials, to men and women distinguished in the arts, literature, academia, business, and/or society, to personal friends of the host and honoree, and to media personalities.
- Interpreters are included when needed and are usually seated behind the person for whom they are interpreting at dinner. If other invited guests speak the language of the foreign guest(s), they are often seated together to make the event more enjoyable for the foreign guest(s).

- It is definitely acceptable to invite government officials one has not previously met to a dinner or luncheon—especially if the person extending an invitation is an ambassador accredited to the United States.

Seating

When the host is a U.S. official or citizen, seating is done by rank, using the U.S. Order of Precedence. This order helps ensure that the dinner or luncheon proceeds smoothly and that no one objects to his or her placement.

In order not to cause seating conflicts, it is advantageous not to invite a person of higher rank than the guest of honor.

It is advisable to contact either the person who represents the honored guest or the government represented (usually the embassy located in the United States) to double-check titles and spelling of names.

Invitations

- Invitations are engraved or semiengraved for official luncheons, receptions, and dinners.
- Invitations are traditionally on white or cream paper with black ink.
- Script is the preferred style for lettering.
- It is important to inquire about postal requirements and sizes in order to avoid costly mistakes in mailing.
- If the host is a high-ranking member of government, the invitation may bear the seal of the host's office. It should be centered at the top of the page.
- The invitation should state the name of the honored guest or guests. Full names are written out.
- The invitation will state the date, time and location, appropriate dress, and response details.
- The lower right-hand corner will often provide dress instructions.

Wording of the Invitation

- The invitation is phrased in the third person: "request the pleasure of your company."

- Courtesy titles are abbreviated: Mr., Mrs., Dr., Jr.
- Religious and professional titles (elected or appointed) are written out in full.
- Military ranks for commissioned officers are never abbreviated.
- Punctuation is used only to separate words on the same line where appropriate: Friday, the first of June.
- Numbers for dates and times are written out: the fifth of June.
- Months and state names are written in full: January or Arizona.
- Addresses are written in full.
- Street numbers are written as numerals (824 Logan Street) unless the number is one through ten (One Hill Road).
- When the envelope is addressed, the state is fully spelled out (i.e., California), though it is acceptable to abbreviate if the length of the copy will destroy the aesthetics of the envelope. In Washington, D.C., the quadrant of the city (e.g., northwest (NW), southeast (SE)) and "District of Columbia" (DC) are abbreviated.
- Times are written out: one o'clock.
- Half hours are written out: half past or half after seven o'clock.
- RSVP is placed at the bottom left-hand corner.
- Dress instructions may be stated at the bottom right-hand corner.

Invitee Bringing a Guest

- Envelope:

The outer envelope states the name of the invited guest only.
Persons that are single, divorced, or widowed are often invited to bring guests.
The inside envelope may state, "(full name) and guest."
If there is only one envelope for an occasion, meaning that an inner envelope is not used, the envelope can state, "(full name) and guest."

- Invitation:

On occasion, as a personalized touch, the invitation itself can state, "(invitee's name) and guest."

High Government Office Addressed

- The host's title should only be used in the event there is only one person with that rank and name: The Secretary of Commerce
- If the invitation is from a couple, the spouse's name is included: The Secretary of Commerce and Mrs. (surname) or Mr. or Ms. (full name)

Foreign Service

The ambassador, minister, chargé d'affaires, consul general, or consul in charge of a post should use his or her title. Other officers use their full names.

Congress

A senator should be addressed as "Senator."

A member of the House of Representatives uses "Mr./Mrs./Ms. (full name)."

The Speaker of the House uses his or her title.

Wording for a White House Invitation

Formal: "(Hosts names) request the pleasure of the company of

_____

    To (state the reason for the function)"

When there is a guest of honor:

    Most formal: "In honor of _____ "

    Formal: "On the occasion of _____ "

    Less formal: "To meet _____ "

    or

    "To bid farewell to _____ "

    or

    "In observation of _____ (such as for Memorial Day or Veteran's Day)"

    or

    "In celebration of _____ (an auspicious occasion)"

More Than One Host

- The name of the person at whose residence the party takes place comes first.
- If an older or more distinguished person is also a host, his or her name may appear first.
- The hosts can be listed alphabetically or according to precedence if the event is held somewhere other than at one of the host's residences.

Invitation by Telephone, Fax, or E-mail

Use of such technologies is not the most desirable way to extend an invitation, but in today's bustling world, it is sometimes the only way to meet a deadline. An invitation by telephone, fax, or e-mail should state all information the guest needs to know and should communicate how and when to reply. If the invitation is extended by this method and the occasion is a more formal event, or if the occasion honors a high-ranking individual, a formal invitation should follow in the mail.

RSVP

An RSVP may be requested in several forms, including "RSVP," "R.S.V.P.," "R.s.v.p.," "Please reply by" (when date is included), or "The favor of a reply is requested." RSVP is an acronym borrowed from the French phrase *Répondez s'il vous plaît*, meaning "Respond if you please" or "Please respond." The request of an RSVP means the invited guest *must* tell the host whether he or she plans to attend. The practical reason for an RSVP is that the host needs a head count for a planned event by a certain date, and it is therefore necessary that guests apprise the host regarding attendance, also by a certain date.

"Regrets only," on the other hand, means that guests should respond only if not planning to attend.

"RSVP" or "Regrets only" should be placed at the bottom left-hand corner of an invitation.

Replying to an Invitation

Handwritten replies are expected unless the invitation has a reply card or provides a telephone number. To reply to a formal invitation, one should use the format and style of the invitation, even indenting the lines just as they are indented in the invitation.

Dr. and Mrs. (full name)
Accept with pleasure [or regret that they are unable to accept]
The kind invitation from
President and Mrs. (surname)
For dinner
On Saturday, the first of January
At eight thirty o'clock

If for some reason your name is misspelled on the invitation, or if you prefer a different title, correct the mistake in your reply, and do not make it an issue.

Attire

It is always important to know exactly what the dress code entails. If you are in the least confused about the attire, call the host or hostess and inquire.

CASUAL

"Casual" has various meanings at different parties in different parts of the United States. Call your host for clarification regarding dress.

INFORMAL

Informal attire can range from jeans to a dressy pantsuit for women and jackets with or without a tie for men. Since informal can have different meanings, if you don't know your host and what he or she intends, call to clarify.

BUSINESS CASUAL

For men: slacks, seasonal sport coat, structured jacket or blazer, optional tie.

For women: matched or unmatched skirt or pantsuit with appropriate top.

BUSINESS

For men: business suit and tie.

For women: business attire; skirt suit or pantsuit; traditional jewelry.

GOOD LOOKING SHOES!

One always wants to look her best and wear the appropriate clothes when attending a dinner hosted by monarchs. I was once invited by a king to make introductions to himself and the queen, along with their chief of protocol, in a receiving line prior to dinner.

King Abdullah and Queen Rania of Jordan had asked me to fly on their airplane from Washington, D.C., to New York City, where I would be a guest at their dinner at the Waldorf Astoria. I took my carry-on luggage for the overnight; I thought it was placed topside in the plane so that I could retrieve it quickly upon arrival and hurry to the hotel to dress for the evening. Upon arrival, I was told that my luggage must have been misplaced in the "hold" of the plane in a container; it was on its way to Jordan!

Trying not to panic, I assured myself that if I hurried, I had time to make it to a department store close to the hotel to select a change of clothes, make-up, and shoes. I hurried, but only had time to buy make-up before clerks in the shoe department informed me that the store was closing and could not stay open late.

Thank goodness I had worn a black pant-suit that was dressy enough to get by at the dinner. However, I had worn my casual black Gucci loafers for comfort. Not having time to buy other shoes, I had no choice but to wear the shoes I had on. His majesty had been told beforehand what had happened to my luggage. As I walked in, we were all laughing about the fact that the best laid plans can go awry.

The king, with his wonderful sense of humor, looked down and said, "Good-looking shoes!"

SEMIFORMAL

For men: dark, dressy, business-type suit, dress shirt, conservative tie, dressy leather shoes, and dress socks.

For women: short afternoon or cocktail dress, long dressy pants or skirt and top.

BLACK TIE

For men: black tuxedo jacket, matching trousers, formal white shirt, black bow tie, black cummerbund to match tie, dressy suspenders to ensure a good fit (optional), black patent leather shoes, and black dress socks; no gloves.

For women: formal, long evening dress, short cocktail dress, or dressy long pants and top; no gloves.

WHITE TIE

For men: black tailcoat, matching trousers with a single stripe of satin or braid, white piqué wing-collared shirt with stiff front, white low-cut waistcoat (waistcoat must not extend below the coat front), white bow tie, black patent leather shoes, and black dress socks. White or gray gloves may be worn.

For women: formal long evening gown. Gloves are worn.

Menu

Menu cards are used at official functions to state what is being served. One should place the card above the plate after reading it. The menu card may be taken upon departure.

Dietary Restrictions

Some guests have dietary restrictions. It is acceptable for the host or hostess to ask if there are dietary restrictions for guests, especially if foreign dignitaries are invited. Such a request is recommended for advance planning; however, most chefs will keep supplies on hand in their kitchens to accommodate restrictions that may arise.

Formal Photograph

The place of honor is to the right of the host; therefore, from the subjects' perspective, the configuration of subjects should be as follows:

Host
Honored guest (to host's right)
Host's spouse (next right)
Honored guest's spouse (next right)

　　　or

Host
Honored guest (to host's right)
Honored guest's spouse (next right)
Host's spouse (next right)

A TURN OF THE SKIRT

After an official luncheon in New York for the United Nations, it was time for an official photograph. Upon standing up from her seat, a presidential cabinet member realized that a stain from the oil and vinegar that topped her salad was fully visible on the front of her skirt. Being the shortest person in the room, among many tall men, she knew she would be placed in the first row for the photograph.

As she later revealed, she had little choice but to take slow steps toward the photographers, turning her skirt inch by inch along the way, until the stain was at her side. Thus, by the turn of her skirt, the appearance that everything was in order was preserved for posterity.

Receiving Line

There are two procedures, the same as for official photographs, for the receiving lines. The one most used is listed next. The place of honor for a guest is to the right of the host.

Host
Guest of honor (to host right)
Host's spouse (next right)
Spouse of guest of honor (next right)

- At the head of the receiving line should be a person who announces or introduces the guest to the host.
- Often, at the end of the line, there should be someone to direct the guest forward so as not to delay the line.
- A guest should not shake hands with the person who is introducing or announcing.
- The receiving line is not for long conversations; greetings should be brief.
- A guest may want to introduce him- or herself by name only to the guest one place farther down the line.
- A guest should never go through a receiving line holding anything in hand. If wearing gloves, the right glove is removed to shake hands.
- If possible, a carpet runner should be placed in front of the receiving line for convenience.
- If older or infirm guests are invited, adequate seating should be available, in case it is needed, depending on the length of the line.
- The guest with the official title or whose name appears first on the invitation should be first in line, contrary to the "ladies first" rule at most unofficial events. In official receiving lines, ladies should not precede their husbands or guests with whom they have arrived unless their official titles are the most prominent or they personally received the invitation.

Greetings and Introductions

A greeting is the acknowledgment of the presence of another. The purpose of an introduction is to convey names and to make each party being introduced more comfortable. These courtesies are observed throughout the world.

If errors are made in introducing one person to another, such errors probably pale in comparison to the discourtesy of leaving a guest or friend wondering who is standing before him or her.

Formal greetings should always be pleasing and may be similar to informal greetings, such as "How do you do, Mrs. Jones" or "Hello,

Mr. Smith." Greetings should always be genuine and may be accompanied by a handshake when appropriate.

Traditionally, the first person named in a greeting is being shown respect based on prominence or seniority. In the diplomatic world, and as a general guideline, it is important to introduce the person of higher rank or prominence to the person of lower rank or prominence.

- The higher-ranking person's name should be mentioned first:

"Mr. President, may I present Mr. Brown."
"Madam Ambassador, may I introduce Mr. (or Mrs.) Jones."

- A younger person is introduced to an older person:

"Aunt Mary, I want you to meet my friend Ann Smith."

- In most situations, men are introduced to women.
- When one does not know or has not seen someone for some time, it is acceptable to say, "Hello, I am Susan Adams."
- When another does introduce him- or herself, one should be sure to return the greeting using *one's* name. "So glad to meet (or see) you, Susan. I am George Smith."

"I'M PEI"

Famous Chinese-born American architect I. M. Pei was awaiting an introduction to the president in an official receiving line. In order to facilitate the introduction, an aide asked Pei for his first and last name.

Pei responded "I. M. Pei," but the aide understood him to say, "I'm Pei." The two volleyed:

"Yes, Pei, but what is your full name?"

"I'm Pei" was all that the aide heard until a third party stepped in to cure the miscommunication.

Toasts

"This custom dates back to the Middle Ages, when people were so distrustful of one another that they weren't above poisoning anyone they perceived as an enemy. As a safeguard, drinkers first poured a bit of wine into each other's glass, acting as mutual tasters.

"Trustworthy friends, however, soon dispensed with the tastings and merely clinked their glasses instead. This custom is said by some to explain why 'to your health' is the most common toast worldwide" (Emily Post 2004, 487).

Regarding the word "toast," "In the ale houses of Elizabethan England, a bit of spiced toast was usually put in the bottom of a cup of ale or wine to flavor it" (Emily Post 2004, 487).

Following the age-old tradition, the host offers a toast to pay tribute to the guest of honor. The toast is usually given at the beginning of the meal, before or after the first course is served; however, it can come after the dessert course. At the White House the toast is offered at the beginning of the meal. The host will stand and raise his or her glass, while offering an expression of good will. For less formal dinners the host may say, "May I have your attention," if necessary. (It is not appropriate to tap on a glass.) The host should stand and propose a toast to the individual and the country at an official dinner. At the White House the guests remain seated during the toast. When guests do stand, the person receiving the toast should remain seated, nod in acknowledgement, and refrain from drinking to his or her own toast. The individual being toasted should then stand, thank the others, and offer a toast in return.

Guests will raise their glasses and drink to the toast. Etiquette calls for guests to participate in the toast, so even nondrinkers should at least raise the glass to their lips. It is not appropriate to "clink" glasses together but only to raise the glass.

Table Etiquette

- Smoking is not considered acceptable inside or at a table almost everywhere in the United States.
- Guests should not sit until the host and hostess are in place and acknowledge seating. Guests should both seat themselves and depart from the left of the chair.

- Guests should not begin to eat until everyone at the table has been served and the host, hostess, or both have put their silverware on their plate or begun eating.
- A considerate guest will speak to the person on his or her right or left who is not engaged in conversation. In times past, and today in foreign countries, the accepted form was first to speak to the person seated to one's right and then to the person seated to one's left, but that form is no longer used in the United States. It is more acceptable to have a table engaged in conversation within acceptable auditory bounds.
- Food is served from the left and removed from the right. (Less formal: plates are prepared in advance, brought to the table, and set before the guest. This is also done when there are time constraints.)
- When eating soup, dip the spoon sideways into the soup at the near edge of the bowl, then skim from the front of the bowl to the back.
- Food, salt, and pepper should be passed counterclockwise to the right, the object being that food moves only in one direction around the table.
- Salt and pepper should be passed together.
- Pitchers or other dishes with handles should be passed with the handle toward the person receiving them.
- The host and hostess will signal when the meal is finished, and guests should leave the table following their host.
- If excusing oneself from the table before the meal is finished and returning to the table, the napkin should be left, lightly folded, in one's chair. When the meal is over, the napkin should be placed where the dinner plate was removed or to the left of the plate on the table, slightly folded.

After-Dinner Entertainment

Unless this is a very formal event with special entertainment, guests usually retire to another room for conversation and after-dinner drinks.

Departing

Guests should be aware of the time frame and not overstay, as most people have early schedules the next morning. Guests should say,

"Thank you and goodnight," to their host, hostess, and honored guests before departing. The honored guest(s) may be the first to depart.

Gifts

Gifts should not be brought to any event or given directly to the host, hostess, or guest.

If a gift is appropriate, it should be sent earlier or the next day with a note from the sender.

If flowers are to be sent, it is advisable to call the host or hostess and ask if flowers are appropriate and when they should arrive. It is also advisable to inquire if certain flowers or colors are inappropriate.

Thank-you Notes

A thank-you note may be written within a few days after the event to the host and hostess to express the guest's appreciation for the invitation.

Receptions

Receptions are a more formal affair than a cocktail party and are usually held in honor of a special guest. The time of the reception can vary, as can the level of formality. The invitation should announce the particulars of the occasion. The host may include a receiving line for guests to meet the guest of honor.

ENTERTAINING CHECKLIST

Event name
    Description
    In honor of
    Contact for event
Host/hostess
Date
Time
Place
    Name of room
    Address

Contact
Date reserved
Date of walk-through
Speaker
    Remarks
    Podium
    Lectern (check speaker's height to lectern's height)
    Stage riser
    Flags
    Interpreter
    Toast
Dress/attire
Invitations
Guest list
Response cards
    Phone line used for responses
    Date for "save the date"
    Date of follow-up phone call
Seating chart
Place cards
Take-in cards
Host/hostess cards
Menu card for table
Name tags
Table numbers for display on tables
Table list for guest reference
Check-in table/chairs
Receiving line
    Participants
Chairs for disabled or infirm guests
Caterer
    Menu
    China, crystal, flatware, finger bowls
    Type of tables
    Type of service (buffet, plated, American, or French)
    Waitstaff
    Equipment
    Rental fees

Delivery
Essential staff
Food for essential staff
Coat check: attendant, umbrella rack
Doorman
Red carpet/awning for bad weather
Map layout of event
Beverages (nonalcoholic and alcoholic)
Linens
Florist/types of flowers
Candles
Dietary restrictions/preferences
Including alcoholic beverages
Allergies to certain foods or flowers
Flower colors or colors not to use
Cultural restrictions
Interpretation required for guests
Technical service
Microphone
Podium
Technician
Pubic address system, microphone, taping program
Music/sound system
Entertainment/piano
Bathroom
Attendant, soap, towels
Accessibility for disabled guests
Elevators
Number of elevators needed/ordered
Accessibility for disabled guests
Contact information for operator(s)
Staffing
Parking
Inclement-weather arrangements
Security
Provide guests names who will arrive with security
Provide details of event to government security
Provide guest list, when possible, if required by security

Photographer
    Contact information
    Date request submitted/to whom
Funding sheet
    Estimated cost of event
Media/press
    Staff responsible
    Date
    Site coordinator
Emergency necessities
    Telephone numbers
    Equipment
    First aid (such as defibrillator)
Postevent:
    Thank everyone involved
    Write thank-you notes as necessary
    Make payments
    Draft notes of event
    Close out file

Chapter 8

Table Seating

Dinner at the White House. Courtesy William J. Clinton
Presidential Library.

FOLLOWING ORDER OF PRECEDENCE

THOSE RESPONSIBLE FOR TABLE SEATING should consult U.S. Order
of Precedence (chapter 3) regarding the rank of each individual on
the precedence list to be seated. The determining factor for seating
arrangements should follow precedence based on official position or
military rank. Any change in the seating rank of a guest should have
an exceptionally good reason that can be readily explained.

Formal official luncheons and dinners require that certain procedures be followed to avoid confusion among government officials,

foreign dignitaries, and distinguished people in international society who are accustomed to being seated by rank. It is very offensive to dignitaries not to be seated in the proper place. Guests have been known to leave dinners because of such an oversight.

Host and Hostess

American custom normally dictates that a host and/or a hostess be seated at each table in use. In the United States the place of honor is to the right of the host or hostess.

The highest-ranking man sits to the hostess's right, and the second-ranking man sits to her left. The highest-ranking woman sits to the host's right, and the second-ranking woman to his left. (Thus, the host and hostess are rarely seated next to each other, unless at a banquet).

This protocol is followed throughout the seating plan, first seating higher-ranking, then lesser-ranking, officials. For more fluid conversation and to accommodate guests' interests, exceptions can be made. Guests of interest and talent or with particular language capabilities can be seated among ranking officials after the seating of the number-two-ranking guests in order to facilitate discussion. Sensitivity to seating arrangements can make the occasion much more enjoyable.

Host and Hostess Seating

The host and hostess may sit at opposite ends or across from each other when one table is used, or they may sit at different tables when using more than one table. When possible, using round tables makes seating and entertaining much less complicated. When round tables are used, the event's host or hostess should be seated facing guests in the room. In other words, the host and hostess table(s) should not be in the center of a room with other tables but at the front of the room. Additional table hosts and hostesses, aside from the event host or hostess, may be seated at other tables for convenience.

Guest of Honor

The host should avoid inviting a guest of higher rank than the guest of honor to allow the guest of honor to sit in the place of honor. If a guest of higher rank than the guest of honor is invited to an event, the host may ask the higher-ranking guest to relinquish his or her place in favor of the guest of honor. If the higher-ranking guest *is* to be seated in the place of honor, the guest of honor must be notified *before* the event to prevent any last-minute disputes. Alternatively, the host may ask the higher-ranking guest to cohost a table when more than one table is in use.

Wife's Rank

When attending an event with her husband, a woman is usually accorded and seated by his rank. When the woman, attending with her husband, holds an official position herself, she would then be seated in her official place. If a nonranking woman attends an event without her husband, she is seated as an invited guest without rank.

Husband's Rank

When a husband without rank attends an event with his ranking wife, as a courtesy, the husband is usually seated according to her rank. If a nonranking man attends an event without his wife who holds rank, he is seated as an invited guest without rank.

Nonmarried Partners

When nonmarried couples who are partners (i.e., are in a committed relationship) attend a function together, the nonranking partner may be seated, as a courtesy, with equivalent rank to the ranking partner.

Guests without Rank

Nonranking guests invited because of their achievements, social prominence, friendships, or interest in the countries involved are seated accordingly after the highest-ranking guest and second-ranking guest have been placed. Such nonranking guests may be seated between ranking guests to further interests and conversation. Priority may also be placed on linguistic ability.

Foreign Country

When Americans host or attend a diplomatic event in a foreign country, the customs may (and often do) vary from those used in the United States. Therefore, it is advisable for Americans, as invited guests, to adhere to the customs of the foreign country. Sometimes, the place of honor will be to the left of the host or hostess in other nations. When Americans entertain abroad and invite citizens of the foreign country to dinner, it is customary to give preference to foreign guests over Americans of comparable rank, with the exception of the American ambassador. Occasionally, other Americans in attendance should be less protocol conscious to achieve the goals of the dinner. Seating should always be arranged with language capabilities taken into consideration.

The host should avoid inviting a guest of higher rank than the guest of honor to allow the guest of honor to sit in the place of honor. If a guest of higher rank than the guest of honor is invited to an event, the host may ask the higher-ranking guest to relinquish his or her place in favor of the guest of honor. If the higher-ranking guest *is* to be seated in the place of honor, the guest of honor must be notified *before* the event to prevent any last-minute misunderstandings. Alternatively, additional tables could be used so that the higher-ranking guest may cohost. One goal of every event is to have all guests enjoy themselves rather than finding themselves flummoxed by restrictive protocol they do not understand.

GUEST PLACEMENT AT TABLES

Seating Two Men or Two Women Together

Seating two men or two women together should be avoided, though it is acceptable. Placement of a woman at the end of a rectangular table is not desirable but sometimes occurs out of necessity and is, at such times, acceptable.

Married and Engaged Couples

Husbands and wives are usually not seated side by side at the same table, but engaged couples may sit together. If there is more than one table, husbands and wives are seated at different tables.

Single Man or Woman

When a single man or woman is the host or hostess, he or she may want to ask a male or female friend to cohost for a more desirable arrangement in seating and conversation. The host or hostess, in this instance, can also ask the highest-ranking man or woman already invited to the event to cohost. If a cohost is at the same table as a host or hostess, he or she should be seated opposite the host or hostess. (See figure 1d.)

Guest Number Divisible by Four

When the number of guests per table is divisible by four (eight, twelve, sixteen, twenty, etc.) and the numbers of men and women are equal, with both host and hostess at the table, the host and hostess may not sit opposite each other without two men and two women being seated adjacently. To rectify this problem, the hostess will balance the table by moving one seat to the left of the seat that is properly hers, with the ranking male guest remaining on her right. This arrangement permits the highest-ranking man to sit to the hostess's right (at the end of the table), which designates the place of honor for the dinner and renders a female-male progression around the table. Seating arrangements are much easier to place if the number of guests per table is not divisible by four. (See figures 3a and 3b.)

Round Tables

When possible, using round tables allows more flexibility at a dinner. There can be more places of honor as the host and hostess can each have a cohost and cohostess at their table. Other high-ranking guests may serve as hosts or cohosts when more than two tables are used. At the White House, when more than one table is used, the president hosts one table, and the president's spouse hosts another table; the vice president may host a table, and still other tables may be hosted by the secretary of state or any high-ranking government official.

Round tables of six, but not more than ten, allow for more convenient conversation. Remember that some guests may have difficulty hearing across the expanse of a larger and/or more crowded table.

Horseshoe or Squared-U Tables

At large ceremonial functions, this table arrangement is used. The host and hostess may be seated side by side, with the hostess to the right of the host. When the guest of honor is a man, he is seated to the hostess's right, and his spouse is seated to the host's left. (See figure 4a).

The host may want to seat a male honored guest to his (the host's) right and the honored guest's spouse to his (the host's) left; such arrangement would place the hostess to the right of the male honored guest. (When facing the table: hostess, honored guest (man), host (in center), honored guest's spouse (woman).) (See figure 4b).

When the guest of honor is a woman, she is seated to the host's right and her spouse is seated to the host's left. This arrangement will place the hostess to the left of the honored woman's spouse, which would therefore place the honored spouse on the hostess's right. (When facing the table: honored guest (woman), host (in center), honored guest's spouse (man), hostess.)

An alternate plan is to use a squared-U table where the host and hostess would sit across from each other. The disadvantage of this plan is that the hostess may have her back to some guests.

Guests Seated on a Dais of Two or More Tiers

The top-ranking guest should be seated on the first (lowest) tier.

Head Tables

Banquets for distinguished foreign visitors and other prominent persons at which a large group gathers will often require a head table. The remainder of the guests should be seated at surrounding tables.

At a head table with official and nonranking guests, important persons representing special interests related to the event may be seated between ranking guests after the guest of honor and second-ranking guest have been placed. When there is a ranking guest, a speaker, and a toastmaster, the host may place these three guests as close to the center of the table as possible. If a guest at the head table outranks the speaker, the speaker may be placed in the second-ranking seat.

Most established groups have had their own seating arrangements firmly in place for many years. (See figures 5a and 5b.)

PRIVATE ENTERTAINING OF OFFICIAL GUESTS

Entertaining a diplomat or high-ranking government official in a private home or at a selected venue should be viewed as an opportunity to entertain him or her in the manner most comfortable for the host or hostess—that is, as long as such entertaining does not violate any rules of diplomatic protocol or general etiquette.

One of the more important aspects of entertaining an official guest is his or her seating; this individual should be seated to the right of the host or hostess. A male official guest should be seated to the right of the hostess, and a female official guest to the right of the host. In the event that there is only a host or a hostess, the official guest might be seated across from the host or hostess. Other official guests should be seated according to their rank. Individual circumstances will sometimes dictate seating, and the detailed information outlined in this chapter will be helpful in making seating arrangements.

When a private dinner includes a receiving line, it should comprise, in this order: the host, the official guest, the host's spouse, and the official guest's spouse. As guests proceed through the line, the host should introduce the official guest; then the hostess introduces the spouse of the official guest. It is important to know how to introduce guests by their correct titles and how to write titles and names on invitations and place cards. (See chapter 5, "Titles and Forms of Address.")

Guest from a Foreign Country

When the official guest is from another country, the host or hostess may be in touch with the embassy of that country in Washington, D.C. The host or hostess may call or write the ambassador's secretary or assistant to obtain pertinent information that will be helpful in arranging a successful event.

The embassy secretary or assistant will be pleased to provide the correct title and spelling of names (both of guests and of the country) and can put the host or hostess in touch with the officer in charge of guests' travel. The secretary or assistant may relay any important information regarding food, beverage, dietary, floral, or color restrictions and/or preferences. (Details regarding how to contact an embassy are located in chapter 17, "Embassy Names and Information.")

More information related to private entertaining of official guests is available in the chapters titled "U.S. Order of Precedence," "Titles and Forms of Address," "Official Entertaining" and "Official Gift Giving."

TABLE-SEATING DIAGRAM OUTLINE

1. Man or woman as host or hostess alone
   a. Hostess without a cohost
   b. Host without a cohost
   c. Alternative seating without cohost or cohostess
   d. Cohost or cohostess designated by host or hostess
2. Traditional lunch or dinner
   a. Host and hostess at ends of table
   b. Host and hostess at center of table
3. Men and women both invited, guest number divisible by four
   a. Equal number of men and women, guest number divisible by four
   b. Round table(s), guest number divisible by four
4. Horseshoe or squared-U tables
   a. Host and hostess seated side by side
   b. Alternative seating for host and hostess
5. Head table
   a. Suggestions for seating in clubs for men or women
   b Official and nonranking guests are both present

TABLE-SEATING DIAGRAMS

1. Man or Woman as Host or Hostess Alone

1a and 1b. Table without a Cohost or Cohostess

When there is no cohost or cohostess, the host or hostess sits at the head of the table. The host or hostess may be hosting alone at one table, or they may be hosting as a couple at two tables. A guest may or may not be seated at the opposite end of the table.

1: Man or Woman as Host or Hostress Alone

1a: Hostess without a cohost

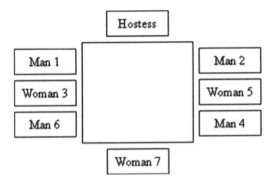

1b: Host without a cohost

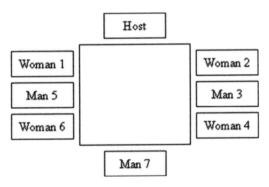

1c: Alternative Seating without Cohost or Cohostess

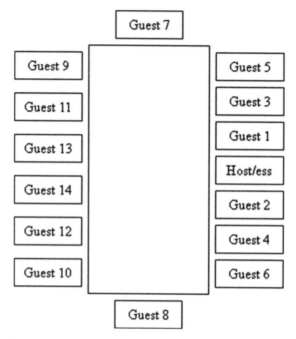

Figure 1c: Alternative seating without cohost or cohostess.

1d: Cohost or Cohostess designated by Host or Hostess

When a man or woman hosts alone, it is often desirable to designate a cohost or cohostess to balance the table. It is appropriate to ask a senior-ranking American to play this role. When foreign guests are invited, it is also appropriate to ask the senior-ranking foreign guest to cohost. If there is a cohost or cohostess, he or she should sit opposite the host or hostess. In figure 1d, depending on the circumstances and whether there is a cohost or hostess, the terms *guest 1*, *guest 2*, and so forth may be changed to *man 1*, *woman 1*, and so on.

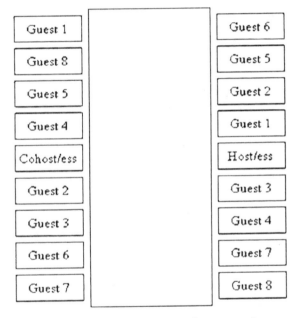

Figure 1d: Host or hostess designates a cohost or cohostess.

2. Traditional Luncheon or Dinner

2a: Host and Hostess at Ends of Table

The host and hostess often sit opposite each other at the end of the table.

If seating a woman at the end of the table is not acceptable to the host or hostess, there is a solution: two women may be seated side by side and the man originally seated between them may be placed at the end of the table. (See figure 2b.)

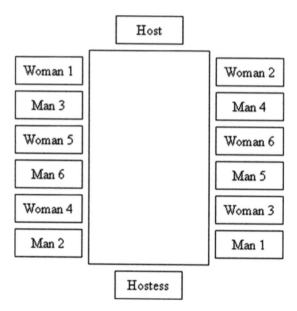

Figure 2a: Host and hostess at ends of table.

2b: Host and Hostess at Center of Table

The host and hostess often sit opposite each other at the center of the table.

If seating a woman at the end of the table is not acceptable to the host or hostess, there is a solution: two women may be seated side by side and the man originally seated between them may be placed at the end of the table as illustrated in the diagram.

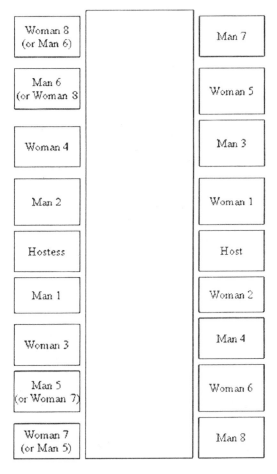

Figure 2b: Host and hostess at center of table.

3: Men and Women Both Invited, Guest Number Divisible by Four

3a: Equal Number of Men and Women, Guest Number Divisible by Four

When a guest number is divisible by four and equal numbers of men and women have been invited, the host and hostess cannot sit at opposite ends of the table without seating two women or two men side by side somewhere at the table. To balance the table, the hostess may move one seat to the left of the seat that is properly hers and place the ranking male guest to her right. (See figures 3a and 3b)

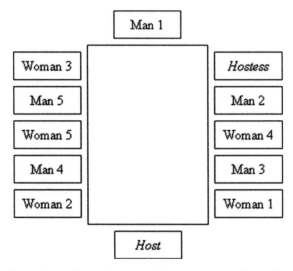

Figure 3a: Equal number of men and women, number of guests divisible by four.

3b: Round Table(s), Guest Number Divisible by Four

When using more than one round table, the host may sit at one table and the hostess at another table, thereby resolving the problem of seating two guests of the same sex side by side. There can be other hosts and hostesses at other round tables in the room.

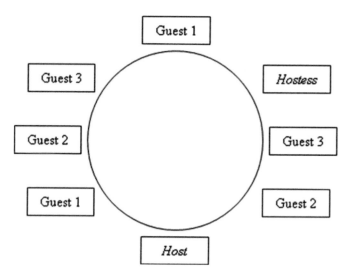

Figure 3b: Round table(s), number of guests divisible by four.

4: Horseshoe or Squared-U Tables

4a: Host and Hostess Seated Side by Side

At large events with horseshoe or squared tables, the host and hostess are often seated side by side. The highest ranking man would sit to the hostess right and the highest ranking woman to the host left.

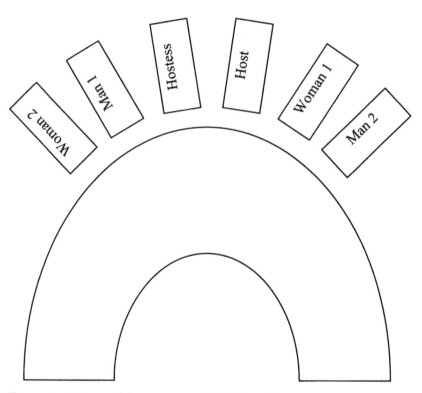

Figure 4a: Host and hostess seated side by side.

4b: Alternative Seating for Host and Hostess

The host may sit between the guests of honor. If there is a hostess, she will sit beside the highest-ranking man. Two women may be seated together to accommodate having a man at the end of the table, if that arrangement is desirable.

This plan shows the man, who is the guest of honor, to the host's right but also gives the host the advantage, at another occasion, of sitting with a *woman guest of honor* to his right. When a woman is the guest of honor, her spouse would then sit to the host's left . Therefore, the hostess will sit beside the spouse of the guest of honor to his left.

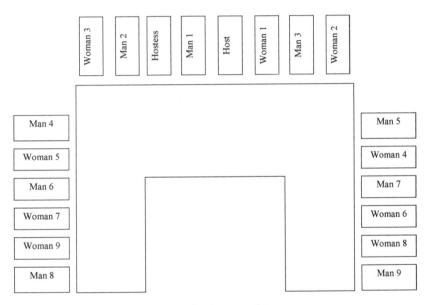

Figure 4b: Alternative seating for host and hostess.

5: Head Table

5a: Suggestions for Seating in Clubs for Men or Women

Seating arrangements for clubs may include those for "mixed groups," "men's only" groups, or "women's only," groups (with or without speakers).

For luncheons or dinners at which club officers and important guests are seated at the head table, Figure 5a illustrates one possible configuration among many. Check with club officials for their own personal club requirements.

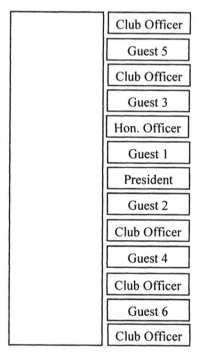

Figure 5a: Clubs for men or women, suggestions for seating.

5b: Official and Nonranking Guests Are Both Present

Citizens representing organizations important to the lunch or dinner may be seated between the ranking guests after the guest of honor and second-ranking official guest are seated.

When couples are seated at the head table, the ranking woman may be seated to the right of the host or chairman of the event. Most clubs and organizations have their own rules concerning how seating should be arranged; therefore, check for group or organization preferences before planning the seating arrangement.

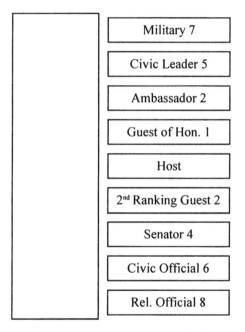

Figure 5b: Official and nonranking guests are both present.

Chapter 9

○

Flag Etiquette

Armed Forces Color Guard, White House South Lawn for a State Arrival Ceremony. Courtesy William J. Clinton Presidential Library.

AMERICAN FLAG

THE AMERICAN FLAG HOLDS GREAT SIGNIFICANCE for U.S. citizens; it is the premier symbol of American patriotism. In fact, those who handle the flag should consider it almost human; it should be treated with the utmost respect, as if it were a person.

U.S. Code Title 36 ("The Flag Code"), the body of federal law governing proper use of the U.S. flag, contains specific instructions concerning its treatment. The Ceremonial Activities Division of the

Military District of Washington provides generally accepted inter-
pretations of Title 36. This division responds to many inquiries from
federal agencies and the general public regarding the proper use and
display of the flag.

Respect for the American Flag

Giving the Flag the Position of Honor

- The U.S. flag is always placed in the position of honor, "to its own
  right." Though, when parsed, this language may seem confusing, it
  means that the flag's position should be to the far right (and, conversely, to the far left when one is facing it).

Dipping the Colors

- U.S. tradition holds that the flag should never be dipped (i.e.,
  angled downward) toward any person or thing. It is not dipped when
  carried past a reviewing stand, even when other flags are dipped.
  The practice of not dipping the flag to any "earthly king" is a long-
  standing custom.
- An exception is made when any ship, under either the U.S. registry
  or that of a nation formally recognized by the United States, salutes
  a ship of the navy by dipping its ensign. Such a salute is answered
  dip for dip. No ship of the navy shall dip the national ensign unless
  in return for such a compliment.

Displaying with Another Flag

- When two or more flags are flown on the same staff, the U.S. flag
  should always be at the peak of the staff. No other flag should be
  flown above the U.S. flag, except during church services conducted
  by naval chaplains at sea. The church pennant may be flown above
  the flag during church services for navy personnel.
- When flown with flags of states, communities, or societies on separate staffs that are the same height and in a straight line, the U.S.
  flag is flown to the right of all others. Flags may be of equal size to
  or smaller than the U.S. flag, but not larger.

- When displayed and grouped with other flags of states, cities, localities, or pennants of societies, the flags are again displayed on separate staffs. The U.S. flag should be at the center and at the highest point.

Putting Fringe on Flag

- It is often customary to place gold fringe on silken (i.e., rayon, silk, or nylon) national flags carried in parades, displayed in offices, or used in official ceremonies. This placement of fringe enhances the aesthetics of the flag. The armed forces, veterans, civic and civilian organizations, and private individuals use and display fringe on flags. Flags displayed on stationary flagpoles customarily do not use fringe.

Raising and Lowering the Flag

- The flag should be raised briskly and lowered ceremoniously and slowly.
- The flag is saluted as it is hoisted and lowered. The salute is held until the flag is unsnapped from the halyard or through the last note of music—whichever is the longest.

Displaying the Flag at Night

- The flag should be illuminated if displayed at night. Otherwise, it should only be displayed between sunrise and sunset.
- The flag should never be displayed, day or night, merely as a convenience.
- Ships under way at sea fly the flag at the gaff night and day.
- Special laws and proclamations authorize the display of the flag twenty-four hours a day at certain locations.

Displaying the Flag in Inclement Weather

- The flag should not be displayed when the weather is inclement unless it is an all-weather flag.

- The code does not prohibit flying the flag in inclement weather but states that the flag should be of all-weather material and should be replaced when it shows signs of wear.

Displaying the Flag Indoors

- The flag is accorded the place of honor, which is always "to its own right." When on a staff, the flag should be placed to the speaker's right on a stage. In a sanctuary or hall, when on the same level as the audience, the flag should be placed to the audience's right.
- When placed not within the area designated as the speaker's area but in that designated as the seating area, the flag should occupy the position of honor to the right of the audience, with any other flag to the audience's left. If the U.S. flag is placed flat, it should be displayed above and behind the speaker.

Displaying the Flag on a Wall

- If the flag is displayed vertically or horizontally against a wall, its union (i.e., stars) should be at the top, to the flag's own right, and to the observer's left.

Displaying Flags with Crossed Staffs

- When one flag is used along with the U.S. flag and the staffs are crossed, the U.S. flag is placed to its own right with its staff in front of the other flag.

Displaying the U.S. Flag Alone in Front of a Building

- As viewed when one is standing in front of a building, the U.S. flag, displayed alone, should be to the observer's left.

Displaying the U.S. Flag Alone over a Street

- When displayed over a street, the flag is suspended vertically, the union to the north on an east-west street and to the east on a north-south street.

Displaying the U.S. Flag Alone over a Sidewalk

- When the flag is suspended over a sidewalk or yard from a rope extending from a house or building to a pole at the edge of a sidewalk, the flag should be hoisted out, union first, from the building.

Displaying the Flag with Other Nations' Flags

Two Flags Displayed

- If only two flags are displayed, the U.S. flag, as the host flag, should be displayed in the position of honor to the right of the other flag.

Several National Flags Displayed

- If several national flags are displayed together, they should be arranged in English alphabetical order using the common country name. When the United States is the host, the U.S. flag stands in its place of honor to the right in the display.

Flags of Nations Displayed as Equal

- International usage forbids the display of one nation's flag above another's in a time of peace.
- Each flag must be displayed from a separate pole of the same height.
- Each flag must be the same size.
- All flags should be raised and lowered simultaneously.
- In the United States, flags of multiple nations should be lined up in English alphabetical order using the common country name.

Displaying the Flags of International Organizations

- Flags of international organizations are grouped in alphabetical order (or in the order designated by the organization) with the U.S. flag displayed accordingly.

Parading and Saluting the Flag

- In a procession, the U.S. flag is carried to the right of the marchers.
- The U.S. flag may be centered in front of other flags or carried to their right.

Viewing the Flag in Procession

- When the flag passes in procession, all should face the flag and salute.

Saluting the Flag

- To salute, all persons stand at attention. Citizens salute by placing their right hands over their hearts.
- Men wearing hats should remove them with their right hand and hold them at their left shoulders, with the right hand over their heart.
- Women wearing casual hats should remove them and hold them at their left shoulders, with the right hand over their heart; however, if women are wearing dressy hats for an occasion, removal is unnecessary.
- Military personnel should give the appropriate formal salute.

Flying the Flag as a Symbol of National Grief

- It is a long-established custom to fly our nation's flag at half-staff as a symbol of national grief.

Flying the Flag at Half-staff

- When flying the flag at half-staff, hoist it to the peak for an instant and lower the flag to a position halfway between the top and bottom of the staff. When lowering the flag, first raise it again to the peak for a moment. The flag is flown at half-staff in mourning for designated, principal government leaders and upon presidential or gubernatorial order.

Only as a National Tribute

- Although neither U.S. Code Title 36 nor Proclamation 3044 (prescribing rules for displaying the flag at half-staff on federal property) prohibits local officials or private citizens from flying the flag at half-staff on appropriate occasions, it is generally believed that our national emblem should not be flown at half-staff except as an emblem of national tribute.

Symbol of Mourning

- A state or community flag (symbolizing a group united in common association) may be lowered to half-staff by local citizens as a symbol of mourning.

Memorial Day

- The code prescribes that on Memorial Day the flag be displayed at half-staff until noon only and then raised to the top of the staff as a special mark of respect for those Americans who gave their lives to protect freedom.

Display on Official Buildings on the Death of Some U.S. Officials

- On the death of the following officials (Proclamation 3044) the U.S. flag should be flown at half-staff on all federal government buildings, grounds, and naval vessels in the District of Columbia and throughout the United States and its territories and possessions for the period indicated:
  - The president or a former president (the flag shall be flown at half-staff for a period of *thirty days* from the date of death). The flag shall also be flown at half-staff (for thirty days from date of death) at all U.S. embassies, legations, and other facilities abroad, including all military facilities and naval vessels and stations.
  - The vice president, the chief justice or a retired chief justice of the U.S. Supreme Court, or the Speaker of the House of Representatives (the flag shall be flown at half-staff for *ten days* from the date of death).
  - An associate justice of the Supreme Court, a member of the cabinet, a former vice president, the president pro tempore of the Senate, the minority leader of the Senate, the majority leader of the House, or the minority leader of the House (the flag shall be flown at half-staff *from the day of death until interment*).
  - A U.S. senator, representative, or territorial delegate or the resident commissioner from the Commonwealth of Puerto Rico (the flag will be flown at half-staff *from the day of death until interment*).
  - A governor (the flag shall fly at half-staff *from the day of death until interment* on all federal grounds and buildings in a state, territory, or possession of the United States).

- Upon the death of other officials, former officials, and foreign dignitaries, with instructions issued by the U.S. president, the flag shall be flown at half-staff.
- When they deem proper, heads of departments and agencies of the government may direct that the U.S. flag be flown at half-staff on buildings, grounds, or aboard naval vessels under their jurisdiction on occasions other than those specified in the Flag Code and that suitable military honors be rendered appropriate.

Flying Other Nations' Flags at Half-staff with the U.S. Flag

- Another nation must give permission before its flag may be flown at half-staff. Unless permission is given on a case-by-case basis, it is recommended that other nations' flags not be flown when the U.S. flag is at half-staff.

Displaying the Flag on Caskets

- To cover a casket, the flag should be placed so that the union is at the head and over the left shoulder of the deceased.
- The flag should not be lowered into the grave.
- The flag should not touch the ground.

Keeping the Flag Clean

- The code states that the flag should never touch anything beneath it: the ground, the floor, the water, or other objects. Such protections are intended to keep the flag from becoming soiled or being torn. If the flag is soiled, it is necessary to have it cleaned; it can be washed by hand or dry-cleaned.

Disposing of Unserviceable Flags

- The flag should not be cast aside or used in any way that is considered disrespectful. If it becomes unusable, it should be destroyed privately, as a whole, preferably by burning or in some other manner that is not considered irreverent or disrespectful. It is suggested, though not mandatory, that such a ceremony be conducted on Flag Day.

right of other flags. An *observer facing a building* would then observe the U.S. flag to his or her left and other flags to his or her right.

2. Flags Displayed in an Open Area with a Speaker

The U.S. flag is displayed on a speaker's platform to the speaker's right, and any other flag is placed to the speaker's left. When the U.S. flag is to be displayed on the same level as the audience, the flag will be to the right of the audience as the audience faces the speaker. Any other flag will be to the audience's left.

When the U.S. flag is displayed flat, it should be above and behind the speaker with the field of stars to the observer or audience's left when the observer or audience is facing the flag.

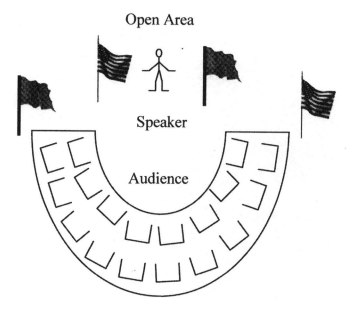

Flags displayed in an open area with a speaker.

3. Flags Displayed with a Raised Platform or on One Level

When the audience is facing the platform and the flag is to be on a level with the audience, the U.S. flag is placed to the audience's right.

Platform

Flags displayed with a raised platform or on one level.

When on the platform with the speaker, the U.S. flag stands in the place of honor to the speaker's right.

When there is a speaker and the speaking level is the same as the level of the audience, the U.S. flag stands in the place of honor to the speaker's right.

4. Flags Displayed in a Classroom

The U.S. flag should always hold the position of supreme prominence, to the teacher, instructor, or professor's right, in advance of students and to their left.

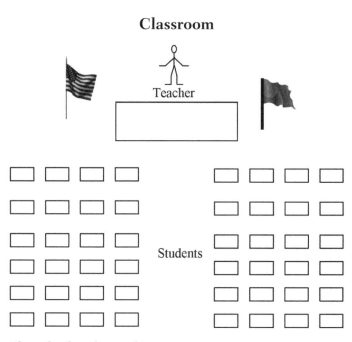

Flags displayed in a classroom.

5. Flags Displayed in a Church

In a church, when flags are displayed in the chancel area, the U.S. flag should be in the position of supreme prominence, to the speaker's right as the speaker faces the audience. Other flags should be placed the speaker's left (to the audience's left).

When flags are to be displayed in the church audience, the U.S. flag should be in the position of supreme prominence to the audience's right in advance of the audience. Other flags should be placed to the audience's left in advance of the audience.

Church

Flags displayed in a church.

NATIONAL ANTHEM

"The Star Spangled Banner," the national anthem of the United States of America, was originally a poem written in 1814 by Francis Scott Key after he witnessed the bombardment of Fort McHenry by Royal Navy ships in the Chesapeake Bay in the midst of the Battle of Baltimore during the War of 1812. It became well-known later as an American patriotic song. Though the song has four stanzas, only the first is commonly sung today.

> O! say can you see by the dawn's early light
> What so proudly we hailed at the twilight's last gleaming?
> Whose broad stripes and bright stars through the perilous fight,
> O'er the ramparts we watched were so gallantly streaming?
> And the rockets' red glare, the bombs bursting in air,
> Gave proof through the night that our flag was still there.
> O! say does that star-spangled banner yet wave
> O'er the land of the free and the home of the brave?

The U.S. national anthem evokes and eulogizes the history, traditions, and struggles of Americans.

Flag Courtesies during the National Anthem

The Flag Code provides that during a rendition of the national anthem, *when the flag is displayed*, all present should stand at attention and place their right hands over their hearts; men should remove their hats and hold them at their left shoulders with their right hand over their heart. Women wearing casual hats should remove them and place them at their left shoulders with their right hand over their heart; however, if women are wearing dressy hats for an occasion, removal is unnecessary. Military personnel in uniform should salute at the first note and maintain that position until the last note (they do not remove their hat).

- *When the flag is not displayed*, all present should face the direction from which the music is being played and repeat the same steps as if the flag were displayed.
- Foreigners as well as U.S. citizens should stand when "The Star Spangled Banner" is played.

- U.S. citizens should stand at attention when a foreign anthem is played. They do not put their hands over their hearts, but they should remove hats.
- The national anthem is to be sung in traditional form and in a respectful manner.
- Although many people clap after the anthem, especially at ball games, *it is not appropriate to clap after the anthem*.

Pledging Allegiance to the Flag

The Pledge of Allegiance to the U.S. flag is an oath of loyalty a citizen takes to the nation of the United States of America. Written in 1892 by Francis Bellamy and revised several times in later years, Congress officially adopted the Pledge of Allegiance under the Flag Code on June 22, 1942.

The Pledge of Allegiance

"I pledge allegiance to the flag of the United States of America, and to the republic for which it stands, one nation under God, indivisible, with liberty and justice for all."

- According to the U.S. Flag Code, one should stand at attention, facing the flag, placing the right hand over the heart, when reciting the pledge of allegiance.
- Hats should be removed and held in the right hand at the left shoulder with hand over heart, unless the hat is a dressy one worn by a woman.
- Those in uniform should face the flag, not removing hats, remain silent, and render the military salute.

Flag of the United States of America

The U.S. flag consists of thirteen equal-width horizontal stripes, alternating red and white. Fifty white five-pointed stars punctuate a blue rectangular field; the stars are arranged in nine offset, horizontal rows containing between five and six stars each. The fifty stars on the flag represent the fifty American states, and the thirteen stripes represent the original thirteen colonies. The flag has several nicknames: the Star-Spangled Banner, Old Glory, and the Stars and Stripes.

The U.S. flag flies over the White House daily. It is also displayed in the Oval Office together with the president's flag behind the president's desk. When one faces the president's desk, as if the president were seated behind it, the U.S. flag is placed to the president's right and the president's flag to the president's left. Both flags remain in this position whenever the president makes an address. Both flags are displayed on Air Force One or on U.S. vessels when the president is aboard. Both flags are flown wherever the president is in residence and at military and naval bases when the president is present.

When the president is abroad, arrangements for the display of flags are made with protocol in the country being visited. The U.S. Embassy displays both the American flag and the president's flag when the president is residing there.

Flag of the President of the United States of America

The president's flag consists of the presidential coat of arms, in proper colors, on a dark blue rectangular background. The blue field appears with fifty white stars surrounding the coat of arms, and the eagle appears in natural color facing "to its own right" and also toward the olive branches of peace, which the eagle holds in its right talon. Arrows, symbolic of war, are held in the eagle's left talon.

Flag of the Vice President of the United States of America

The vice president's flag consists of a white rectangular background on which appears the coat of arms of the vice president in proper colors with four blue stars. The shield displays the breast of an American eagle with inverted wings, holding an olive branch in its right talon, arrows in its left talon, and a yellow scroll inscribed "E Pluribus Unum" (meaning: Out of many one) in its beak. The eagle's head is surrounded by thirteen blue stars in the form of an annulet.

Flag of the Secretary of State of the United States of America

The secretary of state's flag consists of a blue rectangular field with a white disk bearing the official coat of arms of the United States in proper colors. In each of the flag's four corners is a white five-pointed star with one point upward.

Flags of Other Officials of the United States of America

Other U.S. officials are entitled to personal flags, called "standards." Standards are displayed in the office of the official. These personal standards can be flown on official automobiles, aircraft, and ships or at military or naval bases when the official is present; however, standards are seldom used in this manner.

Chapter 10

Ceremonies

President Lincoln delivering his inaugural address on the east portico of the U.S. Capitol, March 4, 1865. Courtesy of the Library of Congress. Photographer: Alexander Gardner

U.S. PRESIDENTIAL INAUGURATION

ON THE DAY THAT A NEW PRESIDENT takes the oath of office in the United States, power passes peacefully from one administration to another. The U.S. Constitution requires that the president be a native-born U.S. citizen, have lived in the United States for at least fourteen years, and have attained the age of thirty-five. While the Constitution specifies the oath of office to which the incoming president swears, it says nothing about the inaugural ceremony.

The newly elected president and his or her family spend a few days prior to the inauguration at Blair House, the President's Guest

House across the street from the White House. The morning of the inauguration, the president-elect and family traditionally attend a worship service at a church of their choice. They proceed to the White House to be welcomed by the outgoing presidential family; from there, the outgoing president, the president-elect, and their spouses ride together in a limousine to the U.S. Capitol.

Over the years, the traditions associated with a presidential inauguration have expanded the ceremonies from a one-day event involving the swearing in into several days of celebration. Since 1937 (with the second inauguration of Franklin D. Roosevelt), inauguration day has occurred on January 20. Since 1981 (with Ronald Reagan's first swearing in), the ceremony has taken place on the West Front of the Capitol overlooking the Mall with the Washington Monument and Lincoln and Jefferson memorials in the background.

The Presidential Inaugural Committee is the legal entity that raises and distributes funds for events (other than the ceremony at the Capitol) such as the inaugural balls and inaugural parade. The Joint Congressional Committee on Inaugural Ceremonies organizes inaugural ceremonies at the U.S. Capitol.

The U.S. military plays a major role in the ceremonies since the president is commander in chief of the armed forces. The Armed Forces Inaugural Committee, called the Joint Task Force–Armed Forces Inaugural Committee, oversees military responsibilities.

Inauguration Day

Inauguration day is a federal holiday only observed by federal employees working in the District of Columbia and surrounding areas. The primary reason for the holiday is to reduce traffic congestion. When inauguration day falls on a Sunday, the address is typically moved to the following Monday. The incoming president will take the oath at noon on January 20 and again the following Monday at the inauguration. The outgoing president usually attends the inauguration along with members of Congress, Supreme Court justices, high-ranking military officers, the diplomatic corps, the Inaugural Committee, and other high-ranking dignitaries.

The vice president takes the oath of office first. The U.S. Constitution does not specify an oath of office for the vice president; therefore, he or she repeats the oath used by other government officials:

I, (state name), do solemnly swear (or affirm) that I will support and defend the Constitution of the United States against all enemies, foreign and domestic; that I will bear true faith and allegiance to the same; that I take this obligation freely, without any mental reservation or purpose of evasion; and that I will well and faithfully discharge the duties of the office on which I am about to enter. So help me God.

This is followed by four ruffles and flourishes, then "Hail, Columbia."

At noon, the new president's term begins. As close to this time as possible, preferably at noon, the president-elect takes the oath of office, traditionally administered by the chief justice of the U.S. Supreme Court. The form mandated in Article II, Section 1 of the U.S. Constitution is used:

I, (state name), do solemnly swear, that I will faithfully execute the office of the president of the United States, and will to the best of my ability, preserve, protect, and defend the Constitution of the United States. So help me God.

The Bible is customarily used for the swearing in, but there is no requirement that any book in particular be used. Immediately following the presidential oath, the band plays four ruffles and flourishes and "Hail to the Chief," followed by a twenty-one-gun salute from howitzers of the Presidential Salute Battery, Third United States Infantry Regiment (The Old Guard).

The new president then gives a speech referred to as an inaugural address. Following the end of the program, the president and vice president are honored at a luncheon hosted by the Joint Congressional Committee on Inaugural Ceremonies. This is the only time that the president, vice president, and both houses of Congress congregate in the same location, with the exception of the State of the Union addresses and state funerals.

Following the luncheon, the president traditionally parades down Pennsylvania Avenue from the Capitol to the White House. Military, collegiate, and high school bands accompany floats from selected states of the union. The jubilant, welcoming parade is long and often ends as darkness is falling. Excited spectators line the route from the Capitol to the White House. The president, vice president, their families, friends, and other invited officials view the parade from an enclosed viewing stand built in front of the White House. The diplomatic corps views the parade from a stand in front of Blair House, where its members and their spouses have been invited for a luncheon following the swearing-in ceremony at the Capitol.

Security is a complex matter involving the Secret Service and many federal law-enforcement agencies, all five branches of the armed forces, the Capitol Police, and the Metropolitan Police Department of the District of Columbia.

Later in the evening the inaugural balls are held at selected hotels and centers in the City of Washington. A good time is had by all until the early hours of the morning.

A new president and family now reside at the White House, and the United States begins a new chapter lasting until the same process repeats itself in four years.

State and Official Funerals

Loss Shared by the Nation

In the United States, state funerals are held to honor deceased presidents, former presidents, and presidents-elect. Another individual may be granted a state or official funeral only if a resolution is passed by the U.S. Congress. For the most part, state and official funerals are open to the public so that the nation has the opportunity to participate in mourning the loss of the deceased leader.

A president's funeral is steeped in tradition and protocol, but the deceased and his or her family have made personal predetermined decisions concerning the arrangements that will take place.

Early Planning

State and official funerals are elaborate events marked by immense detail and careful planning.

Shortly after being inaugurated, a new president meets with a member of the Military District of Washington to discuss his or her wishes for funeral plans. State funerals are ideally planned years in advance; the president or former president may make adjustments to the original plan over the following years.

Spouse of the President

When the spouse of a current or former president dies, the Military District of Washington, Ceremonials Division, will advise and assist the family in planning and coordinating the funeral.

The spouse is authorized the services of armed forces body bearers to carry the casket, and the family may request a military chaplain. These are the only privileges afforded to a spouse. A spouse is not authorized a state funeral.

Announcement of Death

The sitting president announces the death of a former commander in chief and joins the nation in offering condolences. Official notification of the death is sent to all branches of the U.S. government, to foreign governments, and to the public.

The secretary of defense is directed to conduct the funeral on behalf of the nation. The secretary of the army represents the secretary of defense and designates the commanding general for the U.S. Army, Military District of Washington, to execute all responsibilities for the ceremonial arrangements (in Washington, D.C., or elsewhere in the United States). All five branches of the U.S. armed forces serve as support for the implementation of funerary plans.

To execute the sequence of events for the funeral ceremonies, the Military District of Washington follows the state funeral plan document already approved by the deceased as well as accommodates the wishes of the family. The Department of Homeland Security is in charge of national security for special events for these momentous occasions, and the U.S. Secret Service implements security and protection arrangements.

At the State Department, the assistant chief of protocol for diplomatic affairs has the responsibility of notifying foreign embassies in Washington of the death. Ambassadors, in turn, inform their respective governments of both the death and arrangements for funeral services. Members of the diplomatic corps traditionally represent their governments at the Rotunda in the U.S. Capitol and at the funeral service, but occasionally another higher-ranking member of their government will also be present. The assistant chief of protocol for ceremonials makes arrangements for the diplomatic corps, including transportation and seating for the events. Personnel from the Military District of Washington, the Office of Protocol, the U.S. Secret Service (Homeland Security), the White House, Congress, and the National Cathedral (or other church), as well as family representatives, are all involved in meetings from the day of the announcement of death until the interment to ensure arrangements are properly carried out until all services have concluded.

Family of the Deceased

It is tradition that the immediate family of the deceased be accommodated at Blair House, the president's Guest House, during the time of the ceremonies and services held in Washington, D.C.

A STATE FUNERAL SURPRISE AT BLAIR HOUSE

Following the death of one former U.S. president, what was thought to have been a possible security breach at Blair House caused some laughs even during the serious, sad moments. Secret Service approached the manager of Blair House with concern that a "woman of ill repute" had entered the president's guest house without permission.

Upon further inspection, it was uncovered that the woman was actually the daughter of a celebrity, invited by the former first family to attend the state funeral. Though she had security clearance, no one recognized her due in part to her scandalous and revealing outfit.

Military Chaplain

A military chaplain from one of the military branches is assigned to the deceased's immediate family.

Basic Structure of Ceremony Following the Death

Military Escort

The commanding general of the U.S. Army, Military District of Washington, serves as the military escort for the immediate family. The general will serve in this capacity from the time of the official announcement of the death until burial is completed.

When the death takes place outside of Washington, D.C., the Military District of Washington makes arrangements to accompany and transfer the body, as well as to transfer the immediate family of the deceased, to the nation's capital.

Lying in Repose

The body may lie in repose in the East Room of the White House when a president dies in office. The body of a former president may lie in repose in the deceased's home state or at another location in Washington, D.C.

Lying in State

By tradition, for a state funeral, when the deceased has requested and Congress has offered the honor of lying in state in the U.S. Capitol Rotunda, the body of the former leader will be brought to the Capitol for the public to honor.

Body Bearers

A nine-person detail from each of the five branches of the U.S. armed forces carries the casket during a state funeral.

Traditional Honors

Honor Guard

Military District of Washington ceremonial detachments for the army, marines, navy, air force, and coast guard serve as a "guard of honor" as the former president lies in repose or in state.

Twenty-one-Gun Salute

The traditional military honor for a chief of state is a cannon salute of twenty-one rounds.

Flag-Draped Casket

All military veterans are entitled to have the American flag draped over their caskets. The president, as commander in chief of the armed forces, is also entitled to this honor.

Riderless Horse

A riderless horse follows the caisson. A pair of boots is reversed in the stirrups of the empty saddle to symbolize that the warrior will never ride again. During Ronald Reagan's funeral, one of his own boots was reversed in the stirrup of Sergeant York, the horse named to honor World War I soldier Alvin C. York. A riderless horse is also known as a "caparisoned horse," which name refers to its ornamental coverings and their protocol detail.

Military Bands

During each phase of the funeral, a military band will play appropriate music in honor of the former president.

Hail to the Chief

The traditional song played to announce the U.S. president is "Hail to the Chief." For the numerous arrival and departure ceremonies throughout the funeral, four ruffles and flourishes are rendered, followed by "Hail to the Chief," which is performed by a service band.

Ruffles are played on drums and flourishes on bugles. They are sounded together. Four ruffles and flourishes are the highest honor and are played for presidents.

Traditional Components in Washington, D.C., for the Funeral

Procession

A ceremonial funeral procession begins with a caisson in sight of the White House and travels to the Capitol.

Caisson

The caisson is a transport wagon converted for a 75 mm cannon, which transports the remains during the funeral procession in Washington, D.C. The caisson consists of six horses of the same color. Only the three horses on the left are mounted. This tradition dates to a time when one artillery horse in every pair carried provisions instead of a rider. A section chief from the Old Guard Caisson Platoon of the Army's Third United States Infantry Regiment rides a seventh horse separately.

Transfer of the Casket

For former presidents, the casket is transferred to the caisson at Sixteenth Street and Constitution Avenue just before arriving beside the South Lawn; it then moves down Pennsylvania Avenue. For a sitting president, the casket is transferred at the Pennsylvania Avenue Entrance in front of the White House before moving down Pennsylvania Avenue to the Capitol. The procession comprises the five branches of the armed forces, represented by the National Guard, including active-duty, academy, and reserve personnel. A riderless horse follows the casket. A service band precedes each unit. Traditionally, the procession ends at the East Entrance of the Capitol. Exceptions have been made in the past for the procession to end at the Capitol's West Entrance.

U.S. Capitol

Upon arrival, the body will be taken to the Rotunda of the Capitol building, and a short service will ensue, attended by members of Congress and the deceased's family. The body will then lie in state in the Rotunda of the Capitol for public viewing until one hour before the departure ceremony for the memorial service. Members of each of the armed services compose the honor guard, which maintains a vigil over the remains throughout the period they lie in state.

In 1865, Abraham Lincoln became the first president to lie in state in the Rotunda of the Capitol. Funerals thereafter, most notability that of John F. Kennedy in 1963, were based somewhat on the Lincoln state funeral. For Lincoln's funeral, a rough, pine-board catafalque was built as a raised bier to support the casket. Known as the "Lincoln catafalque," this black-cloth-covered bier is used to support the remains of U.S. presidents to this day. The Lincoln catafalque is on display in the Exhibition Hall at the U.S. Capitol Visitors Center.

National Cathedral

A national funeral service, typically at the National Cathedral in Washington, D.C., is conducted with family, representatives of the U.S. government, foreign dignitaries, friends of the family, media, and often (when seats are available) members of the general public. According to the wishes of the deceased, the service may be held at another church or cathedral. The Office of Protocol arranges and directs seating for American and foreign government officials using the Order of Precedence.

Final Resting Place

Immediately after the service is concluded, the body and family travel by military arrangement to the final resting place, where the private service and interment take place. In recent times, the body and family have traveled to and from Washington by one of the military jets used in the presidential fleet. Arrivals and departures are normally met with a twenty-one-gun salute, an honor guard, and a service band as the coffin is loaded onto and unloaded from the aircraft.

Taps

This bugle call is sounded over the grave at interment. Taps dates back to the Civil War.

Firing of Three Volleys

A military rifle party of seven service members fires three volleys (which do not constitute a twenty-one-gun salute). The interment service is then concluded.

THE CUSTOM OF THREES

The custom of "threes" is thought to have been taken from writings about ancient Rome when describing mourners casting dirt on a coffin three times, calling the name of the dead three times, and declaring farewell three times as they left the tomb.

Military custom dictated, when in battle, that fighting would pause for removal of the dead. When the dead were removed, three volleys then signaled that the battle could resume.

Table of Funeral Entitlements

Official				Funeral					
Official	State	Official	Special Military	Armed Forces Full Honor	Special Full Honor	Full Honor (Company)	Full Honor (Platoon)	Simple Honor	
President of the United States*	•								
Former president of the United States*	•								
President-elect of the United States*	•								
Other persons designated by the president*	•								
Vice president of the United States*		•							
Chief justice of the United States*		•							
Cabinet members*		•							
Other government officials designated by the U.S. president*		•							

(Continued)

Table of Funeral Entitlements (Continued)

Official	State	Official	Special Military	Armed Forces Full Honor	Special Full Honor	Full Honor (Company)	Full Honor (Platoon)	Simple Honor
Foreign civil dignitaries designated by the U.S. president*		•						
Deputy secretary of defense*			•					
Former secretary of defense*			•					
Secretary of the army, the navy, and the air force*			•					
Chairman, Joint Chiefs of Staffs			•					
Five-star generals and admirals			•					
Chief of staff, U.S. Army			•					
Chief of naval operations			•					
Chief of staff, U.S. Air Force			•					
Commandant, U.S. Marine Corps			•					
Commandant, U.S. Coast Guard			•					
Other persons designated by the secretary of defense*			•					
Foreign military personnel designated by the U.S. president*			•					
Former deputy secretary of defense*				•				

Official				Funeral				
	State	Official	Special Military	Armed Forces Full Honor	Special Full Honor	Full Honor (Company)	Full Honor (Platoon)	Simple Honor
Former chairman, Joint Chiefs of Staff (not a five-star general or admiral)				•				
Assistant secretary of defense*				•				
Former secretary of the army, the navy, and the air force*					•			
Former chief of staff, U.S. Army and U.S. Air Force; former chief of naval operations					•			
Undersecretary of the army, the navy, and the air force*					•			
Four-star generals and admirals					•			
Lieutenant general, vice admiral, major general, rear admiral, brigadier general, colonel, and captain						•		
Officers below grade of colonel and captain							•	
All other military personnel								•

* These persons are not entitled to burial in a national cemetery simply by virtue of this position.

AWARDS AND DECORATIONS

Military awards and decorations in the United States recognize the service and personal accomplishments of members of the armed forces. The word "award" is all-inclusive, incorporating any decoration, medal, badge, ribbon, or appurtenance bestowed on an individual or unit. Civilian awards and decorations are bestowed by various agencies of the U.S. government and are usually issued for sustained meritorious service rather than for a specific heroic act. Certain government awards may be issued to armed forces personnel and may be worn in conjunction with awards and decorations of the U.S. military. The word "ribbon" is also all-inclusive and describes that portion of the suspension ribbon of a service medal or decoration worn instead of the service medal or decoration and made in the form of a ribbon bar; a ribbon is $1^{3}/_{8}$" long by $^{3}/_{8}$" wide. Service and training ribbons are included in this description.

The first American order was established by Gen. George Washington in 1782: the Purple Heart. Although this medal ranks lower on the list today, the bravery and self-sacrifice of Washington's soldiers ranked highest in the hearts of Americans at the time.

The coveted Medal of Honor is the highest military medal that can be bestowed upon anyone. It was once awarded to a female surgeon, Mary Walker, who exhibited great courage at Gettysburg during the Civil War. Walker is the only female to have received this honor.

Order of Precedence for U.S. Military Decorations

A military decoration is awarded to an individual for an act of gallantry or meritorious service. U.S. military decorations authorized for wear on an armed forces uniform are listed below in order of precedence:

1. Medal of Honor (army, navy, air force)
2. Distinguished Service Cross
3. Navy Cross
4. Air Force Cross
5. Defense Distinguished Service Medal
6. Distinguished Service Medal (army, navy, air force, coast guard)
7. Silver Star
8. Defense Superior Service Medal
9. Legion of Merit

10. Distinguished Flying Cross
11. Soldier's Medal
12. Navy and Marine Corps Medal
13. Airman's Medal
14. Coast Guard Medal
15. Bronze Star Medal
16. Purple Heart
17. Defense Meritorious Service Medal
18. Meritorious Service Medal
19. Air Medal
20. Joint Service Commendation Medal
21. Army Commendation Medal
22. Navy Commendation Medal
23. Air Force Commendation Medal
24. Coast Guard Commendation Medal
25. Joint Service Achievement Medal
26. Army Achievement Medal
27. Navy Achievement Medal
28. Air Force Achievement Medal
29. Coast Guard Achievement Medal
30. Prisoner of War Medal
31. Combat Action Ribbon

For information regarding armed forces regulations for wearing decorations, service medals, badges, unit awards, and appurtenances, contact the Department of Defense. Alternatively, one may review a military website regarding the particular decoration in question.

Nonmilitary Decorations

Various branches of the U.S. government and other organizations award nonmilitary decorations too numerous to list. Each must be worn according to the Order of Precedence, which should be referenced prior to an occasion. Nonmilitary decorations may be worn on uniforms when accompanied by one or more U.S. military decorations.

Awards and Decorations Given by the President of the United States

• Presidential Medal of Freedom
• Presidential Citizens Medal

- Public Safety Officer Medal of Valor
- President's Award for Distinguished Federal Civilian Service
- Presidential Award for Excellence in Mathematics and Science Teaching
- Presidential Award for Leadership in Federal Energy Management
- Preserve America Presidential Award
- President's Environmental Youth Award

BASIC GUIDELINES FOR WEARING DECORATIONS

- Military and civilian decorations may be worn at prestigious non-military ceremonial functions, providing the invitation specifically calls for them. Decorations may be worn when an invitation states, "White Tie and Decorations" or "Black Tie and Decorations".
- The host or hostess responsible for a function decides if it is fitting for decorations to be worn.
- Whoever issues the decoration governs the protocol for the wearing of the decoration.
- The decorations of one's own country are given precedence over foreign decorations, as are the decorations that accompany one's military rank.
- When the person wearing the decorations has more orders than may be worn at once, that person should wear the most senior order.
- There are no regulations for wearing civilian lapel buttons or rosettes, but general guidelines discussing buttons and rosettes are helpful: miniature replicas of ribbons made in the form of lapel ribbons and rosettes may be worn on the left lapel of civilian clothes with the exception of civilian evening dress.

White Tie with Decorations

Men in White Tie

- The broad riband (sash) with a badge of the senior order is to be worn in the correct manner, normally running from the right shoulder to the left hip across the body. The order of the badge may dictate the shoulder over which the riband should be worn. This riband may be replaced by a shortened riband, which is more convenient with evening dress. Such a riband is fastened at one end to two buttons at the front of the arm hole of the waist coat, and the other end to a button on the bottom of the waistcoat in such a manner that the bow rests on the hip. The riband is always worn under the tail coat but over the waist coat.

- A total of four stars may be worn on the left breast of the tailcoat.
- Only one neck badge may be worn. The riband of the senior order should be of miniature width and worn just below the bow tie.
- Miniature badges of orders, decorations, and medals may be worn on the jacket's left lapel and are often mounted on a bar brooch in the correct order.

Women in Long Evening Dress

- A total of four stars may be worn on the left side of the dress.
- The full-size broad riband of the senior order may be worn.
- A woman wears the badge, which a man wears as a neck badge, suspended from the riband and formed into a bow on the left side of her dress. The badge would be worn above stars of orders and above miniature orders, decorations, and medals.
- Miniatures of all orders, decorations, and medals should be mounted on a bar brooch in the correct order on the left side of the dress.

Black Tie with Decorations

Men in Black Tie

- Only one star may be worn on the left breast of the coat.
- One neck badge suspended on a miniature ribbon of an order may be worn.
- One neck badge suspended on a miniature ribbon of an order may be worn below the bow tie.
- Miniatures of all orders, decorations, and medals are worn on a medal bar on the jacket's left lapel in the correct order.

Women in Long Evening Dress

- Miniatures of all orders, decorations, and medals should be mounted on a bar brooch in the correct order on the left side of the dress.

- Badges of orders may be worn mounted on a bow directly below the medal bar.
- One star only may be worn on the left side of the dress directly below bow orders.

Business Suit

Men in Business Suit

- The invitation should indicate whether decorations should be worn.
- Full-size insignia, suspended from a medal bar, may be worn on the left side of the coat.
- Only one neck badge should be worn, suspended from a full-width ribbon. The ribbon is worn under the shirt collar so that the badge rests on the tie immediately below the knot.
- The stars of orders should not be worn.

Late-Afternoon Suit or Cocktail Dress

Women in Late-Afternoon Suit or Cocktail Dress

- The invitation should indicate whether decorations should be worn.
- At a daytime event to which men are wearing lounge/business suits, women may wear full-size insignia, suspended from a medal bar.
- For an evening function, miniatures should be worn.
- One full-size badge (that would be worn at a man's neck) should be worn on a bow attached to the dress immediately below the medal bar.
- The stars of orders should not be worn.

Daytime Occasions

For special gatherings and services during the day, such as Memorial Day services, guests are often expected to wear medals with suits. It is acceptable to wear miniatures rather than full-size medals at evening functions for these events.

The invitation to the event should indicate that medals are to be worn.

Uniformed Members

Both men and women of uniformed organizations should wear their insignia as set out in their respective dress regulations.

Those persons in military uniforms should consult their respective services for guidance.

U.S. Merchant Marine medals may be worn on uniforms following all other U.S. decorations and service medals.

U.S. decorations, medals, and ribbon bars, with the exception of the Medal of Honor (which is worn around the neck), are worn on the left breast pocket of a soldier's uniform coat or jacket and are pinned or sewn from the wearer's right to left in order of precedence.

Medal of Honor

The Medal of Honor is worn with the neck-band ribbon placed around the neck outside the shirt collar and inside the coat collar, the medal itself hanging over the necktie near the collar. If a foreign neck decoration is worn with the Medal of Honor or with the Presidential Medal of Freedom, the foreign decoration should be beneath the Medal of Honor.

Foreign Awards with U.S. Decorations

Foreign awards are worn following all other U.S. decorations and medals. Foreign awards that are dissimilar to, or must be worn in a manner different from, U.S. awards may be worn only as a courtesy to the awarding country. Such awards are worn when the recipient is attending a public function in the house of, or in honor of, an official or citizen of the country of origin of the decoration. The invitation to an event should read "with decorations" if decorations are appropriate.

No foreign award is worn on a uniform unless at least one U.S. award is worn at the same time.

It should be noted that strict regulations govern the acceptance of foreign awards and decorations. Armed service personnel should seek the approval of the Department of Defense, and civilians should contact the Office of the Chief of Protocol, Ceremonials Division, Department of State, regarding their acceptance.

Decorations Worn in Europe

Throughout most of Europe, white tie is considered the only attire formal enough to display one's honors. When the attire for an occasion in Europe is black tie, one should consider confining the decorations to a rosette or (less traditionally) to a maximum of six miniature medals. Check that the occasion calls for decorations.

Foreign Service Personnel

Miniature war service decorations and civilian medals may be worn by Foreign Service personnel at official and social functions with formal day or evening clothes, when they are appropriate and the invitation calls for decorations. Miniature service decorations are worn on the left lapel or over the breast pocket.

The protocol officer of the mission concerned will advise on the propriety of whether or not awards should be worn on any particular occasion.

General Notes on the Wearing of Decorations

When in a foreign country to which he or she is accredited, a diplomat should wear the decorations given to him or her by that country when an invitation states "with decorations." A diplomat present at the embassy or legation of a country that has decorated him or her should give preference to those decorations.

Diplomatic officers do not wear insignia of a higher order than that worn by their superiors.

Chapter 11

Conduct of Diplomacy

President Ronald Reagan greeting Ambassador Shirley Temple Black during the White House visit of Lee Kuan Yew, Prime Minister of the Republic of Singapore, October 8, 1985. Courtesy of the Reagan Presidential Library. Ambassador Black was Ambassador to Czechoslovakia (1989–1992), Chief of Protocol (first woman, 1976–1977), Ambassador to Ghana (1974–1976), Delegate to the United Nations (1969).

ROLE OF PROTOCOL IN DIPLOMACY

THE RULES OF PROTOCOL MAY BE FAR-REACHING and affect numerous aspects of day-to-day life in governmental and official circles. However, these rules and customs have perhaps their greatest influence and impact when it comes to relationships between governments, particularly in the conduct of diplomacy.

For centuries, nations and their representatives at home and abroad have observed rules of etiquette designed for various purposes. Such rules may serve to further a nation's self-interest by showing respect and deference or may simply help to avoid misunderstanding and conflict by establishing a transparent, commonsense system for conducting affairs. In some cases, these practices were born of necessity; in others, they reflect the adoption of practices already in existence for years. In any event, with the passage of time, a body of rules developed, and eventually was recorded, that provided guidance for personal and official conduct in many different situations. Indeed, with the existence of a readily available code of conduct, breaches of protocol have become less common. On the other hand, when they do occur, there are fewer excuses.

Perhaps the first recognition of the need for a code of conduct among societies arose before man grouped into civilized societies. It has been said that when people roamed the earth—moving from place to place seeking food and water for themselves and grazing land for their animals—the various tribes would communicate through messengers. On occasion, when the news being delivered wasn't positive, disappointment was taken out on the deliveryman, resulting in his injury or death. It didn't take long to learn that messengers had to be given protection to promote communication between groups and to ensure that vital information was exchanged.

Throughout the millennia, the system for communication between nations, and the status and protections accorded messengers, has been refined. However, commonsense rules still form the basis for the conduct of diplomacy.

Over time, people established permanent settlements. As these centers became more populated and evolved into cities and states with definable borders, strategic assets, businesses, and national identities, the need to interact with neighboring centers (sometimes friendly, sometimes hostile) became increasingly important, and delegations routinely traveled from one to the other to deliver messages, negotiate matters, or take part in official ceremonies. Eventually, delegations took up residence and established a presence in the country.

Today, relations between countries are established by mutual agreement, in accordance with international law, treaties, and customary practice.

ESTABLISHING DIPLOMATIC RELATIONS

It is in nation's interests to establish diplomatic relations with one another. In addition to facilitating communication between governments and foreign leaders on issues of mutual importance, such as security, trade, and possible areas of cooperation, the presence of a diplomatic mission in a foreign country may lend credibility or prestige to both sending and receiving states. It also may provide opportunities for better understanding of the government, way of life, culture, or politics of a particular country.

Under international law, there are no hard and fast rules for establishing diplomatic relations between countries, except that relations must be established by mutual consent. One country cannot force diplomatic relations upon another. Once the parties have negotiated an agreement to establish relations, it may be memorialized by an exchange of treaties or diplomatic notes, by a letter from one leader to another or between foreign ministers, or simply by a handshake.

After establishing diplomatic relations, nations customarily exchange ambassadors, each of whom serves as the personal representative of his or her country's sovereign or leader. An ambassador is the personification of his or her leader in the country where accredited and is the point of contact between the host country and the sending state. In the United States, most ambassadors travel to Washington and reside there for a period of years when carrying out their responsibilities. However, some ambassadors are "nonresident" and live elsewhere (either in another country where they also serve as ambassador or in their home country), traveling to Washington occasionally throughout the year to conduct business or represent their governments at important events.

Another step that follows the establishment of diplomatic relations is the opening of an embassy. The word "embassy" describes two types of buildings: the *chancery*, which is the building or suite of offices where an ambassador and staff work, and the *residence*, which is the home of the ambassador. Before embassies in the United States may be occupied, the U.S. State Department must approve the location of the office as well as the contract for the sale or lease of the property.

In addition to sending an ambassador, most governments will wish to send a number of diplomats of varying ranks to carry out a variety of functions on its behalf.

AMBASSADORS

The highest-ranking diplomat sent by one country to represent it in another is its ambassador. While there are no universal job qualifications for ambassadors—the sending state may nominate anyone it chooses to represent it—the majority of ambassadors are career diplomats who have acquired a broad range of experience during the course of their careers and have served their countries in increasingly responsible positions, both abroad and at home. By the time they are appointed to serve in Washington, many ambassadors have held ambassadorial positions in at least one other country or at an international organization. It is not uncommon for ambassadors to the United States to be drawn from foreign governments' highest levels, having served as foreign ministers or in other senior positions in the foreign ministry. In a few cases, former presidents and prime ministers have been sent to Washington to represent governments. In most cases, ambassadors appointed from outside their governments' career service have distinguished themselves in other fields, such as business or education.

Agrément

No matter what the person's background, the Vienna Convention on Diplomatic Relations, the international law governing the conduct of diplomacy, stipulates that the sending state must secure the advance approval of the receiving state before sending an ambassador to represent it. The term describing this procedure is *agrément*, which is the French word for "agreement."

The purpose of the procedure is to ensure that the designated ambassador is acceptable to the receiving state. This has less to do with whether the person has the experience necessary to handle the job (because it is believed that governments should have broad discretion in appointing their ambassadors) and more to do with whether the person possesses the character, integrity, and standing to serve effectively as the sovereign's representative in the country and as the channel of communication between the two. While it is rare for one country to refuse *agrément*, people have been turned down because they were known (or suspected) to have engaged in illegal activity, advocated positions far beyond the mainstream, or been overly critical of the receiving country.

The *agrément* procedure is always conducted confidentially in order to avoid embarrassment to the sending government and the nominee in the event the request is refused, which happens rarely. In the few cases where *agrément* is not granted, the refusal often is not issued formally. Instead, the receiving state may delay responding on the theory that the sending state eventually will "get the message." If this approach is not successful, after a while, an informal meeting may be arranged between representatives of both governments and word passed that the appointment of another candidate might be viewed more favorably.

Requests for *agrément* may be transmitted in a number of different ways. The most common method is for the sitting ambassador to deliver the request for his or her successor personally to the foreign ministry. In this case, the embassy prepares a diplomatic note to the ministry requesting *agrément* and encloses the curriculum vitae of the nominee. In other cases, the foreign ministry of the sending state may transmit the same documents through the receiving state's embassy. When the request for *agrément* is approved, a diplomatic note is sent via the same channel through which the original request was made. Often, the note is preceded by a telephone call.

Ambassadors at Post

When the time comes for the new ambassador to take up his or her post, the sending state notifies the receiving state of the ambassador's travel plans. Upon arrival at post, the ambassador will be met at the airport and welcomed by host-country representatives. Thereafter, arrangements are made for presentation of credentials by the ambassador to the country's head of state. This ceremony is the host country's formal recognition that the ambassador has been accepted and is empowered to function on behalf of his or her government.

Presentation of Credentials

The formality of the ceremony varies from country to country. In the United States, ceremonies are arranged several times during the year. A number of ambassadors are invited with their immediate family members to visit the White House on a given day to present credentials to the president. They are escorted from their residences by protocol officers in State Department–supplied limousines, which fly the flags of the United States and the ambassador's country. A police escort is provided to facilitate the trip.

At the White House, the limousines are arranged in precedence order, based on the date of the ambassador's arrival in the United States (with the ambassador who arrived earliest in the group going first). A military honor guard lines the driveway, and as each ambassador's vehicle makes its way to the Diplomatic Entrance, a fanfare is played.

The chief of protocol greets each ambassador and accompanying family members, who then are escorted to the West Wing to meet the other newly arrived ambassadors and their families and to enjoy refreshments.

The president receives each ambassadorial party individually for a meeting in the Oval Office. During that time, the ambassador presents his or her credentials to the president, and there is a short conversation. There is also an exchange of written remarks between the president and the ambassador. An official photograph of the president and the ambassador will be taken. After the ceremony, the ambassador is escorted to his or her residence.

Because there may be delays of up to two months between the time the ambassador arrives in the United States and presentation of credentials to the president, a less formal interim ceremony takes place at the State Department shortly after the ambassador comes to Washington. In that case, a courtesy call is made by the ambassador upon the secretary of state (or, in the secretary's absence, upon a senior State Department official), who receives copies of the documents the ambassador will present to the president. Although the ambassador is not considered to be "fully credentialed" until the White House ceremony, the call to the State Department enables the ambassador to begin carrying out many of his or her duties.

Unlike the arrival, there is no formal procedure when an ambassador departs the United States. Most will make arrangements to visit the State Department or other government agencies to say good-bye to working-level friends and associates. In some cases, appointments may be made to bid farewell to senior U.S. government officials. Only rarely will the ambassador meet with the president.

Role of the Ambassador

A foreign ambassador residing abroad is the personal representative of his or her sovereign. As such, an ambassador personifies the sovereign in the host country and deals with host-country officials on behalf of the sovereign. Ambassadors carry out responsibilities, make decisions, and act in matters based on instructions from, and consultations with, their governments. An ambassador's primary duty, as is the case with all personnel working under his or her direction, is to promote the interests of the represented country. The ambassador's performance will be judged on how well these responsibilities have been carried out.

Ambassadors should seek to develop relationships with high-ranking officials in the host country. A personal relationship with the leader of the country to which he or she is assigned is particularly desirable. Such a relationship places the ambassador in the position of exercising influence at the highest level. However, in most countries, for most ambassadors, this level of access is not feasible. Nevertheless, it is advantageous to form close ties to other ranking members of the government, particularly in agencies with a direct impact on the ambassador's government's national interest. For example, if one country is looking to another for military aid and support, the ambassador will focus on the country's defense agencies. If it is seeking financial aid and support, the treasury and foreign aid agencies will be of greatest importance. Naturally, the ambassador will want to develop a network within these agencies at both the senior and the working levels in order to build a broad network of contacts from which to draw.

In addition to making contacts in these areas, an ambassador should become acquainted with others in the host country who may influence the government and its policies. While in some countries there is little input from outside the government, in others many entities have a hand, either formally or informally, in shaping policy. In the United States, a savvy ambassador will befriend key senators and congressmen, leaders of think tanks and advocacy organizations, and journalists whose work helps to shape public opinion.

Such contacts and attention to news reports, journals, and other sources of information, including the occasional rumor, will enable the ambassador to perform another important duty, which is to report on political and economic goings-on, as well as a wide range of other events in the host country. It is important for the ambassador not only to describe what is happening at the time but to report to his or her government regarding trends and to provide analysis to guide his or her government in shaping future policies.

The ambassador also may be called upon to negotiate resolutions of important issues between the countries, deal with issues related to business relationships, help promote the sale of his or her country's goods, assist in promoting foreign investment in his or her nation's enterprises, address issues relating to his or her nation's citizens living in the host country, organize visits of government officials traveling to the host country, and participate in official visits.

As the ranking member of his or her government in the host country, the ambassador also serves as governmental spokesperson, appearing on media broadcasts, talking with journalists and authors, and participating in symposia. The ambassador's activities may include travel throughout the host country to speak before various groups, meeting with members of the home nation's community, and becoming acquainted with local officials in areas that have a relationship with his or her country.

The ambassador will serve as the home country's representative at official and social events given by host-country officials and other ambassadors and will host numerous breakfasts, lunches, dinners, coffees, teas, and receptions at the embassy or residence.

Usually an ambassador will have professional diplomats and support staff, as well as chefs, butlers, and chauffeurs, to help carry out responsibilities on his or her government's behalf.

Ambassadors Representing Their Governments at Major National Events

As noted previously, a large portion of an ambassador's time is spent performing representational responsibilities. When not hosting events on behalf of his or her government, an ambassador is often attending events (or "showing the flag," in diplomatic parlance). Generally, the most important business or social occasions for an ambassador are those sponsored by the head of state or host country at which the ambassador represents his or her government.

In the United States, perhaps the most significant occasion for an ambassador to represent his or her government is at the inauguration ceremony of the U.S. president. Because it is primarily a national, not an international, occasion—and because in modern times it would be logistically impossible to accommodate a large contingent of foreign officials and their entourages for the event—the U.S. government follows the practice of inviting the foreign ambassadors accredited to Washington to represent their governments at the inauguration and related ceremonies. Although there have been frequent requests from abroad in the past, foreign leaders are not invited to the event, and inquirers are politely told to send their ambassadors. At times, this may be awkward for the ambassador, but the rule is followed strictly. Every four years, the Office of Protocol issues a diplomatic note to all of the embassies in Washington reiterating the policy. This issuance is helpful in deterring higher-level solicitations for invitations and gives the ambassador an official statement for reference when delivering the unpleasant news to an unhappy sovereign. Even so, it is believed that in one instance a hapless ambassador lost his job because he could not procure a seat at an inauguration for his Third World leader.

The chiefs of missions' involvement in each president's inaugural celebration may vary from administration to administration. But every occasion shares some common elements. All foreign ambassadors and their spouses are invited to attend the swearing-in ceremony at the Capitol on January 20. Because of their high rank and standing in the U.S. Order of Precedence, foreign ambassadors are included on the platform with the incumbent president and vice president, the president-elect and vice president–elect, Supreme Court justices, senators, congressmen, and numerous other dignitaries. Because of space limitations, however, their spouses are seated elsewhere. Following the ceremony, the ambassadors and their spouses attend a luncheon reception at Blair House, the president's Guest House, directly across from the White House on Pennsylvania Avenue. In years when a new president is being inaugurated, the president-elect and his or her family will have resided at Blair House for a short stay leading up to the inauguration and will have vacated the premises just hours before. Following the reception, the ambassadors and spouses can view the inaugural parade from bleachers set up just outside Blair House's front door. That evening, as a group, they are invited to one of the inaugural balls held at venues throughout the city.

More solemn, but significant, events requiring the ambassador's presence are the state ceremonies following the death of a current or, more often, former U.S. president. On those occasions, foreign ambassadors are invited to represent their governments at the formal lying-in-state ceremony, when the president's casket is brought to the rotunda of the U.S. Capitol. Ambassadors are included as a group among the official mourners at the funeral services a few days later. In this instance, however, foreign governments also may send a senior official from abroad to participate in the church services, and many governments choose to do so. Ambassadors' spouses are not included in these events.

Another example of an important host-country event at which foreign ambassadors represent their governments is the annual State of the Union address given by the president before a joint session of Congress. In this case, the chiefs of mission are seated on the floor of the chamber of the U.S. House of Representatives, along with the senators, congressmen, Supreme Court justices, and cabinet members attending. Similarly, they are invited to attend joint meetings of the Congress convened when a foreign leader or other distinguished individual addresses the legislature. Sometimes, too, official Washington gathers to seek comfort and guidance, such as at the ceremonies at the Washington National Cathedral in the aftermath of the terrorist attacks of September 11, 2001. The chiefs of mission lent the condolences and support of their governments on this occasion as well.

Although they are not official U.S. government events, every four years foreign ambassadors and their spouses eagerly accept invitations from both political parties to attend their presidential nominating conventions. In these cases, the chiefs of mission travel at their own expense. However, attending the conventions affords them the opportunity to experience the hustle and bustle of a political convention, to observe the political process firsthand, and to meet political leaders and a cross section of political activists in both parties.

Role of the Ambassador's Spouse

Most ambassadors are accompanied to their postings by their spouses. Although an ambassador's duties are many, varied, and clearly understood, in most cases, there is no "position description" for the ambassador's spouse. While the ambassador will receive a detailed set of instructions upon taking up the new posting and will undoubtedly engage in frequent and lengthy consultations with the foreign ministry during the his or her tour of duty, most ambassadorial spouses receive no such guidance. Surprisingly, however, at one time in the U.S. Foreign Service, a diplomat was rated not only on his (as most diplomats at that time were men) own performance, but on how well his spouse carried out her responsibilities too!

The spouse's role is crucial to the ambassador's success. A spouse provides an extra pair of eyes and ears to help the ambassador take in all that is going on and an alter ego when the ambassador cannot attend two functions at the same time.

Operating without portfolio, most ambassadors' spouses learn the job as they go along, relying on advice and guidance from spouses of more senior ambassadors and their own wits and good judgment. In the broadest sense, the spouse is there to support the ambassador in promoting his or her government's interest and foreign policy. Generally, this means running the official residence; ensuring that the household staff functions effectively and efficiently; ensuring that the house and grounds are well maintained, presentable for functions, and attractive to visitors; and hosting a multitude of events from intimate dinners for elite groups to receptions for hundreds. An effective spouse, when a woman, will have the grace and style of the best hostesses to carry out these duties. Many men who are spouses tend to pursue their own careers, and therefore many duties regarding the residence and entertaining must be placed in others' portfolios.

In the process, an ambassador's spouse must learn "who's who" in the local hierarchy, who is up-and-coming and who is on the way out. While expected to accompany the ambassador to major events and to travel around the country as necessary, the spouse also may be required to speak at events on the ambassador's behalf, appear at functions that the ambassador cannot attend, and host groups in the ambassador's absence. A spouse will find him- or herself involved with certain obligatory memberships in various groups important to his or her government. In addition, the ambassador's spouse should develop a network of his or her own, including the spouses of other ambassadors as well as of senior government officials, legislators, and business, cultural, academic, and social leaders. Many successful ambassadorial spouses have supplemented their husband or wife's network of contacts with an array of their own, giving them a larger circle of friends and a greater sphere of influence.

DIPLOMATIC CORPS

In its broadest sense, the term *diplomatic corps* encompasses the hundreds of diplomats working at their various governments' embassies in host countries. Generally speaking, however, the term is understood to include the chiefs of diplomatic missions residing in a given country. The corps includes foreign ambassadors and chargés d'affaires. The chargés are in charge of the embassy when the ambassador is away or when the ambassadorial position is unfilled. Events hosted for the diplomatic corps are usually those to which the chiefs of diplomatic missions and their spouses are invited.

Dean of the Diplomatic Corps

The dean of the diplomatic corps represents the entire corps on occasions when it is not practical to invite all chiefs of mission. When the corps is assembled as a group, the dean precedes all others and, when necessary, speaks for the corps. Today, in most countries, the deanship automatically goes to the ambassador who has served longest in the host country. However, in some countries with a strong Roman Catholic tradition, the papal nuncio serves as dean. The second-ranking ambassador is known as the vice dean and substitutes for the dean when he or she is not available. Sometimes, when the diplomatic corps is gathered for an occasion and neither the dean nor vice dean is present, the senior-most ambassador will substitute and may be referred to as the "acting dean."

As noted, the dean of the corps traditionally represents his colleagues at official functions and serves as the spokesman for the group. The dean also represents the corps in meetings with host government officials where the perspective of the corps is solicited and, conversely, may meet with host-country officials when the corps as a group wishes to make its opinion known on a matter. Customarily, newly arrived ambassadors pay a courtesy call upon the dean and, on other occasions during the course of their postings, may solicit his or her advice and guidance.

In more recent times, as the diplomatic corps has increased in size and regional groupings have become more active, a subset of deans has evolved. They perform functions on behalf of their regional colleagues similar to those performed by the dean on behalf of the entire diplomatic community. Thus, there are now regional deans among the African, Asian, and Latin American ambassadors. The ambassador of the country that holds the presidency of the European Union (EU) speaks on behalf of all of his or her EU colleagues.

Who May Serve as a Diplomat?

In most cases, persons entering the diplomatic service of their countries receive little formal diplomatic training. Instead, it is preferred that persons with diverse interests, backgrounds, and life experiences be recruited, then subsequently receive training in languages, area studies, and other subjects related to specific assignments. Over time, with experience in foreign and domestic assignments, additional training, exposure to more experienced colleagues, periodic performance evaluations, and counseling, people rise to more senior positions with increased responsibilities.

For the most part, nations do not impose educational or professional requirements for those who would serve as foreign diplomats within their countries. Instead, the acceptance requirements for diplomats are typically minimal and general. To be recognized as a diplomatic agent by the United States, for example, a person must be over twenty-one years of age, be a national of the sending state, possess a recognized diplomatic title, carry a diplomatic passport from his or her government (or provide a statement explaining the lack thereof), hold a diplomatic visa issued by the U.S. government, and be performing diplomatic duties full time (as opposed to clerical or staff duties) at the country's embassy in Washington. A formal registration from the sending state attesting to the above is submitted to the Protocol Office, Department of State, after the person's arrival, entitling him or her to, and qualifying family members for, diplomatic accreditation.

Role of a Diplomat

A diplomat's primary functions include representing his or her government in the receiving state; protecting the interests of his or her country and its nationals; carrying on negotiations with the host country; learning about conditions and developments in the country and reporting on them to his or her own government; performing consular functions; promoting economic, cultural, and scientific ties; and generally promoting friendly relations.

In broad terms, a diplomat's role is to support the ambassador in promoting the home government's foreign policy and maintaining friendly relations. And, like an ambassador, he or she will be expected to host and attend social events, appear and speak on behalf of the government at various occasions, and so forth. However, unlike the ambassador, who has broad-ranging responsibilities, most diplomats focus their attention on a narrower set of duties. For example, almost every embassy has divisions to handle political, economic, press, cultural, consular, and embassy-management responsibilities. These sections have varying numbers of diplomats and staff members. In addition, a military section, comprising military officers who are also accredited as diplomats, will be liaising with the host-country military establishment.

As in the military, various titles within the diplomatic service indicate the rank and status of the individual. The highest-ranking diplomat at an embassy is the ambassador. Below him are the ministers, who generally serve as division heads. Next are the minister-counselors, counselors, first, second, and third secretaries, and finally the attachés. When there is no ambassador at the embassy, either because he is out of the country and unable to carry out his responsibilities or because no ambassador has been appointed, the next-ranking diplomat is designated to run the embassy and is referred to as the chargé d'affaires. Very often, persons assigned to embassies as attachés are not career diplomats but are attached to the embassy for a one-time posting. The military attaché, for example, is a career military officer serving in an occasional diplomatic posting, and the finance attaché may be a civil servant from the ministry of finance who has been sent to the host country to work on a special project.

Role of a Diplomat's Spouse

Although most diplomats' spouses host functions and attend events with their husbands or wives, they do not have the responsibilities of the ambassador's spouse. Today, many diplomatic spouses chose to pursue their own careers while abroad. In many countries, rules that formerly prohibited their employment have been liberalized, and in a modern global economy, there are many opportunities for spouses to work for either a host-country business or a foreign business with offices in the host country. Some spouses have portable careers, such as journalist or professor; others may be more limited in the duties they can perform.

Living in a foreign country for an extended period also affords many opportunities that both diplomats and their spouses will want to take the time to explore. Most capital cities have fine cultural institutions, museums, and universities (all of which have interesting programs for continuing education). Diplomats will benefit from any opportunity to learn more about the history and culture of the country they are visiting, including taking the time to travel and learn about other regions.

Chancery and Residence

Generally speaking, a country's embassy in a foreign country comprises the office or offices where the ambassador and diplomats work and the home where the ambassador resides. The chancery, which also may be referred to as the embassy, is the main office. It will house the ambassador and most, if not all, of the other officials and departments. If more space is required, the ambassador's government will buy or rent additional facilities. These offices, while still considered part of the embassy, are known as annexes. It is not uncommon for the consular or cultural section of the embassy to be located in another building, called the consular annex or cultural section. The ambassador's residence, which also comes under the umbrella of the embassy, may be located many miles away. Nevertheless, it is in integral part of the country's representation since it is used for many of the events hosted to promote the government's foreign policy.

MISSIONS TO THE UNITED NATIONS AND ORGANIZATION OF AMERICAN STATES

For centuries, diplomatic relations were conducted primarily on a bilateral basis (that is, directly between one country and another) through diplomats serving at embassies (or, in earlier times, legations) in capitals throughout the world. However, in more recent times, particularly since the end of World War II, nations have placed greater emphasis on conducting their foreign policy through multilateral organizations such as the United Nations (UN) and the Organization of American States (OAS). As a result, a new class of diplomats has evolved—those who represent their governments to an organization, not to another government. Thus, countries have established missions to the UN in New York City, which serves as UN headquarters, in much the same way as they have established embassies in Washington. Each country sends an ambassador, known as a permanent representative, to the UN, along with a host of diplomats and staff members to support the operation. The ambassadors are accredited to the UN, and the ambassador presents his or her credentials to the secretary-general. UN ambassadors are accorded diplomatic status and, for the most part, are treated similarly to their counterparts at embassies in Washington. Nevertheless, their work is not interchangeable, and with limited exceptions, they are admitted into the United States to perform one or the other function—especially since diplomats assigned to the UN must live in the New York City area and work at their UN missions on a full-time basis.

The arrangement with the OAS in Washington is similar. In most cases, governments have established missions to the OAS in Washington, separate and apart from their bilateral embassies, to carry out their OAS business. The exception to the rule is that a few countries with small foreign service staffs have combined embassy and OAS mission staffs, with the personnel handling both bilateral and multilateral duties.

Consulates and Consular Officers

Whereas embassies are established in a nation's capital for the conduct of diplomatic relations between two countries, consulates are established in cities other than the capital to perform promotional activities on behalf of a country and to provide services to its nationals living in the area. Although embassies may have consular sections that perform consular functions, consulates do not perform diplomatic functions.

The Vienna Convention on Consular Relations sets out the duties of a consular office in detail. These duties can be divided into two general categories: promotion and services. Consulates promote tourism, help to develop trade and commercial relations between countries, foster scientific, cultural, and educational exchanges, and generally seek to develop friendly relations between people. They also issue visas to persons wishing to travel to their country, issue passports, birth certificates, and other official documents, and provide notarial services for their nationals living in the area. Further, they look after their nationals by visiting prisons and assisting people in distress.

The senior consular staff members are officers with titles such as consul general, consul, vice-consul, and consular agent. Usually members of their governments' diplomatic service, they, like diplomats, are sent abroad for a tour of duty ranging from three to four years. They are assisted by the consular staff, which may also be sent from abroad or hired locally.

Honorary consuls are nationals of the host country who perform consular functions for a foreign government on a part-time basis, while pursuing a full-time career in another area, such as business, law, or teaching. They are appointed by foreign governments wishing to have a consular presence in a given area but unable to establish a consulate because of the small size of their foreign service or because employing a full-time consul is not cost-effective.

As with an embassy, a foreign government must secure permission in advance from the State Department before opening a consular office, be it career or honorary. Generally, the government will send a written request explaining the need for consular services in the area and requesting approval to buy or lease a specific site for the office. Once the department has approved the request in writing, personnel subsequently assigned to the office must be registered with the Office of Protocol in much the same manner as diplomats in Washington.

DIPLOMATIC IMMUNITY

A fundamental principle guiding relations between governments is that diplomats of one country are immune from jurisdiction when serving in another. For the most part, they may not be arrested, detained, or prosecuted in the host country. That does not mean that they are "above the law," as some people erroneously believe. Rather, it reflects the commonsense understanding that in order for diplomats to perform their duties effectively on behalf of their governments, they must be able to work free from concern about interference from the host country. This is particularly important when they are assigned to countries that might have unfriendly relations with their own or in which the judicial systems may not offer the protections and safeguards commonly observed by other countries.

The principle of extending immunity to diplomats is not new; governments have observed it for centuries. As noted previously, the basis for this arrangement can be traced back to the roots of human civilization; it was created to keep open the channels of communication between groups and to enable their representatives to carry out their duties effectively for the common good.

Today, in countries throughout the world, when a diplomat and family members arrive to take up their assignment, their government's embassy will notify the protocol office of the foreign ministry of their arrival and provide whatever additional information the host country requires to accredit them with privileges and immunities. Thereafter, they will be issued diplomatic identification cards, and the names of the diplomat and spouse will be added to the diplomatic list along with all other diplomats at the embassy. In addition to identification cards, they will be given special license plates for their cars and, on a reciprocal basis, cards exempting them from payment of sales taxes on goods and services.

Although diplomats are granted diplomatic immunity to afford them complete freedom, independence, and security in carrying out their duties, under international law, they have an obligation to respect the laws of the host country. If they are caught committing a crime, particularly one that would endanger others or themselves, they may be deterred and subsequently detained for long enough to confirm their status with host-country officials. If necessary, they may be held until they can be released into the custody of an official from their embassy. In cases involving violent crimes, arrangements have been made between countries for offenders to be incarcerated while the matter is reviewed and agreement as to next steps can be reached. The same rule applies to spouses and children of diplomats.

Most incidents involving diplomats and their family members involve crimes that are not considered serious. In the United States, in such cases, once the authorities have verified entitlement to immunity, a report of the incident is sent to the State Department's Office of Protocol. The local prosecutor is contacted and asked if, in the absence of immunity, the case would be brought to trial. Subsequently, the diplomat's ambassador is advised in writing of the incident. If the prosecutor wishes to pursue the matter, the ambassador will be asked if his or her government will waive the person's immunity so that prosecution may proceed. The request for the waiver is made to the government rather than to the individual diplomat because the immunity belongs to the government, not the individual; it is extended to the diplomat so that he or she can carry out duties on behalf of the government, not as a personal benefit for the ambassador or his or her family. In a case involving a nonserious incident, if immunity is not waived, the State Department will maintain a record of the offense and will take stronger action if the person is involved in subsequent incidents. However, upon learning of the incident, the diplomat's government may, and often does, take disciplinary action on its own.

In cases that are considered serious (i.e., mostly felony offenses), the same procedure is followed. However, if the foreign government does not grant a waiver of immunity so that the offender may be prosecuted, the offender is expelled from the country, and an arrest warrant is issued so that return is not permitted unless the individual agrees to address the charges.

BREAKING DIPLOMATIC RELATIONS

Occasionally, but not often, nations will break diplomatic relations with one another. This most commonly happens when they go to war. However, there may be other occasions, such as the 1979 Iran hostage crisis, when one government's actions are so offensive to another that they cannot carry on business as usual. Usually, a written communication, coupled with a public announcement of the break, will be made. Subsequently, each government will remove its diplomatic personnel from the other's territory, usually within a few weeks' time.

While it is possible to withdraw most of the embassy staff, wind down the administration of the embassy, and secure the building within a short time, ongoing tasks may have to be performed. For example, the embassy complex will need looking after, personal effects and vehicles may need to be shipped, and an assortment of other administrative functions may have to be performed on an ongoing basis. Therefore, a government will often ask another government that maintains an embassy in the country to serve as its protecting power. In those cases, the protecting power will look out for the interests of the departing nation, particularly in regard to the embassy and any residences left behind.

There may be occasions, especially after some time has elapsed since the break in relations, when a government requires a presence in the country but is not prepared to reestablish full diplomatic relations. In those cases, the country requiring a continued presence may arrange with a third government to establish an interests section under the auspices of that country's embassy. It will then send its own diplomats to staff the office, but they will be accredited as diplomats from the third country's embassy.

Chapter 12

○

Blair House

His Majesty King Abdullah II, King of the Hashemite Kingdom of Jordan, signing the guest book at Blair House. Observing are Faisal al-Fayez, Chief of Royal Protocol, and Mary Mel French, U.S. Chief of Protocol. Author's collection.

The President's Guest House

MANY STORIES HAVE BEEN TOLD about Blair House, and many have attempted to explain its purpose, but to most, this historic house remains a mystery. Because Blair House is not open to the public, very few people have been inside the historic buildings that make up what is known today as "the president's guest house."

Located at 1651 Pennsylvania Avenue, just across from the White House, Blair House is the official Washington residence for foreign chiefs of state and heads of government visiting Washington, D.C., at the invitation of the U.S. president. This includes reigning monarchs and family members traveling with them. It is also used as a temporary residence for incoming U.S. presidents and has provided a comfortable place to stay for the families of deceased former presidents while they are in Washington for official state funeral ceremonies. President Harry Truman and his family also stayed at Blair House while the White House was being renovated from 1948 to 1952.

The primary purpose of Blair House is to make foreign leaders feel "at home" while they are in Washington. Blair House becomes a de facto diplomatic mission of the guest's home nation, and the guest's national flag flies over the house while he or she is in residence. An invitation to stay at Blair House—a vital part of any foreign leader's official visit—is considered an honor and a gesture of U.S. diplomatic goodwill toward a foreign nation's leader. Guests are made to feel as welcome as possible, and all efforts to ensure the highest level of service are considered essential to the visit's success. What happens behind the scenes at Blair House can be as much a part of the outcome of the visit as the official meetings and public ceremonies in which the leaders participate.

Blair House, as it exists today, is actually comprised of four interconnected houses that have been acquired and renovated over the years. From the exterior, the divisions of the house remain visible, but the interior conveys the impression of one elegant house. The entire complex is larger than the White House, although the rooms are smaller and not on the same grand scale. Blair House has 119 rooms, including 1 principal suite and 13 other guest bedrooms, 35 bathrooms, 4 dining rooms, several kitchens, a laundry, an exercise room, a hair salon, a flower shop, and gardens. The Blair House staff does its best to provide a visiting dignitary with all the services needed for a comfortable, secure, and discreet visit.

History of Blair House

The original Blair House was built in 1824 by Dr. Joseph Lovell, the first surgeon general of the United States, and is referred to as Blair House because it became the home of Francis Preston Blair and his family in 1836. Francis Blair, a member of President Andrew

Jackson's "Kitchen Cabinet," founded and published *The Congressional Globe*, which exists today as *The Congressional Record*. He also served as an advisor to Presidents Martin Van Buren and Abraham Lincoln. Francis Blair's two sons, Montgomery and Frank, were also very politically influential in Washington. Montgomery, Blair's eldest son, was the defending counsel in the *Dred Scott* case and later served as postmaster general under President Lincoln. Frank, a U.S. senator from Missouri, is credited with persuading that state to remain in the Union. Frank became a general in the Union army.

In 1859, Francis Preston Blair built the red-brick Lee House next door for his daughter Elizabeth and her husband, Union navy admiral Samuel Phillips Lee, cousin of Col. Robert E. Lee. At Blair House in the spring of 1861, Blair, on behalf of President Lincoln, offered Colonel Lee command of the Union forces. Colonel Lee declined and three days later resigned his commission from the Union army, taking command of all forces in Virginia (his home state). Lee later became a general in the Confederate army, then commander of all Confederate forces. Another prominent figure in the Civil War, Gen. William Tecumseh Sherman, had been married years earlier in Blair House.

With the support of President Franklin D. Roosevelt, Blair House was officially designated a place of national historic interest in 1940. Following U.S. entry into World War II, there was an increase in the visits of foreign leaders traveling to Washington for frequent bilateral meetings at the White House. In April 1942, the Blair family began leasing the house to the Department of State as a convenient and accommodating place for foreign leaders to reside during their stay in Washington. President Manuel Prado of Peru, King George of Greece, and Foreign Minister Vyacheslav Molotov of Russia were early guests. On December 11, 1942, the U.S. government purchased Blair House for $150,000 and most of its furnishings for an additional $33,000. After renovations were completed, the State Department assumed stewardship of Blair House as the nation's official guest house in February 1943.

"Truman White House"

At the time that President Truman occupied Blair House during the White House's renovation, Blair House and Lee House (the adjacent house purchased earlier than Blair House by the government in 1942) were merged by cutting doorways through the adjoining walls, creating the "Truman White House."

While living at Blair House, President Truman used the Lee Dining Room for cabinet meetings, and many important decisions were made around the table in this historic room. The Foreign Assistance Act of 1948, which enabled the Marshall Plan, had its origins in the Lee Dining Room, and the policy behind the Truman Doctrine also developed as a result of meetings in this room. After a series of Blair House meetings, President Truman signed a declaration declaring, on June 30, 1950, the North Korean invasion of South Korea a national emergency and authorizing the commitment of U.S. troops to the Korean conflict.

On November 1, 1950, during President Truman's residence at Blair House, two Puerto Rican nationalists, Oscar Collazo and Griselio Torresola, stormed the front door in an attempt to assassinate him. A gun battle on the steps of Blair House left three White House policemen injured, one of whom, Pvt. Leslie Coffelt, died later that day as a result of his wounds. Coffelt killed Griselio Torresola before he himself was wounded, and his badge is displayed at Blair House to this day in honor of his service and bravery. President Truman was upstairs at Blair House at the time of the shootings but escaped unharmed.

Preservation of Blair House

The two Jackson Place townhouses, built next to Blair House around 1860, were purchased and became part of the Blair House complex in 1970. Funded by a partnership between the federal government and the Blair House Restoration Fund, the house was completely renovated between 1982 and 1988. The government continues to fund the maintenance of the complex, and the Blair House Restoration Fund raises the monies necessary to preserve and expand its collections of furniture and American fine and decorative arts, as well as to maintain the décor of this historic residence.

The Blair House collections represent American Federal, English Regency, Victorian, and Colonial Revival tastes. Included in these treasures are paintings by American masters Gilbert Stuart, Thomas Sully, Thomas Moran, and John Singer Sargent; eighteenth- and nineteenth-century English and Chinese export porcelain; American glass and silver; and over fifty early lighting fixtures.

The Blair House Library contains a variety of books. They are in large part American, but many others have been received as gifts from foreign delegations who have stayed as guests at Blair House. A selection of these special gifts is always available as a symbol of the house's numerous visitors.

Today, four different State Department offices—Protocol, Diplomatic Security, Facilities Management, and Fine Arts—partner with the private Blair House Restoration Fund to manage, protect, maintain, conserve, and renew Blair House to serve the president and the American people by extending our finest diplomatic hospitality to official guests visiting the United States.

Chapter 13

Official Gift Giving

President Harry S. Truman (seated, left) receives a doll from Korean educator Dr. Helen Kim (seated, right). Dr. John Myun Chang, Ambassador of the Republic of Korean to the United States (standing, left) and Dr. Frederick Brown Harris, Chaplain of the Senate (standing, right) look on. Photograph courtesy of Harry S. Truman Library.

FIVE WORDS OF ADVICE

QUESTIONS RECEIVED BY THE OFFICE OF PROTOCOL about gift giving are almost always posed with noticeable insecurity and trepidation. Significant anxiety often accompanies gift giving, especially at the highest levels of government, such as when a president or other government official must present a gift to a foreign leader. The meaning and significance of these gifts increase exponentially in such a context; items passed from one nation's leader to another are rendered promises of a new relationship or become symbols of an existing relationship. There is always an implication that official gifts should be of the most unique, one-of-a-kind type when given at the presidential level. When gifts fail to match the occasion or the level of the relationship, diplomatic relationships may fail along with them.

Mastering the art of gift giving is not easy; recognition of the nuances of official giving comes with experience and knowledge of how to approach the process. There are those in the Office of Protocol, and others who have a background in the official gift-selection process, with creative knowledge not only of what to give but of how gifts should be presented for certain occasions. Their knowledge can be extraordinarily helpful to those without experience in this area. Consulting such people could save those needing to select official gifts who have not been involved in gift giving at the diplomatic level much time, frustration, and embarrassment. Official gift choices, after all, are quite different from the personal gift choices one makes when giving gifts to friends.

In a diplomatic context, gifts have tremendous potential for forging friendships, establishing ties, easing tensions, and sometimes simply saying thank you. To find the perfect symbol for that diplomatic occasion, some reliable steps can guide choices.

The Office of Protocol can follow guidelines that have proven effective in the past in order to select a gift to be given by the U.S. president, the vice president, the secretary of state, or their spouses. The protocol gift officer researches the background of the leader receiving the gift and presents a detailed list of one or more appropriate gifts to the official giving the gift. The official makes the selection, and the gift officer makes arrangements for obtaining the gift and gift card and for preparing the gift for presentation. Five simple words are useful when applied to the gift-selection process: occasion, background, creativity, sources, and elegance.

Occasion

If a gift is to be given to mark a special occasion (for example, a state visit, a treaty signing, or an inauguration), it is always advisable to choose one that can be interpreted as directly symbolic of that occasion. A personal gift is not appropriate in this context: in these cases, the gift is generally presented on behalf of one country to another rather than by one leader to another.

DAYTON PEACE ACCORD — PARIS, FRANCE

After grueling diplomatic negotiations, a peace treaty had been agreed upon between the presidents of Bosnia, Croatia, and Serbia. The signing ceremony was to take place in Paris, France. The United States had been a central player in forging the peace treaty. To commemorate the occasion and the significance of the event, an elegant bronze statue of three ballerinas dancing together, called Pas de Trois, was given as a symbol of the three warring countries now choosing to dance together in peace and harmony.

Background

If it is determined that a gift should be more personal in nature rather than ceremonial or symbolic, researching the background of the recipient to uncover his or her interests and hobbies is always a helpful tool in the gift-selection process. Discovering a key piece of information about the recipient that will resonate through a gift will invariably demonstrate how much effort and thought went into the selection.

SOUTH AFRICAN PRESIDENT NELSON MANDELA'S GIFT ON THE OCCASION OF HIS FIRST STATE VISIT TO THE UNITED STATES

After reaching out to U.S. Embassy officials in Johannesburg, South Africa, for background information on newly elected president Nelson Mandela, the gift officer discovered that Mandela was a boxer in his youth. Mandela was enthralled with

(Continued)

SOUTH AFRICAN PRESIDENT NELSON MANDELA'S GIFT ON THE OCCASION OF HIS FIRST STATE VISIT TO THE UNITED STATES (CONTINUED)

the sport and would often listen to boxing matches on the radio while growing up in South Africa. As an adult, Mandela would meet privately with U.S. boxing champions when he visited the United States.

With this information, the gift officer created a compilation of original letters from all of the living U.S. boxing champions addressed to President Mandela. After contacting the retired boxers, protocol received some heartfelt notes congratulating Mandela on becoming the new president. Some of the letters were sophisticated and others were not, but together they created a poignant tapestry. Many used metaphors such as fighting for freedom against apartheid, tying sports metaphors to Mandela's personal journey and to the journey of all blacks in South Africa.

These letters were compiled in a large hand-bound leather book with an inscription from the United States president to President Mandela. Black-and-white fighting stance photos of all of the boxers who wrote letters were included, as was a poem by American poet Langston Hughes, called "Question and Answer," in which the poet used boxing metaphors to describe South African apartheid. Last, an original ticket was located to the famous boxing match between Joe Louis and Max Schmeling, the German boxing world champion, in which Joe Louis beat the German in a match at Yankee Stadium in 1938. Louis's victory became symbolic of the United States' victory over Nazism and Adolf Hitler. Mandela had listened to this match on the radio as a child.

This gift was presented to President Mandela on the first day of his state visit to Washington. President Mandela, with his tall, wiry frame, was jumping up and down like a little boy upon receiving the gift. It was a special moment; the gift was a hit.

Creativity

Good gift ideas are the result of both inspiration and diligence. The Office of Protocol must be very careful with the amount of money spent on any gift. Creativity is the key to finding a unique gift at the right price.

GIFT FOR THE KING OF THAILAND

For this foreign trip, the protocol gift officer researched King Bhumibol's background and found that he was an accomplished alto saxophone jazz musician and composer. When he was just thirty-two years old, the king became the first Asian composer awarded honorary membership in the Academy of Music and Dramatic Arts in Vienna. In his travels, the king had played with such American jazz legends as *Benny Goodman, Jack Teagarden, Lionel Hampton, Maynard Ferguson,* and the *Preservation Hall Jazz Band.*

Knowing this information helped the gift officer narrow the gift possibilities. Through research, the gift officer contacted famous American photographer Herman Leonard, who, for over fifty years, had photographed all of the great American jazz musicians. Leonard agreed to develop some of his most famous black and white photographs in a large-scale format from his original negatives. The images of jazz legends like BB King, Louis Armstrong, and Etta James, to name a few, were compiled and placed in a special presentation box with an inscription.

His majesty was impressed by the fact that the president of the United States thought to present something so personal and that the president also had a personal interest in jazz. The two leaders made an instant connection through their love of jazz which simultaneously helped foster their diplomatic relationship.

WHAT CAN HAPPEN WHEN CREATIVITY IS LACKING?

Gift giving and receiving, by protocol standards, is generally accomplished in private. It is not proper diplomatic etiquette to give a gift directly; therefore, when protocol is in charge of the gift, it is delivered from one protocol officer to another protocol officer. There are always exceptions to the rule however, especially in the Middle East.

Gifts in Middle Eastern countries ruled by monarchs are often displayed in a room where the leaders of both countries will gather to view their gifts. The gifts from a chief of state are many times ornate and expensive. Since the U.S. government has very definite rules about funds spent on a gift, it is essential for the gift officer to do extensive research to uncover a unique idea that will please the recipient and not look out of place when viewed alongside more expensive items.

The gift officer from Protocol learned a valuable lesson on this first trip to the Middle East. One of the stops was to the Hashemite Kingdom of Jordan where the king and queen hosted a lovely private dinner for the American presidential couple. During the dinner, the U.S. gift officer was ushered into a room in the palace set up to display the gifts from the king and queen intended for the first couple. The instructions were to lay out the gifts being presented to their majesties along with the gifts their majesties were presenting.

After dinner, the two couples entered the room and admired the gifts. The gifts displayed from the king and queen were the most exquisite the gifts officer had ever seen. They were indigenous to the country, which was entirely appropriate in the context of developing personal relationships. The table was filled with bedouin jewelry, richly woven rugs, throws, tapestries in rich colors, and hand-forged silver chalices. Clearly much thought had gone into the selection. The gift officer was in panic mode.

The Americans would only be presenting a crystal eagle and a sterling silver bowl. Both were from well-established American companies and were suitable gifts, but they did not match the occasion that day. The gifts officer learned a valuable lesson—

always have a list developed of creative gifts that can measure up against gifts that are more costly and elaborate. Study the interests, hobbies, talents and collections of the leader and spouse to whom the gifts will be given so that under any circumstances the gift will be appropriate and suited to the occasion.

Sources

The Internet offers boundless options for gift ideas, as anyone who peruses it will see. It is helpful to develop a good list of options ahead of time so ideas are on hand when the time for gift giving arrives. In the Protocol Office, the task is to look for American-made items that represent the best of America and have a certain quality that makes them appropriate presidential gifts within the gift budget. The protocol gifts officer is advised to take trips to the National Archives and to speak to White House historians to better understand the symbols in and around the White House. The gifts officer may find it useful to compile a file of symbols to be used to identify an item as presidential without always using the presidential seal to convey that message. Artists throughout the country are generally willing to work with the Protocol Office to develop unique gift ideas under temporal and budgetary constraints.

GIFTS THAT FULFILL NEEDS

Some foreign trips require not only ceremonial gifts for officials, but also require gifts of a medical and educational nature for villages. The gift officer developed a comprehensive list of the items these sites desperately needed. Some of those items included computers, school supplies, encyclopedias, and medical equipment. Working with American embassies in the foreign countries, as well as with the United States Agency for International Development, it was possible to arrange for American companies to donate and ship these items to the villages ahead of the visit.

The villagers were tremendously appreciative of the effort that was made. These gifts made a difference to the villages and were truly gifts that kept on giving because they would continue to serve the villagers for years and provide the seeds for change.

Elegance

The final quality used when considering diplomatic gifts is elegance. After the occasion has been noted, the background research completed, options drawn from sources, and creative ideas developed, the final test is whether the potential gift choice has a certain stately quality. In other words, is it presidential enough? A gift given in a diplomatic context must have a definite *je ne sais quoi*. The more experience one has with a variety of gifts and options, the more one recognizes the gift that reaches a higher level of grace and resonance.

STATE VISIT OFFICIAL GIFT

In the beginning of a new administration, it is often decided that a gift should be created that will be presented only at state visits for visiting chiefs of state. The protocol gift officer may meet with notable American silver and crystal manufacturers to discuss a variety of designs appropriate for state gifts. Design elements and historical symbols of the White House may be used in the creation of the gift for these state occasions.

During the Clinton administration, Tiffany & Co. designed a large oval sterling silver cache-pot. The ceiling cornice design of the Oval Office was etched on its outer rim and the design on the front was taken from fireplace moldings built for the State Dining Room. It was inscribed to the receiving leader from the president of the United States. Only twenty of these cache-pots were made and presented to kings, presidents, and prime ministers; they were numbered so that a history could be recorded on each of these unique pieces.

Some gifts simply must be timeless treasures, and an official gift for a state visit is no exception.

GIFT RECOMMENDATIONS

- *Indigenous gifts*: Diplomatic gifts, both foreign and domestic, that reflect something about the giver's culture and background are appreciated. The key is to find one or two items that highlight a particular hometown, state, or country and to make those standard gifts.

  Examples: A coffee-table book with photographs featuring a particular city, state, region, or country; a locally made textile; a framed pencil sketch of a scene from a well-known area

- *Gifts with inscriptions*: Inscribing or engraving a gift will make even the most generic item unique to the recipient. However, care must be taken not to devalue the gift. Often, a card from the giver is more appropriate than an inscription or engraving.

  Example: A silver picture frame with the principal's picture and signature

- *Small gifts*: Even when a large or expensive gift may be unnecessary, a small gift is still a thoughtful gesture. The quality of a gift is a factor not to be overlooked when making a gift choice.

  Examples: Money clips, handmade wooden boxes, key rings, writing pens, coins, and stamps for collections

Gifts to Avoid

- *Alcohol*: Cultural considerations, as well as potential pitfalls in someone's personal background, make this gift a risky choice.
- *Gifts that are logistically difficult for the recipient to handle*: When the gift given is more of an inconvenience than a benefit, it should be avoided (i.e., flowers brought to a host without a vase, requiring the recipient to stop and place them in water; flowers should be sent the day before or after an event).

THE GIFT OF A HORSE

Sometimes gifts cannot be wrapped in boxes with ribbons; such was the case with the gift President William Jefferson Clinton was to receive in a South American country. The Protocol Office had made a decision at the beginning of the new term not to accept live animal gifts from foreign countries because of the cost burden to our country and the problems associated with quarantining the animals. Evidently, this information never reached the president.

The president had heard from some unnamed source that he was to receive two horses at a horse show in his honor. He also heard that the head of protocol in the host country had told the horse show officials that the U.S. chief of protocol was reluctant to accept the horses. The president was furious—he wanted those horses! (Never mind that they could not be his personally, but would have to go the National Park Service or a National Zoo.)

At the evening rodeo where the horses were to be trotted out, the president's closest advisor sat down beside me and said, "You are in big trouble if those horses are not the gift presented to the president tonight. What is your backup plan if he receives a different gift?"

I replied, "I plan to put a note under his door that says, 'Mr. President, I owe you two horses,' and run as fast as I can."

Gift giving and receiving is rarely a simple job.

- *Certain flowers*: Red roses (for their romantic significance) and white flowers (because they are a funeral flower in some countries) should be avoided.
- *Paintings*: What is considered appropriate and tasteful art in one country may not be viewed favorably in another. Portrait paintings and art depicting people, especially, can be inappropriate because the artist's interpretation of the subject might be off-putting.

- *Wrapping papers*: Colors should be chosen carefully; certain wrapping-paper colors may be associated with negative emotions or may be offensive in some countries.
- *Objects with alternate meanings*: Clocks may represent time running out on a life, or a knife may be considered a symbol of aggression.

Be on the Safe Side

It is crucial to become educated regarding country customs and traditions relating to any gift given. Some research will ideally prevent mistakes that could ruin an event, dampen a trip, or even strain diplomatic relations with another country.

Chapter 14

Presidential Advance and Government Officials Information

President-elect John F. Kennedy shakes hands with Father Richard J. Casey, the pastor, after attending Mass at Holy Trinity Church prior to inauguration ceremonies. Courtesy of the Library of Congress.

ADVANCE FOR THE PRESIDENT AND OTHER OFFICIALS

ADVANCE TEAMS ARE RESPONSIBLE FOR PREPARING for and planning trips and public events for the president, the president's spouse, and high government officials. The advance team literally goes *in advance* to ensure that trips and events are aesthetic, public relations, and media successes. The advance team will set the tone for the event leading up to the appearance of the principal, and this is the team's opportunity to humanize the principal.

The conduct of advance teams can have a serious impact on the principal's image, as well as on that of other officials and Americans in general. Advance teams must recognize that their behavior can have either a positive or a disastrous affect on the public's view of their principal. It is not an exaggeration to say that an advance person may change an individual's, group's, or country's attitude toward the president, the president's spouse, or any government official representing the United States. Further, how Americans treat foreigners on domestic soil may affect how Americans are treated abroad.

Volunteers

Advance is a tough job; it requires smart, well-educated people with solid common sense. Many advance people are volunteers. Volunteers need adequate training, preferably gained by working with a very thorough and conscientious *lead advance*. When the lead advance has been in the job for some time and has considerable experience, he or she can provide invaluable training and advice to the volunteer. Good people often volunteer for jobs with advance hoping for a position on the permanent team. A volunteer often wonders, Why am I doing this seemingly unappreciated work for nothing? If he or she can learn the skills of a successful advance person and has the patience to persevere, the reward is often reaped not only in obtaining the desired permanent job or title but in having learned the skills requisite to being a representative of the United States.

Team Members

To be a good advance person for the principal, every person on the advance team should observe certain national and international courtesies. Advance team members will be scrutinized and judged not only by those with whom they work but also by the American and foreign publics. As representatives of the principal, advance team members should always remember that their conduct reflects on the principal and on this country.

At the presidential level, the advance team will work under the direction of the advance team leader. The lead (team captain), site lead, leads for the crowd, press lead, motorcade lead, and remain-overnight lead will have daily countdown meetings to ensure that information flows to everyone involved. These meetings, especially when in foreign countries, will also involve not only advance persons but the principal's scheduler, others on the principal's staff, military personnel, communications staff, press for the principal, protocol officers, agents of the Secret Service and Diplomatic Security, and representatives of the National Security Council, the State Department, and the American Embassy.

Working with American and Foreign Embassies

When a principal directs that a foreign trip be planned, several advance trips are made to the designated foreign country. Advance personnel will work with many counterparts to ensure the trip's success. Advance personnel cooperate with others in selecting sites and hotels, plan events, and work with the media, as well as with security from the United States and the host foreign country. U.S. Embassy personnel arrange the initial meetings and provide information to each group of contacts; from then on the groups will work together closely throughout the visit.

The advance person should recognize quickly that both American and foreign embassy personnel must understand how to participate in the visit and what each person's job description entails. This information will help immensely in obtaining a balance when working abroad with those involved in the visit. The embassy personnel consist of Foreign and Civil Service staff, political appointees, contract personnel, volunteers, and foreign nationals. The advance person has a job to do, but so too does the embassy representative. The U.S. ambassador to the country visited and his or her staffs have been working directly in the country involved and will understand the unique customs and special requirements of that country. The advance person has to learn how to achieve harmony in all these areas in order to plan and execute a favorable trip for the principal.

In the world of diplomacy, it is important to understand that many diplomats have been in their jobs for years and appreciate respect, courtesy, manners, and order. U.S. teams can learn a great deal from diplomats' experience.

Showing respect to those with whom one is working lends great creditability to advance team members, enabling them to influence others to cooperate with them. Such attributes contribute to understanding and forge friendships that may prove helpful in the future to an individual advance person, to the advance team, or to the administration and the country.

Relationship to Protocol

In the U.S. government—and in every government around the world—defined protocol provides a tried-and-true structure for accomplishing goals. It is crucial for advance team members to study and understand this protocol in order to fulfill their duties. Following are a few areas of protocol that members of advance teams should consider. This list is not exhaustive, and individual chapters of this book should be consulted for more detailed information.

Order of Precedence

The U.S. Order of Precedence will clarify, by title, officials who come first at events. It is important to know that there is a correct place to sit, walk, and stand when arranging meetings, dinners, and other events for officials of the highest level. The Order of Precedence will identify ranking for government officials. (See chapter 3, "U.S. Order of Precedence.") This book will provide examples of how the Order of Precedence functions in practice. For example, the president will normally arrive last and depart first from an event, and the U.S. ambassador assigned to a country, as a courtesy, relinquishes his or her protocol position to the U.S. secretary of state when the secretary is also in country. Such examples will be useful to the advance team.

Correct Forms of Address

Chapter 5, "Titles and Forms of Address," will guide team members regarding how to write a letter and how to speak to almost anyone. It will explain that the president is referred to as "the president" (never by a given name) or as "the president of the United States." *Only* when abroad should the president be referred to as "the president of the United States of America."

U.S. government officials may be addressed, as a courtesy, as "The Honorable," but the foreign counterpart normally is "His/Her Excellency." Occasionally, when abroad, an American official will be referred to as "His/Her Excellency" by a foreign person, as is his or her custom; this courtesy title does not require correction at the moment it is uttered if it is incorrect. What is important is that one understands the correct usage of "The Honorable" and "His/Her Excellency."

Each part of this book will have something to offer for the success of trips important to the U.S. government.

GUIDANCE FOR ADVANCE AND GOVERNMENT OFFICIALS

- The office of the presidency is more important than the person who occupies it and deserves the respect of every citizen regardless of political affiliation.
- All government officials represent the United States; others scrutinize their personal words and actions as examples for the country as a whole.
- A person on an advance team represents the president, a presidential candidate, or another principal.
- The place of honor for the president's guest, when the president is the host of an event, is to the president's right.
- When in a foreign country, the U.S. president should walk to the right of the leader of the foreign country, unless the United States is the host.
- The place of honor for a guest is to the right of an American host or hostess.
- The majority of foreign countries have a chief of protocol who represents his or her country.
- When representing the United States, one should always be aware and respectful of the customs of foreign countries.
- The president is often referred to in "scenarios" (day-to-day schedules) and on toe cards as "Potus" (president of the United States). The first lady is called "Flotus" (first lady of the United States).

- Appearance is important; clothes appropriate to the job at hand, the occasion, and the customs of the country being visited should be worn. Pantsuits are ideal for women in public life due to the need to get in and out of automobiles and airplanes and up and down stairs, as well as to be seated on stages where photographs are often taken. The view is more appropriate and less likely to result in embarrassment.
- Solid-color clothing (as opposed to fabrics patterned with prints, dots, or stripes) is advantageous if photographs are to be taken. A competing background might render the photograph unbecoming over the years.
- Chewing gum is indecorous. One only has to see someone chewing gum on television to understand that the behavior is distracting and unflattering.
- It is generally helpful to observe others on television in considering one's own appearance.
- Great care should be taken to ensure that microphones are turned off until it is time for one to speak.
- Shake hands when introduced to another person unless in a country where it is specifically stated that a hand should not be extended unless another person's hand is extended first. In some countries, women do not shake hands at any time.
- When waving, it looks more appropriate to move one's hand from side to side or to simply hold it in the air rather than "shaking" the hand in a fast, back-and-forth manner. This movement is more becoming for the principal also, if the advance person has influence in that area.
- People should not clap for themselves. When a person is on a stage and people are clapping for him or her, the individual being recognized should not clap for him- or herself but should wave a hand slightly or nod to acknowledge the praise.
- Notice that when the principal shakes hands with people in a rope line, they are more flattered when he or she takes some time and looks at the person being greeted instead of trying to move through the line too rapidly.
- It is helpful and important to think about the words one uses in a given situation. For example, "children" often sounds better than

"kids"; "people" may be more appropriate than "folks"; colloquial phrases such as "take a listen" may not be pleasing to most. Advance team members should remember that they, as well as their principal, are role models for speech as well as conduct.

- When traveling, team members and officials should learn the proper rules and courtesies in a foreign country so that they will not embarrass themselves or the government. There are plenty of briefing books and published volumes to study about the country being visited. For example, most people in foreign countries kiss on both cheeks as a greeting or do not kiss at all—it is important to know the customs.
- Customs related to public touching of another person should be reviewed and observed.
- Pleasant introductions make good first impressions.
- Exercise good judgment and common sense.
- Be a good manager and organizer; pay attention to detail!
- When there is a lectern, and another person is speaking before or after the president, plan for that person's height at the lectern also so that the media or audience has an appropriate view of the other speaker. A small stool may be placed beneath the lectern to be pulled out at the appropriate moment to adjust for height differences.
- Plan for emergencies.
- Get all permissions necessary.
- Be sure to return borrowed belongings.
- Be prepared—do the homework!
- Make a list and check it off. Read and reread it to ensure no detail is overlooked.
- Work as a team to get the most out of the job.
- Be on time! No one likes to wait.
- When eating in a restaurant, remember to tip the waitstaff. They are working too.
- Learn how to give good directions, attending to all details.
- Share information! Doing so can only make one more effective and important.
- Try to be flexible; there is often more than one way to accomplish a goal.
- Value the rights and feelings of others.
- Develop patience.

Remember that what is said is not always what is heard. Put information on paper so that everyone understands the same instructions, directions, and so forth. It is often advantageous to have someone sign off on information given as "correct" so that there is documentation to fall back on when things go wrong. On the other hand, one need not be obsessive concerning self-protection.

Actions to Avoid

- Gesturing with fingers (pointing, peace sign, etc.)
- Winking, which some cultures find offensive
- Yawning
- Blowing nose in public
- Crossing legs when sitting, although it is appropriate to cross feet at the ankles
- Showing the bottoms of one's feet
- Patting a visitor's shoulder or back
- Touching a visitor's head
- Bowing, one can embarrass oneself and others if customs are not understood. It is appropriate to slightly bow if that is the accepted custom
- Eating while standing or walking
- Using a toothpick in public
- Putting one or both hands below the table while eating is offensive in some countries
- Making fun of anyone, which not only hurts feelings but diminishes the speaker

Avoid Revealing Confidential Information

When eating out in restaurants or with friends, it is tempting to discuss the day's events or to bring up something that elevates one's status because one has been privy to discussions by or between "important" persons. *Never, never talk about such things when confidentiality cannot be ensured—which it rarely, if ever, can.* One does not know what or whom the other person will tell concerning what has been said. Waitstaff may overhear when restaurant conversation is loud (or even when it is not). Waitstaff and customers nearby in a restaurant have ears and can and will repeat what they hear. Tempting as these conversations may be, *talking* could result in job loss or mistrust by colleagues or employers. Remember that the danger of leaving papers or notes exposed in a hotel or meeting room is that waitstaff or others may see, read, or even make copies of them!

Hotels

Advance team members and other officials should not leave rooms "messy" (wet towels on the floor, bed rumpled, or furniture draped with dirty clothing). Not only does such behavior constitute bad manners, but hotel staffs vote and in foreign countries voice observances to others. They judge candidates, officials, and the president by team actions. These actions may influence many people never considered.

Someone on the team should be designated to pen *hand-written* thank-you notes to the hotel manager, domestic or foreign staff who were especially helpful, vendors, and so forth. Someone should ensure the note is delivered or mailed the day of departure. Advance teams should have notes, good pens, writing papers, and stamps in their supplies. It is not appropriate to e-mail a thank-you—time should be taken to demonstrate the best manners.

Events

Trash generated at an event should be picked up and disposed of. Arrangements should be made for the site to be well cleaned after any event; reputations follow actions.

Rentals should be returned in proper condition and on time. Ample time should be allowed to accomplish tasks. Bills should be paid and tickets signed. Someone can always discover the culprit, so be upfront from the beginning if a mistake is made.

When the national anthem is played, the following practices should be observed:

- Everyone should stop immediately and stand at attention with hand placed over heart.
- Hats should be removed and held over the left shoulder. Military personnel salute but do not remove hats.

- No one should clap after the anthem.
- When another country's anthem is played in the United States or abroad, everyone should stop wherever they are and stand at attention.

Flag Etiquette

Chapter 9, "Flag Etiquette," should answer most questions regarding proper flag-related decorum. Any unanswered questions may be directed to the Military District of Washington, Ceremonials Division. Ensure information is correct and current because it is embarrassing if the wrong flag is hoisted (countries do change flags occasionally) or a flag is placed in the wrong position or upside down.

U.S. Secret Service and the Bureau of Diplomatic Security

The U.S. Secret Service and Bureau of Diplomatic Security should be contacted immediately when a visit or a foreign trip is first being planned.

The Secret Service and Diplomatic Security must both be cooperated with in every possible way; these men and women are well trained and have a wealth of knowledge that will be helpful and could even save lives. They deserve the respect of everyone working with them.

Advance and government officials should take time to review early on what they have been assigned to accomplish in conjunction with their security counterparts and to develop good working relationships. There are times when new advance people, new government officials, and new security agents have not had the experience needed to work with each other; therefore, that relationship must be developed. Everyone involved should realize the importance of team work and strive for the advantage of the other to accomplish jobs successfully without undue tension. There is plenty of strife in other areas to go around.

Traveling Out of the Country

Always remember that foreign countries often do not have the same customs as the United States. Every country has its own protocol, rules of personal conduct, and notions of right and wrong. Pay attention to the other country's customs and abide by them when in that country.

The White House Medical Unit reminds persons traveling overseas to take certain dietary precautions and provides the following suggestions regarding food and beverages in foreign countries:

- Consume bottled, rather than tap, water. (Often it is necessary to brush teeth with bottled water as well.)
- Avoid eating food sold by street vendors.
- To be on the safe side, eat only peelable fruits.
- Do not eat anything raw or rare meat.
- Salads are of concern outside of four- or five-star hotels.

It pays to take precautions as it is not great fun to wake up sick when you are in charge.

WHAT DOES STOP MEAN?

As chief of protocol, I was once riding in a car with a foreign driver. The event to which we were driving was in a country with much traffic and few traffic rules. The driver went through every stop sign without stopping. He narrowly veered around the oncoming and side approaching cars.

After several of these mishaps, I asked the driver why he did not stop for stop signs. His reply was, "They are only suggestions."

Remember that the laws adhered to in one country are not necessarily followed in another.

Gifts

It is gracious to give a small gift to your foreign counterpart. Refer to chapter 13, "Official Gift Giving" for many items that are appropriate and inappropriate. The advance team lead often has a box of trinkets to give as gifts to those with whom advance team members have worked especially closely. Be sure to ask the lead if he or she has trinkets or gifts that team members may use.

Flowers

In many countries, giving flowers of certain colors or types is not considered appropriate. White flowers or chrysanthemums, for example, are often used solely for funerals. Check the country's information on customs regarding flowers.

Pride in Advance Work

To be part of an advance team, especially at the presidential level, is an honor. One should always conduct oneself in a manner that will make the president and the country proud.

Chapter 15

────────○────────

Internet Protocol

So-called etiquette is etiquette for Internet users. Though every cybersituation is unique and must be evaluated objectively, some guidelines may assist in making decisions in an increasingly digital world.

Social Planning and E-mail

Technology and Tradition

When using today's technology in connection with social events, traditions and standards must still be maintained. While modern technologies such as e-mail can certainly make the process of social planning much more convenient and efficient for all parties, they should not be used to the detriment of social courtesy and (especially for very formal events, such as a dinner at the White House) social elegance.

Invitations Are Personal

One of the hallmarks of invitations is that they are personal. Mass e-mails are not appropriate for important events because they seem impersonal. Just as a written invitation would be addressed by a calligrapher to individual invitees, so should an e-mail address each invitee individually with his or her proper name, title, and so forth. For most formal events, an e-mail invitation may be sent as a guest convenience followed by a formal mailed invitation; however, an e-mail should never serve as a substitute for a formal mailed invitation.

If two types of invitations are used, the event host must be as clear as possible about the desired mode of response and RSVP to avoid guest confusion regarding attendance and event-related questions.

E-mail Mailing Lists

For some events, a host may wish to send information by e-mail to a group. Hosts should always use caution when e-mailing a group. Using the "undisclosed recipients," or "bcc" (i.e., blind carbon copy), features ensures privacy. Most e-mail programs can be configured to reply directly to the host and to exclude the remainder of the list. Many people desire that their e-mails remain private and do not want to be identified publicly to a group. This desire should be respected by employing one of the features mentioned above.

E-MAIL AND PROFESSIONALISM

It has happened to us all: either we hit the "reply" button intending to respond only to the sender (only to discover later that our e-mail has been distributed to an entire list), or a scathing e-mail is sent or copied to the wrong recipient (even—dread of all dreads—the person being scathed).

In the world of near-instant communications, it is vital that Internet, blog, and e-mail users pause to double and triple check intended recipients and carefully consider contents before clicking items away into cyberspace. The virtual world becomes infinitely more real when an Internet blunder causes a rift in one's professional and social relationships.

E-mail Rules of Thumb

(This list, or applicable parts of it, may be copied and used as a ready reference or checklist for important e-mails.)

- *Avoid generic usernames.* To establish credibility more firmly, use an e-mail prefix that clearly identifies the sender. For example, "happygirl41@aol.com" not only comes across as unprofessional but also fails to identify the sender by name.

- *Create a signature line.* Signature lines help recipients by providing pertinent information for identification (such as full name and title) and multiple modes through which to contact the sender. Senders may elect to include their full names and middle initials, their titles, their physical address (and/or mailing address if different), their phone numbers, facsimile numbers, and even cell phone numbers where appropriate. E-mail programs can be set up to generate signature lines automatically so that this courtesy takes no additional time for users.

- *Reply promptly.* It is bad business practice (not to mention bad etiquette) to keep someone waiting for a response—especially if the e-mail relates to an important and/or time-sensitive matter. If necessary information is unavailable, or if one must speak with someone else or research a topic in order to respond, one should let the sender know the e-mail has been received and will receive a response as soon as the answer has been discovered.

- *Use "out-of-office" replies.* If you are out of the office during normal business hours for more than one day, use the automatic "out-of-office" reply rather than keeping senders waiting for a response.

- *Include all pertinent information and attachments.* Though accidental omissions are sometimes unavoidable, it is most professional and considerate of others' time to include all information in one e-mail. E-mails related to events should contain all pertinent event information, including time, place, attire, and any link to the event website. When sending an important message, one may find it easiest to get it right the first time by writing the e-mail, providing attachments, and setting the e-mail aside for a few minutes before sending. Such an approach gives the sender's brain a cognitive break and may reveal errors or omissions that would have gone unnoticed at first glance.

- *Provide a subject.* It is most discourteous to leave a subject line blank. Inappropriate labels can be just as frustrating as blank ones. Providing adequately descriptive subject lines enables recipients to prioritize, categorize, organize, and (later) locate e-mails.

- *Choose the appropriate level of formality.* A good rule for business e-mails (or for those directed to someone the sender does not know well) is to treat an e-mail as if it were a letter. Unlike letters, however, e-mails have a tendency (perhaps due to their rapid volley) to turn casual quickly. If you are communicating with a superior or writing an e-mail that may be duplicated as a record, it is a good idea to choose a more formal approach and to permit the superior to control any lowering of formality standards.

- *Keep it short.* E-mails should be kept as succinct as possible while still conveying key information. Droning on unnecessarily or embellishing needlessly will only irritate recipients and detract from the intended message.

- *Don't type in capitals.* Such typing is not only difficult to read but is considered as offensive as shouting. It may unintentionally incense recipients and should never be used for an entire e-mail (though using it for headings, subheadings, or to draw attention to certain words may be acceptable).

- *Consider context and tone.* Attention not only to *what* is said but to *how* it is said is especially important in e-mail communications, considering that no social cues from body language or tone of voice will be available to the recipient. Ample contextualization for any potentially sensitive statements should be provided to minimize their negative impact. A highly emotional tone (including excessive use of exclamation marks) should be tamped down and saved for more informal e-mailing to friends. It is usually best to keep extreme personal excitement and woes to oneself. Exclamation marks should be used sparingly (if at all), and it is best that "smiley" or "frowney" faces never be used in professional communications.

- *Use discretion.* It is almost always in the best interest of the sender *not* to forward e-mails containing inciting or gossipy information. There is always the chance that such e-mails may be mishandled down the line, and such forwarding only serves to fan workplace or social flames. Similarly, especially in political arenas, e-mail that could jeopardize the security of an individual (or even of the nation) should be handled with the utmost care. If such sensitive information arrives in the hands of someone unsure of what to do with it, the best approach is to ask (face-to-face, without forwarding the e-mail) a superior who may know how to approach the situation, rather than to risk the e-mail's falling into the wrong hands.

  Discretion should be exercised in setting e-mails as "high priority." Crying wolf by using false labels may cause the sender to lose credibility among colleagues. Further, an important e-mail may not take priority when it really counts.

  Using foul language is also ill advised.

- *Avoid bombardment.* When e-mailing someone multiple times per day, it is considerate to save two or three questions and send them in one e-mail rather than filling the recipient's inbox with multiple e-mails. Not bombarding the recipient with too many e-mails may prevent exhaustion and annoyance with required responses and, perhaps most importantly, with the sender.
- *Trim the fat.* If forwarding e-mails from multiple recipients or a long trail of e-mails between two or more persons, "trim the fat" by deleting any irrelevant messages so that the new recipient need not wade through bogs of useless text in order to uncover the pertinent information.

Greeting: Comma or Colon?

Generally, colons punctuate greetings addressed in business settings, whereas commas are reserved for social situations. An addressee may fill both roles, and personal judgment can be used, but it is always better to err on the side of formality.

In work-related e-mails (or those seeking favors, advice, or information from another, especially someone whom the sender does not know), consider always using a colon after the greeting (i.e., "Dear Mr. Jones:" or "Mr. Jones:").

THE PSYCHOLOGY OF E-MAILING

Think Before You Click

Consider parking an angry e-mail in the drafts folder overnight to permit time to reflect on its damage potential and possible repercussions before it is too late. Once the "send" button is clicked, fate is no longer in the sender's control; the e-mail is not retractable, and it is subject to being forwarded, duplicated, or published at the recipient's will. Its specter may return to haunt the sender personally or professionally.

E-mail as a Tool for Avoidance

While we may prefer to deal with some things through "detached" modes of communication, think carefully about using e-mail as a substitute for face-to-face or personal interaction. Discussing a salary issue or increase with a superior, attempting to douse a work-related fire, or consoling an associate who has lost a loved one, for example, may be more appropriately handled in person than via e-mail.

Always Consider Audience and Purpose

Ask two questions prior to sending an e-mail: (1) to whom should this e-mail be addressed, and (2) what will sending it achieve?

The first answer may, upon initial glance, seem obvious; a couple of scenarios, however, prove that the addressee should be carefully considered. First, if you are working with "high-powered" or extraordinarily busy people (even if you yourself are one), ask whether a lower-ranking person might answer the e-mail. Such a choice may avoid frustrating superiors or colleagues unnecessarily by engaging them in an interaction that someone else could have handled. Second, e-mail addressees may, by the mere fact of their inclusion in the "to" or "cc" lines, send messages. For example, is a superior being copied on an e-mail directed to a colleague to chastise that colleague for having done something wrong or inappropriate? If so, the colleague is likely to become annoyed that the situation was not handled outside the superior's presence rather than accepting the message as "constructive criticism."

The later consideration bleeds into the second question: what will sending this e-mail achieve? Is its purpose to communicate to achieve a positive result? Or is it something more underhanded? Practically everyone who has sent an e-mail has had his or her words misinterpreted at one time or another. Though misinterpretation may be unavoidable, purposeful attacks (even if subtle) rarely achieve the desired result in the long run and tend to build walls rather than bridges between people. If a sender has concerns that an e-mail may fall into the malicious category and wants to avoid this, he or she should ask if the purpose of the e-mail is to do any of the following:

- *Shift blame away from the sender and toward another*: While not sending such an e-mail may subject the sender to some negative consequences, he or she should be sure that the long-term reward outweighs the short-term desire for approval.

- *Criticize a colleague or superior openly*: Again, what gain may the criticism bring about? Is it being done for the good of the organization, company, government, citizenry, and so forth, or for personal gratification?
- *Obtain credit that may have otherwise gone ungiven*: It has been said that the mark of a good leader is the willingness to forfeit credit for good deeds. If good deeds become a pattern, others will doubtless recognize them; there is no need to attempt to force the opinion or response of another by calling attention to achievements or accomplishments (however small or large).

SOCIAL-NETWORKING SITES AND PERSONAL INFORMATION

Users of social-networking sites such as Facebook, Twitter, and MySpace know that along with their benefits (such as networking with business associates, reconnecting with old friends, learning more about new friends, and sharing more easily and intimately over long distances) come potential hazards and pitfalls. If planning to become "friends" with colleagues or business associates on such sites, it is worthwhile either (1) to monitor every status update or tweet added, or (2) to limit access such persons may have through privacy controls. If frequently in the social, political, or business "spotlight," one may also wish to disable the "wall" feature on Facebook and Myspace in order to prevent the publication of undesired information.

SAVE INTERNET PLAY FOR PRIVATE COMPUTERS

Especially for employees of federal and state governments, it is important to remember that computers are subject to the Freedom of Information Act. Thus, subjects or materials that users may consider private should not be accessed through, or added to, federal and state-owned computers. Always remember that employees are being paid for their time. Playing card games or launching inappropriate websites at work or from a work computer is not only ill advised but could lead to the loss of work privileges or the loss of a job altogether.

Chapter 16

———————◯———————

Valuable Information

Former U.S. President's (back row, left to right): George H. W. Bush, William J. ("Bill") Clinton, Gerald R. Ford, James E. ("Jimmy") Carter. Front row, left to right): Barbara Bush, Claudia Alta ("Lady Bird") Johnson, Hillary Rodham Clinton, Betty Ford, Rosalynn Carter. Courtesy of the William J. Clinton Presidential Library.

Facts about Presidents of the United States

	President	Party	Spouse	Birth and Death (Age) Burial	Vice President
1	George Washington (April 30, 1789, to March 4, 1797)	(none)	Martha Dandridge Custis	1732–1799 (67) Mount Vernon, VA	John Adams
2	John Adams (March 4, 1797, to March 4, 1801)	Federalist	Abigail Smith	1735–1826 (90) United First Parish Church Quincy, MA	Thomas Jefferson
3	Thomas Jefferson (March 4, 1801, to March 4, 1809)	Democratic-Republican	Martha Wayles Skelton	1743–1826 (83) Monticello Charlottesville, VA	Aaron Burr George Clinton
4	James Madison (March 4, 1809, to March 4, 1817)	Democratic-Republican	Dorothy "Dolley" Payne Todd	1751–1836 (85) Montpelier Estate Orange, VA	George Clinton (vacant) Elbridge Gerry (vacant)
5	James Monroe (March 4, 1817, to March 4, 1825)	Democratic-Republican	Elizabeth "Eliza" Kortright	1758–1831 (73) Hollywood Cemetery Richmond, VA	Daniel D. Tompkins
6	John Quincy Adams (March 4, 1825, to March 4, 1829)	Democratic-Republican National Republican	Louisa Catherine Johnson	1767–1848 (80) United First Parish Church Quincy, MA	John C. Calhoun

#	President	Party	Wife	Life/Burial	Vice President
7	Andrew Jackson (March 4, 1829, to March 4, 1837)	Democratic	Rachel Donelson Robards	1767–1845 (78) The Hermitage Nashville, TN	John C. Calhoun (*vacant*) Martin Van Buren
8	Martin Van Buren (March 4, 1837, to March 4, 1841) ·	Democratic	Hannah Hoes	1782–1862 (79) Kinderhook Cemetery Kinderhook, NY	Richard Mentor Johnson
9	William Henry Harrison (March 4, 1841, to April 4, 1841) (*died in office*)	Whig	Anna Symmes	1773–1841 (68) North Bend, OH	John Tyler
10	John Tyler (April 4, 1841, to March 4, 1845)	Whig (*none*)	Letitia Christian Julia Gardiner	1790–1862 (71) Hollywood Cemetery Richmond, VA	(*vacant*)
11	James Knox Polk (March 4, 1845, to March 4, 1849)	Democratic	Sarah Childress	1795–1849 (53) Tennessee State Capitol Nashville, TN	George M. Dallas
12	Zachary Taylor (March 4, 1849, to July 9, 1850) (*died in office*)	Whig	Margaret Smith	1784–1850 (65) Zachary Taylor National Cemetery Louisville, KY	Millard Fillmore

(*Continued*)

	President	Party	Spouse	Birth and Death (Age) Burial	Vice President
13	Millard Fillmore (July 9, 1850, to March 4, 1853)	Whig	Abigail Powers Caroline Carmichael McIntosh	1800–1874 (74) Forest Lawn Cemetery Buffalo, NY	(*vacant*)
14	Franklin Pierce (March 4, 1853, to March 4, 1857)	Democratic	Jane Means Appleton	1804–1869 (65) Old North Cemetery Concord, NH	William R. King (*vacant*)
15	James Buchanan (March 4, 1857, to March 4, 1861)	Democratic	(*unmarried*)	1791–1868 (77) Woodward Hill Cemetery Lancaster, PA	John C. Breckinridge
16	Abraham Lincoln (March 4, 1861, to April 15, 1865) (*assassinated*)	Republican National Union	Mary Todd	1809–1865 (56) Oak Ridge Cemetery Springfield, IL	Hannibal Hamlin Andrew Johnson
17	Andrew Johnson (April 15, 1865, to March 4, 1869)	Democratic National Union	Eliza McCardie	1808–1875 (66) Andrew Johnson National Cemetery Greeneville, TN	(*vacant*)
18	Hiram "Ulysses S." Grant (March 4, 1869, to March 4, 1877)	Republican	Julia Dent	1822–1885 (63) Grant's Tomb New York, NY	Schuyler Colfax Henry Wilson (*vacant*)

#	President	Party	Spouse	Life / Burial	Vice President
19	Rutherford Birchard Hayes (March 4, 1877, to March 4, 1881)	Republican	Lucy Ware Webb	1822–1893 (71) Spiegel Grove Fremont, OH	William A. Wheeler
20	James Abram Garfield (March 4, 1881, to September 19, 1881) (assassinated)	Republican	Lucretia Rudolph	1831–1881 (49) Lakeview Cemetery Cleveland, OH	Chester A. Arthur
21	Chester Alan Arthur (September 19, 1881, to March 4, 1885)	Republican	Ellen Lewis Herndon	1830–1886 (57) Albany Rural Cemetery Albany, NY	(vacant)
22	Stephen "Grover" Cleveland (March 4, 1885, to March 4, 1889)	Democratic	Frances Folsom	1837–1908 (71) Princeton Cemetery Princeton, NJ	Thomas A. Hendricks (vacant)
23	Benjamin Harrison (March 4, 1889, to March 4, 1893)	Republican	Caroline Lavinia Scott / Mary Scott Lord Dimmick	1833–1901 (67) Crown Hill Cemetery Indianapolis, IN	Levi P. Morton
24	Stephen "Grover" Cleveland (March 4, 1893, to March 4, 1897)	Democratic	Frances Folsom	1837–1908 (71) Princeton Cemetery Princeton, NJ	Adlai E. Stevenson

(Continued)

Facts about Presidents of the United States (Continued)

	President	Party	Spouse	Birth and Death (Age) Burial	Vice President
25	William McKinley (March 4, 1897, to September 14, 1901) (*assassinated*)	Republican	Ida Saxton	1843–1901 (58) McKinley National Memorial and Museum Canton, OH	Garret Hobart (*vacant*) Theodore Roosevelt
26	Theodore Roosevelt (September 14, 1901, to March 4, 1909)	Republican	Alice Hathaway Lee Edith Kermit Carow	1858–1919 (60) Young Memorial's Cemetery Oyster Bay, NY	Charles W. Fairbanks
27	William Howard Taft (March 4, 1909, to March 4, 1913)	Republican	Helen Herron	1857–1930 (72) Arlington National Cemetery Arlington, VA	James S. Sherman (*vacant*)
28	Thomas "Woodrow" Wilson (March 4, 1913, to March 4, 1921)	Democratic	Ellen Louise Axson Edith Bolling Galt	1856–1924 (67) National Cathedral Washington, D.C.	Thomas R. Marshall

#	President	Party	First Lady	Life/Burial	Vice President
29	Warren Gamaliel Harding (March 4, 1921, to August 2, 1923) (*died in office*)	Republican	Florence Kling DeWolfe	1865–1923 (57) Marion Cemetery Marion, OH	John "Calvin" Coolidge Jr.
30	John "Calvin" Coolidge Jr. (August 2, 1923, to March 4, 1929)	Republican	Grace Anna Goodhue	1872–1933 (60) Notch Cemetery Plymouth Notch, VT	(*vacant*) Charles G. Dawes
31	Herbert Clark Hoover (March 4, 1929, to March 4, 1933)	Republican	Lou Henry	1874–1964 (90) Herbert Hoover Presidential Library and Museum West Branch, IA	Charles Curtis
32	Franklin Delano Roosevelt (March 4, 1933, to April 12, 1945) (*died in office*)	Democratic	(Anna) Eleanor Roosevelt	1882–1945 (63) Home of Franklin D. Roosevelt National Historic Site Hyde Park, NY	John Nance Garner Henry A. Wallace Harry S. Truman
33	Harry S. Truman (April 12, 1945, to January 20, 1953)	Democratic	Bess Wallace	1884–1972 (88) Harry S. Truman Presidential Library and Museum Independence, MO	(*vacant*) Alben W. Barkley

(*Continued*)

FACTS ABOUT PRESIDENTS OF THE UNITED STATES (CONTINUED)

	President	Party	Spouse	Birth and Death (Age) Burial	Vice President
34	Dwight David Eisenhower (January 20, 1953, to January 20, 1961)	Republican	Mamie Geneva Doud	1890–1969 (78) Dwight D. Eisenhower Presidential Library and Museum Abilene, KS	Richard M. Nixon
35	John Fitzgerald Kennedy (January 20, 1961, to November 22, 1963) (assassinated)	Democratic	Jacqueline Lee Bouvier	1917–1963 (46) Arlington National Cemetery Arlington, VA	Lyndon B. Johnson
36	Lyndon Baines Johnson (November 22, 1963, to January 20, 1969)	Democratic	Claudia Alta "Lady Bird" Taylor	1908–1973 (64) Lyndon B. Johnson National Historical Park Johnson City, TX	(vacant) Hubert H. Humphrey Jr.

#	President	Party	First Lady	Dates / Library	Vice President
37	Richard Milhous Nixon (January 20, 1969, to August 9, 1974) (*resigned*)	Republican	Thelma Catherine "Pat" Ryan	1913–1994 (81) Richard Nixon Presidential Library and Museum Yorba Linda, CA	Spiro T. Agnew (*vacant*) Gerald R. Ford
38	Gerald Rudolph Ford (August 9, 1974, to January 20, 1977)	Republican	Elizabeth "Betty" Bloomer Warren	1913–2006 (93) Gerald R. Ford Presidential Library and Museum Grand Rapids, MI	(*vacant*) Nelson A. Rockefeller
39	James Earl "Jimmy" Carter Jr. (January 20, 1977, to January 20, 1981)	Democratic	Rosalynn Smith	1924–	Walter F. Mondale
40	Ronald Wilson Reagan (January 20, 1981, to January 20, 1989)	Republican	Jane Wyman Nancy Davis	1911–2004 (93) Ronald Reagan Presidential Library and Museum Simi Valley, CA	George H. W. Bush
41	George Herbert Walker Bush (January 20, 1989, to January 20, 1993)	Republican	Barbara Pierce	1924–	James Danforth "Dan" Quayle

(*Continued*)

FACTS ABOUT PRESIDENTS OF THE UNITED STATES (CONTINUED)

	President	Party	Spouse	Birth and Death (Age) Burial	Vice President
42	William Jefferson "Bill" Clinton (January 20, 1993, to January 20, 2001)	Democratic	Hillary Rodham	1946–	Albert Gore Jr.
43	George Walker Bush (January 20, 2001, to January 20, 2009)	Republican	Laura Welch	1946–	Richard B. "Dick" Cheney
44	Barack Hussein Obama (January 20, 2009)	Democratic	Michelle LaVaughn Robinson	1961–	Joseph R. Biden Jr.

Facts about States of the Union

State	Capital	Nickname	Tree	Flower	Bird
Alabama	Montgomery	The Yellowhammer State	Longleaf pine	Camellia	Yellowhammer
Alaska	Juneau	The Last Frontier	Sitka spruce	Forget-me-not	Willow ptarmigan
Arizona	Phoenix	The Grand Canyon State	Palo verde	Saguaro cactus blossom	Cactus wren
Arkansas	Little Rock	The Natural State	Pine	Apple blossom	Mockingbird
California	Sacramento	The Golden State	Coast redwood, giant sequoia	California poppy	California valley quail
Colorado	Denver	The Centennial State	Colorado blue spruce	Rocky Mountain columbine	Lark bunting
Connecticut	Hartford	The Constitution State	White oak	Mountain laurel	Robin
Delaware	Dover	The First State	American holly	Peach blossom	Blue hen chicken
*District of Columbia	—	—	Scarlet oak	American Beauty rose	—
Florida	Tallahassee	The Sunshine State	Sabal palm	Orange blossom	Mockingbird
Georgia	Atlanta	The Peach State	Live oak	Cherokee rose	Brown thrasher
Hawaii	Honolulu	The Aloha State	Candlenut tree, kukui	Pua aloalo	Nene
Idaho	Boise	The Gem State	Western white pine	Syringa mock orange	Mountain bluebird
Illinois	Springfield	The Prairie State	White oak	Purple violet	Cardinal

(Continued)

State	Capital	Nickname	Tree	Flower	Bird
Indiana	Indianapolis	The Hoosier State	Tulip poplar	Peony	Cardinal
Iowa	Des Moines	The Hawkeye State	Oak	Wild prairie rose	Eastern goldfinch
Kansas	Topeka	The Sunflower State	Eastern cottonwood	Sunflower	Western meadowlark
Kentucky	Frankfurt	The Bluegrass State	Tulip poplar	Goldenrod	Cardinal
Louisiana	Baton Rouge	The Pelican State	Bald cypress	Magnolia	Eastern brown pelican
Maine	Augusta	The Pine Tree State	Eastern white pine	Eastern white pine tassel and cone	Chickadee
Maryland	Annapolis	The Old Line State	White oak	Black-eyed Susan	Baltimore oriole
Massachu- setts	Boston	The Bay State	American elm	Mayflower	Chickadee
Michigan	Lansing	The Great Lakes State	Eastern white pine	Apple blossom	Robin
Minnesota	St. Paul	The North Star State	Red pine	Pink and white ladyslipper	Common loon
Mississippi	Jackson	The Magnolia State	Magnolia	Magnolia	Mockingbird
Missouri	Jefferson City	The Show Me State	Flowering dogwood	Hawthorn	Bluebird
Montana	Helena	The Treasure State	Ponderosa pine	Bitterroot	Western meadowlark
Nebraska	Lincoln	The Cornhusker State	Eastern cottonwood	Goldenrod	Western meadowlark
Nevada	Carson City	The Silver State	Singleleaf pinyon pine, bristlecone pine	Sagebrush	Mountain bluebird

State	Capital	Nickname	Tree	Flower	Bird
New Hampshire	Concord	The Granite State	Paper birch	Purple lilac	Purple finch
New Jersey	Trenton	The Garden State	Northern red oak	Violet	Eastern goldfinch
New Mexico	Santa Fe	The Land of Enchantment	Pinyon pine	Yucca	Roadrunner
New York	Albany	The Empire State	Sugar maple	Rose	Bluebird
North Carolina	Raleigh	The Tar Heel State	Longleaf pine	Flowering dogwood	Cardinal
North Dakota	Bismarck	The Peace Garden State	American elm	Wild prairie rose	Western meadowlark
Ohio	Columbus	The Buckeye State	Ohio buckeye	Scarlet carnation	Cardinal
Oklahoma	Oklahoma City	The Sooner State	Eastern rosebud	Mistletoe	Scissor-tailed flycatcher
Oregon	Salem	The Beaver State	Douglas fir	Oregon grape	Western meadowlark
Pennsylvania	Harrisburg	The Keystone State	Eastern hemlock	Mountain laurel	Ruffed goose
Rhode Island	Providence	The Ocean State	Red maple	Violet	Rhode Island red
South Carolina	Columbia	The Palmetto State	Sabal palmetto	Yellow jessamine	Great Carolina wren
South Dakota	Pierre	The Mount Rushmore State	Black Hills spruce	Pasque flower	Ring-necked pheasant
Tennessee	Nashville	The Volunteer State	Tulip poplar	Iris	Mockingbird
Texas	Austin	The Lone Star State	Pecan	Texas bluebonnet	Mockingbird
Utah	Salt Lake City	The Beehive State	Blue spruce	Sego lily	Common American gull
Vermont	Montpelier	The Green Mountain State	Sugar maple	Red clover	Hermit thrush

(Continued)

FACTS ABOUT STATES OF THE UNION (CONTINUED)

State	Capital	Nickname	Tree	Flower	Bird
Virginia	Richmond	The Old Dominion State	Flowering dogwood	Flowering dogwood	Cardinal
Washington	Olympia	The Evergreen State	Western hemlock	Coast rho- dodendron	Willow goldfinch
West Virginia	Charleston	The Mountain State	Sugar maple	Rhododen- dron	Cardinal
Wisconsin	Madison	The Badger State	Sugar maple	Violet	Robin
Wyoming	Cheyenne	The Equality State, The Cowboy State	Plains cottonwood	Indian paintbrush	Western meadowlark

*Not a state of the union.

ADDRESSES FOR THE PRESIDENT'S CABINET AGENCIES

Department of Agriculture (USDA)

Mailing address:
    1400 Independence Avenue, SW
    Washington, DC 20250
Telephone:
    Various subject-matter directories are available through the website's "Contact Us" tab.
Website: www.usda.gov

Department of Commerce

Mailing address:
    1401 Constitution Avenue, NW
    Washington, DC 20230
Telephone:
    Main: (202) 482-2000

Website: www.commerce.gov

Department of Defense

Mailing address:
    1400 Defense Pentagon
    Washington, DC 20301-1400
Telephone:
    Pentagon switchboard: (703) 545-6700
Website: www.defenselink.mil

Department of Education

Mailing address:
    400 Maryland Avenue, SW
    Washington, DC 20202
Telephone:
    General inquiries: (800) USA-LEARN (872-5327)
    Switchboard: (800) 872-5327
    D.C. metropolitan area: (202) 401-2000
Website: www.ed.gov

Department of Energy

Mailing address:
    1000 Independence Avenue, SW
    Washington, DC 20585
Telephone:
    Toll-free: (800) dial-DOE (342-5363)
    Switchboard: (202) 586-5000
Website: www.energy.gov

Department of Health and Human Services (HHS)

Mailing address:
    200 Independence Avenue, SW
    Washington, DC 20201
Telephone:
    Toll-free: (877) 696-6775

Website: www.os.dhhs.gov

Department of Homeland Security

Mailing address:
    To reach the secretary:
        Secretary (full name)
        Department of Homeland Security
        U.S. Department of Homeland Security
        Washington, DC 20528
    For other department staff:
        U.S. Department of Homeland Security
        Washington, DC 20528
Telephone:
    Operator number: (202) 282-8000
    Comment line: (202) 282-8495
Website: www.dhs.gov

Department of Housing and Urban Development (HUD)

Mailing address:
    451 Seventh Street, SW
    Washington, DC 20410
Telephone:
    (202) 708-1112
Website: www.hud.gov

Department of the Interior

Mailing address:
    1849 C Street, NW
    Washington, DC 20240
Telephone:
    (202) 208-3100
Website: www.doi.gov

Department of Justice

Mailing address:
    950 Pennsylvania Avenue, NW
    Washington, DC 20530-0001
Telephone:
    Switchboard: (202) 514-2000
Website: www.usdoj.gov

Department of Labor

Mailing address:
    200 Constitution Avenue, NW
    Washington, DC 20210
Telephone:
    (866) 4-USA-DOL (487-2365)
Website: www.dol.gov

Department of State

Mailing address:
    2201 C Street, NW
    Washington, DC 20520
Telephone:
    (202) 647-4000
Website: www.state.gov

Ceremonials Division, Office of Protocol

Mailing address:
    Ceremonials Division, Office of the Chief of Protocol
    2201 C Street, NW.
    Room 1238
    Washington, DC 20520
Telephone:
    For protocol questions: (202) 647-1735
Website: www.state.gov/s/cpr/index.htm

Department of Transportation

Mailing address:
    1200 New Jersey Avenue, SE
    Washington, DC 20590
Telephone:
    (202) 366-4000
Website: www.dot.gov

Department of the Treasury

Mailing address:
    1500 Pennsylvania Avenue, NW
    Washington, DC 20220
Telephone:
    Switchboard: (202) 622-2000
Website: www.ustreas.gov

Department of Veterans Affairs

Mailing address:
    810 Vermont Avenue, NW
    Washington, DC 20420-0002
Telephone:
    (202) 273-5400
Website: www.va.gov

U.S. Mission to the United Nations in New York

Mailing address:
    799 United Nations Plaza
    New York, NY 10017
Telephone:
    Opinion and comment line: (212) 415-4062
Website: www.usunnewyork.usmission.gov

U.S. Secretaries of State

The secretary of state serves as the president's chief foreign affairs advisor, working through the State Department and the Foreign Service to carry out American foreign policy. The secretary of state is appointed by the president and confirmed by the Senate.

Former Secretaries of State

Thomas Jefferson	(1790–1793)
Edmund Jennings Randolph	(1794–1795)
Timothy Pickering	(1795–1800)
John Marshall	(1800–1801)
James Madison	(1801–1809)
Robert Smith	(1809–1811)
James Monroe	(1811–1817)
John Quincy Adams	(1817–1825)
Henry Clay	(1825–1829)
Martin Van Buren	(1829–1831)
Edward Livingston	(1831–1833)
Louis McLane	(1833–1834)
John Forsyth	(1834–1841)
Daniel Webster	(1841–1843)
Abel Parker Upshur	(1843–1844)
John Caldwell Calhoun	(1844–1845)
James Buchanan	(1845–1849)
John Middleton Clayton	(1849–1850)
Daniel Webster	(1850–1852)
Edward Everett	(1852–1853)
William Learned Marcy	(1853–1857)
Lewis Cass	(1857–1860)
Jeremiah Sullivan Black	(1860–1861)
William Henry Seward	(1861–1869)
Elihu Benjamin Washburne	(1869–1869)
Hamilton Fish	(1869–1877)
William Maxwell Evarts	(1877–1881)
James Gillespie Blaine	(1881–1881)
Frederick Theodore Frelinghuysen	(1881–1885)

Thomas Francis Bayard	(1885–1889)
James Gillespie Blaine	(1889–1892)
John Watson Foster	(1892–1893)
Walter Quintin Gresham	(1893–1895)
Richard Olney	(1895–1897)
John Sherman	(1897–1898)
William Rufus Day	(1898–1898)
John Milton Hay	(1898–1905)
Elihu Root	(1905–1909)
Robert Bacon	(1909–1909)
Philander Chase Knox	(1909–1913)
William Jennings Bryan	(1913–1915)
Robert Lansing	(1915–1920)
Bainbridge Colby	(1920–1921)
Charles Evans Hughes	(1921–1925)
Frank Billings Kellogg	(1925–1929)
Henry Lewis Stimson	(1929–1933)
Cordell Hull	(1933–1944)
Edward Reilly Stettinius	(1944–1945)
James Francis Byrnes	(1945–1947)
George Catlett Marshall	(1947–1949)
Dean Gooderham Acheson	(1949–1953)
John Foster Dulles	(1953–1959)
Christian Archibald Herter	(1959–1961)
David Dean Rusk	(1961–1969)
William Pierce Rogers	(1969–1973)
Henry A. (Heinz Alfred) Kissinger	(1973–1977)
Cyrus Roberts Vance	(1977–1980)
Edmund Sixtus Muskie	(1980–1981)
Alexander Meigs Haig	(1981–1982)
George Pratt Shultz	(1982–1989)
James Addison Baker	(1989–1992)
Lawrence Sidney Eagleburger	(1992–1993)
Warren Minor Christopher	(1993–1997)
Madeleine Korbel Albright	(1997–2001)
Colin Luther Powell	(2001–2005)

Condoleezza Rice   (2005–2009)
Hillary Rodham Clinton   (2009–)

U.S. Chiefs of Protocol

The Department of State first established a Division of Protocol on February 4, 1928. All chiefs of protocol since 1961 have held the rank of ambassador. The Office of Protocol has been part of the Office of the Secretary of State since July 12, 1965. The chief of protocol serves as the protocol officer for the U.S. government and advises the president, the vice president, the secretary of state, and other high-ranking officials on all aspects of diplomatic protocol.

Former Chiefs of Protocol

James Clement Dunn	(1934–1935)
Richard Southgate	(1935–1937)
George T. Summerlin	(1937–1944)
Stanley Woodward	(1944–1950)
John F. Simmons	(1950–1957)
Wiley T. Buchanan	(1957–1961)
Angier Biddle Duke	(1961–1965)
Lloyd Nelson Hand	(1965–1966)
James W. Symington	(1966–1968)
Angier Biddle Duke	(1968–1968)
Tyler Abell	(1968–1969)
Emil Mosbacher Jr.	(1969–1972)
Marion H. Smoak	(1974–1974)
Henry E. Catto Jr.	(1974–1976)
Shirley Temple Black	(1976–1977)
Evan S. Dobelle	(1977–1978)
Edith H. J. Dobelle	(1978–1979)
Abelardo L. Valdez	(1979–1981)
Leonore Annenberg	(1981–1982)
Selwa Roosevelt	(1982–1989)
Joseph Verner Reed Jr.	(1989–1991)

John Gifford Weinmann   (1991–1993)
Mary M. Raiser   (1993–1997)
Mary Mel French   (1997–2001)
Donald Burnham Ensenat   (2001–2007)
Nancy Goodman Brinker   (2007–2009)
Capricia Penavic Marshall   (2009–)

AMERICAN PATRIOTIC SONGS

"The Star Spangled Banner" (U.S. National Anthem)

Lyrics by Francis Scott Key, 1814

> Oh, say can you see by the dawn's early light
> What so proudly we hailed at the twilight's last gleaming?
> Whose broad stripes and bright stars through the perilous fight,
> O'er the ramparts we watched were so gallantly streaming?
> And the rockets' red glare, the bombs bursting in air,
> Gave proof through the night that our flag was still there.
> Oh, say does that star-spangled banner yet wave
> O'er the land of the free and the home of the brave? . . .

John Stafford Smith composed the music for "The Star Spangled Banner" in the mid-1760s. The piece was commissioned by London's Anacreontic Society (so named in honor of the ancient Greek poet Anacreon) for material written by its president, Ralph Tomlinson.

In September 1814, Francis Scott Key was detained on a British ship, where he witnessed the failed British attempt to bombard Fort McHenry, which, had it succeeded, would have been a significant step in taking Baltimore. This experience inspired him to ask, "Does that star-spangled banner yet wave?"

On July 26, 1889, the secretary of the navy designated "The Star Spangled Banner" the official tune to be played while raising the American flag. During the administration of Woodrow Wilson, the song was chosen to be played whenever a national anthem was appropriate.

Amid some controversy over its violent tone and difficult vocal leaps, in 1931, famous American composer John Philip Sousa showed his support for the song, calling Key's poem "soul stirring" and further stating that "it is the spirit of the music that inspires." On March 3, 1931, President Herbert Hoover signed the act establishing Key's poem and Smith's music as the official anthem of the United States.

"My Country 'Tis of Thee"

Also known as "America"; lyrics by Samuel Francis Smith, 1831

> My country, 'tis of thee,
> Sweet land of liberty,
> Of thee I sing;
> Land where my fathers died,
> Land of the pilgrims' pride,
> From every mountainside
> Let freedom ring! . . .

The origin of this melody remains a mystery, but it has been used as the British national anthem, as well as the national anthem of several other countries. The song served as the de facto national anthem of the United States before the adoption of "The Star Spangled Banner."

"America the Beautiful"

Lyrics by Katharine Lee Bates, 1893

> O beautiful for spacious skies,
> For amber waves of grain,
> For purple mountain majesties
> Above the fruited plain!
> America! America!
> God shed his grace on thee
> And crown thy good with brotherhood
> From sea to shining sea! . . .

Katharine Lee Bates, a professor of English, scribbled the words to the first four verses of "America" during a lecture trip to Colorado in 1893 after climbing Pike's Peak.

On July 4, 1895, the weekly journal *The Congregationalist* first published Bates's poem. Today, "America" is sung to a melody by Samuel Augustus Ward, a Newark, New Jersey, church organist who composed it for another hymn in 1882 (a decade before Bates's poem was even written). Previously "America" had been sung to different musical accompaniment, and Ward's melody was often contested. In 1926, for example, the National Federation of Music Clubs sponsored a contest for new music to accompany Bates's poem. As the federation failed to find a winner, Ward's music became the default melody and has remained so since.

"God Bless America"

Lyrics by Irving Berlin, 1938.

Irving Berlin became a U.S. citizen in 1918. After being inducted into the army, he wrote the original "God Bless America" to raise both spirits and money as part of a musical comedy review. Feeling that the song was too solemn for the event, he put it aside for twenty years. In 1938, as war threatened Europe, Berlin felt stirred to write a peace song. When he recalled the unpublished poem languishing in his trunk, he shaped it into "God Bless America." The final version of the song was drafted that year.

Kate Smith, singing for CBS radio, asked Berlin for a patriotic song to be broadcast from the New York World's Fair on November 10, 1938; following Smith's rendition, "God Bless America" became an instant hit.

Berlin assigned his royalties to charity, the revenues going to the Boy and Girl Scouts of America. Irving Berlin lived for 101 years.

"Hail, Columbia"

Composed by Philip Phile (Pfeil), lyrics by Joseph Hopkinson (1798)

> Hail, Columbia, happy land!
> Hail, ye heroes, heav'n born band . . .

This tune, originally known as "The President's March," was played during George Washington's tour following his inauguration. After writing its lyrics in 1798, Joseph Hopkinson sent them to Washington in a letter, and the song debuted at Philadelphia's New Theatre later that year to raucous applause; the audience supposedly demanded repeated encores. Until the 1890s, "Hail, Columbia" served as America's national anthem.

"Hail to the Chief"

The origins of "Hail to the Chief" lie in Sir Walter Scott's poem "The Lady of the Lake." Published on May 8, 1810, Scott's poem brought him international acclaim, selling a record-breaking twenty-five thousand copies in eight months. In 1812, Mr. J. A. Jones selected a tune of James Sanderson's, "Hail to the Chief," written for a London production, to be part of an opening in Philadelphia's New Theater. Jones set some of the words of Scott's "Lady of the Lake" to Sanderson's music.

"Hail to the Chief" was first associated with a chief executive in 1815 when it was played to honor both George Washington and the end of the War of 1812.

In Case He Can't Be Spotted, "Hail to The Chief!"

President James K. Polk's wife, Sarah, grew tired of the fact that no one noticed when her husband entered a room; due to his average height, he often went undetected. Some announcement became necessary to avoid the embarrassment of his entering the room without recognition. Thus, at large affairs, the band rolled the drums and played a march to clear the way for Polk's arrival. "Hail to the Chief" is now played every time the president enters a room.

President John Tyler's wife, Julia, first asked that the song be played to announce the president on official occasions. But it was President James Polk's wife, Sarah, who ritualized its use.

When the U.S. president arrives at any formal occasion, "Hail to the Chief" sounds forth to announce his or her presence. When asked his favorite song, John F. Kennedy once quipped, "I believe that Hail to the Chief has a nice ring."

"Yankee Doodle"

Yankee Doodle went to town
A-riding on a pony,
Stuck a feather in his cap
And called it macaroni . . .
Chorus:
Yankee Doodle, keep it up,
Yankee Doodle Dandy,
Mind the music and the step,
And with the girls be handy.

Conflicting accounts surround of the origin of "Yankee Doodle." Thought to stem from the French and Indian War, it may have served as a way for the British to mock the colonial "Yanks," whom they viewed as disheveled and disorganized. A "doodle" was a silly person or country bumpkin. Conversely, a "dandy" was a gentleman. "Macaroni" referred to foppishness (a fancy style of dress), not to the pasta today associated with the word. By sticking a feather in his cap and calling it "macaroni," Yankee Doodle was declaring himself a "dandy," proudly proclaiming himself a gentleman, not a country bumpkin.

The first verses of "Yankee Doodle" were likely penned in 1755 by Dr. Richard Schackburg, a British surgeon. By 1777, "Yankee Doodle" was thought of as an unofficial American anthem. Following the Revolutionary War, "Yankee Doodle" surfaced in stage plays, classical music, and operas, and it remains immensely popular today.

"Battle Hymn of the Republic"

Early lyrics by William Steffe, 1856; current lyrics by Julia Ward Howe, 1861

Mine eyes have seen the glory of the coming of the Lord
He is trampling out the vintage where the grapes of wrath are stored
. . .

The early lyrics and tune, written by William Steffe in 1856, were popularized as a Methodist camp meeting song. New verses were added to the song around 1859 after John Brown's acts at Harper's Ferry rendered him an abolitionist martyr. Later, active abolitionist Julia Ward Howe and her husband witnessed a Union/ Confederate skirmish and heard troops sing the tune. Ward then wrote lyrics she deemed more uplifting in November 1861, and they were first published in the *Atlantic Monthly* on February 1, 1862. Her poem quickly became the song known as "The Battle Hymn of the Republic."

"Stars and Stripes Forever" (American National March)

Written by John Philip Sousa in 1896, "Stars and Stripes Forever" was declared the national march of the United States in 1987.

MILITARY SONGS

Each branch of the U.S. armed forces maintains its own marching song to inspire troops and preserve tradition. Military bands, once an integral element on the battlefield, now perform these songs as a ceremonial function. Each band represents the individual history and traditions of its respective branch of the U.S. armed forces.

U.S. Army: "The Army Goes Rolling Along" (1956 Version)

First to fight for the right,
And to build the Nation's might,
And The Army Goes Rolling Along
Proud of all we have done
Fighting till the battle's won,
And The Army Goes Rolling Along

Then it's Hi! Hi! Hey!
The Army's on its way.
Count off the cadence loud and strong

The "Caisson Song" was written by field artillery 1st Lt. Edmund L. Gruber (later Brigadier General Gruber) at Fort Stotsenburg in the Philippines, where he was stationed in 1908. The song was never designated as the official U.S. Army song. The official song today retains Gruber's music, but the lyrics have been rewritten.

U.S. Navy: "Anchors Aweigh"

> . . . Anchors Aweigh my boys
> Anchors Aweigh
> Farewell to college joys [or Farewell to foreign shores]
> We sail at break of day day day day
> Through our last night on shore
> Drink to the foam
> Until we meet once more
> Here's wishing you a happy voyage home!

"Anchors Aweigh" was composed in 1906 by Charles A. Zimmerman with lyrics by Alfred Hart Miles. Over the years, the lyrics have been rewritten. The song was first played for the Army–Navy football game on December 1, 1906, at Franklin Field in Philadelphia.

The first verse begins, "Stand Navy out to sea, Fight our battle cry," but the second verse is recognized immediately today: "Anchors Aweigh my boys/Anchors Aweigh . . ."

Another line, "Farewell to college joys," also appears in some versions as "Farewell to foreign shores." The word "aweigh" (often believed to be "away") is a nautical term meaning that the anchor is just free from the sea floor.

U.S. Navy Hymn: "Eternal Father, Strong to Save"

> Eternal Father, strong to save,
> Whose arm hath bound the restless wave,
> Who bidd'st the mighty ocean deep
> Its own appointed limits keep;
> Oh, hear us when we cry to Thee,
> For those in peril on the sea! . . .

"Eternal Father, Strong to Save" is a musical benediction found in many Protestant hymnals. The original words were written around 1860 as a hymn by the Rev. William Whiting, a clergyman of the Church of England. The words have been changed numerous times since the publication of the original hymn.

U.S. Air Force: "Into the Wild Blue Yonder"

Capt. Robert MacArthur Crawford wrote the lyrics and music to "Into the Wild Blue Yonder" in 1939. The song and current title were officially adopted in 1979 by Gen. Lew Allen Jr., chief of staff of the Air Force.

U.S. Marine Corps Hymn

> From the Halls of Montezuma
> To the shores of Tripoli
> We fight our country's battles
> In the air on land and sea.
> First to fight for right and freedom
> And to keep our honor clean;
> We are proud to bear the title
> Of United States Marines . . .

It is believed that the melody of the Marines' Hymn was taken from the aria in *Geneviève de Brabant* by French composer and conductor Jacques Offenbach (1819–1880). Tradition holds that an officer wrote the first verse of the song during the Mexican–American War (1846–1848), set to the tune of the Offenbach aria.

U.S. Coast Guard: "Semper Paratus" ("Always Ready")

Lyrics (1922) and music (1927) by Capt. Francis S. Van Boskerck

> From Aztec shore to Arctic zone,
> To Europe and Far East.
> The Flag is carried by our ships,
> In times of war and peace.
> And never have we struck it yet,
> In spite of foe-men's might,

Who cheered our crews and cheered again,
For showing how to fight.
We're always ready for the call,
We place our trust in Thee.
Through surf and storm and howling gale,
High shall our purpose be.
"Semper Paratus" is our guide,
Our fame, our glory too.
To fight to save or fight to die,
Aye! Coast Guard, we are for you!

Many stories surround the choosing of "Semper paratus" as the Coast Guard's motto. It is certain that Capt. Francis S. Van Boskerck rendered the motto a song by adding lyrics and music. The words were written in 1922 in the cabin of the *Yamacraw*, the cutter Van Boskerck commanded. While stationed in Savannah, Georgia, Van Boskerck's charge was to drive rum runners from the coasts of Florida and the Carolinas. Five years later, Van Boskerck composed the accompanying music on a rickety piano while stationed in Alaska.

AMERICAN AND RELIGIOUS HOLIDAYS

The following are American federal holidays or common national observances. Federal holidays are noted as such next to the holiday's name and date. Many other religious and ethnic celebrations are not included in this list. Federal and state offices, tourist locations, and businesses may be closed during these holidays; those wishing to visit or conduct business during a holiday may wish to call ahead in case of closure. The holidays appear below in date order to the extent that dates are fixed. Those with movable dates are noted.

New Year's Day: January 1 (Federal Holiday)

New Year's Eve (December 31) launches this federal holiday. In celebration of the New Year, Americans congregate to wish each other a joyous and prosperous year. Many make New Year's resolutions, through which they resolve to accomplish personal goals or make personal changes.

Chinese New Year: A Day between January 20 and February 20

Also called Lunar New Year, Chinese New Year traditionally begins on the first day of the first month of the Chinese calendar and continues until the fifteenth of the month, when the moon is typically the brightest.

Martin Luther King Day: Third Monday in January (Federal Holiday)

The Martin Luther King holiday commemorates the life and accomplishments of Rev. Martin Luther King Jr., an African American clergyman and civil rights leader who advocated struggling for equal rights for all through nonviolent means.

Groundhog Day: February 2

Believing it to foreshadow the continuance of winter or the emergence of spring weather, Americans await the appearance of a ground hog (a type of rodent) called "Punxsutawney Phil" from his burrow in Punxsutawney, Pennsylvania. If Punxsutawney Phil sees his shadow, six more weeks of winter weather can be predicted. This holiday has been celebrated since 1887.

Valentine's Day: February 14

Named after a Christian martyr, St. Valentine, Valentine's Day is celebrated with gifts of cards, candy, flowers, and so forth, to loved ones. The holiday has become an enormous commercial boom since valentine cards were first mass-produced in the 1840s.

Washington's Birthday or President's Day: Third Monday of February (Federal Holiday)

This holiday honors the birthday of George Washington, the first U.S. president. Many groups use this holiday to celebrate the legacy of past presidents.

Mardi Gras: The Day before Ash Wednesday

Celebrated the last three days before Lent, "Fat Tuesday" (called Mardi Gras in France), marks the end of the carnival season. It is observed in several American cities—most notably, New Orleans, Louisiana—and is characterized by parades and overindulgence in food and spirits.

Ash Wednesday: First Day of Lent

Ash Wednesday is a Christian day of public penance on which penitent's foreheads are marked with ashes of palms burned and blessed during the previous year. The holiday marks the beginning of the forty days of Lent.

St. Patrick's Day: March 17

Characterized by parades and the wearing of green clothing (as tradition goes, the nonwearer will be pinched), St. Patrick's Day celebrates St. Patrick, the patron saint of Ireland.

April Fool's Day: April 1

Though the origins of this holiday are unclear, Americans enjoy engaging in hijinks, such as telling false tales to others, for the purpose of tricking gullible "fools."

Passover (Pesach): A Spring Day (Varies Each Year)

This holiday commemorates the Jews' exodus from Egypt after four hundred years of slavery and is celebrated on the fifteenth day of the Jewish month *Nissan*. Passover lasts for seven days (eight days outside of Israel) and culminates in a seder, or dinner, that is a time to eat and practice rituals with family and friends.

Good Friday: The Friday before Easter

This Christian holiday commemorates the crucifixion of Jesus Christ, the story of which is retold during services from the Gospel according to St. John. Many Christians fast on Good Friday.

Easter: A Sunday in Spring (Varies Each Year)

A Christian holiday, Easter marks the day Christians believe Jesus Christ was resurrected. For Christians, it is typically a time to attend religious services and spend time with family. Many Americans follow old traditions of dying hard-boiled eggs and hiding them outdoors for children to "hunt" and of giving baskets of candy to children.

Orthodox Easter (Pascha): A Sunday in Spring (Varies Each Year)

Those who are Greek Orthodox celebrate Easter according to the Orthodox calendar (also known as the Julian calendar, as opposed to the Gregorian calendar used to calculate the Western Christian Easter). Part of the Easter celebration includes Holy Saturday, a vigil service that starts after sundown the day before Easter Sunday and continues overnight until early morning (postsunrise). Many Greek Orthodox fast prior to Easter and do not eat foods such as butter, milk, meat, and olive oil. The Greek Orthodox also dye Easter eggs, but they only use the color red.

Earth Day: April 22

This holiday was designated to mark the inception of the modern American environmental movement in 1970. It has inspired legislation such as the Clean Air and Clean Water acts. It is intended to advance respect for the planet, to promote regard for the environment, and to focus on land, air, and water pollution.

Arbor Day: Last Friday in April (Can Vary from State to State)

Arbor Day celebrates the planting of trees, which was associated with Nebraska settlers and homesteaders in 1872, when they were encouraged to plant trees where there were few. It was officially declared a holiday by President Richard Nixon in 1970 and may be celebrated at different times from state to state, depending on the weather.

Mother's Day: Second Sunday in May

This holiday observes the vital role of mothers in the lives of Americans. It began in 1914 when President Woodrow Wilson asked Americans to publicly express their gratitude to and reverence for their mothers.

Memorial Day: Last Monday in May

Originally intended to honor those who died during the American Civil War, Memorial Day now honors those killed in all American wars. The American flag is displayed for this holiday, and ceremonies and services are held in public meeting places, cemeteries, and churches.

Flag Day: June 14

On Flag Day, the public is encouraged to display the American flag in observance of the history and tradition it represents. Since 1916, this holiday has been a presidentially proclaimed observance.

Father's Day: Third Sunday in June

Though Lyndon Johnson issued a proclamation honoring fathers in 1966, the holiday began in Spokane, Washington, in 1909. There, a daughter desired a day designated to honor her father, a Civil War veteran who raised his children after the death of his wife.

Independence Day: July 4 (Federal Holiday)

Honoring the signing of the Declaration of Independence on July 4, 1776, and the birth of America, this holiday is typically celebrated with fireworks, parades, outdoor eating, flying of the American flag, and all things patriotic.

Ramadan: Ninth Month of the Islamic Calendar

A Muslim holiday focusing on spiritual purification through prayer, fasting, and self-sacrifice, Ramadan is celebrated each day from sunrise to sunset. The month-long holiday concludes with the "Eid" or "Eid ul-Fitr," a three-day festival to break the fast.

Labor Day: First Monday of September (Federal Holiday)

Honoring the contributions of America's working people to the stability, strength, and plentitude of the nation, Labor Day is often celebrated with parades and flag displays. For many, this holiday marks the end of summer and the beginning of the school year.

Patriot Day: September 11

Patriot Day is an annual observance on September 11 to remember those who were injured or killed during the terrorist attacks against the United States on September 11, 2001. Many Americans refer to Patriot Day as 9/11 or September 11.

Rosh Hashanah (Jewish New Year): Usually in September or October (Varies Each Year)

The Jewish New Year opens the Ten Days of Penitence that close with Yom Kippur (Day of Atonement). The Jewish day stretches from sundown to sundown; consequently, all holidays begin at sundown of the day preceding the stated date and end at sundown on the last day stated.

Yom Kippur (Day of Atonement): Usually in September or October (Varies Each Year)

The holiest day of the Jewish year, Yom Kippur is celebrated on the tenth day of the Hebrew month *Tishrei*. It is a day of self-denial and repentance during which fasting is practiced. This day marks the end of the Ten Days of Penitence that begin with Rosh Hashanah. Services at synagogues begin the preceding sundown, resume the next morning, and continue until sundown.

Columbus Day: Second Monday in October (Federal Holiday)

This holiday, proclaimed by President Franklin D. Roosevelt in 1937, commemorates the day on which Italian explorer Christopher Columbus landed in the New World.

Halloween: October 31

This holiday is celebrated with the donning of costumes and taking children "trick-or-treating" (i.e., going door to door to request candy), typically in one's neighborhood. Neighbors generally respond by giving "treats" of candy. Carved pumpkins, witches, black cats, and spiders are also associated with Halloween.

Election Day: First Tuesday in November

An 1845 act of Congress made the first Tuesday in November the date for choosing presidential electors. A legal holiday in some states, it is also the day most state elections are held.

Veterans Day: November 11 (Federal Holiday)

Veterans Day now honors veterans of all U.S. wars, though it formerly recognized those veterans who served in World War I and was originally called Armistice Day. Parades sponsored by veterans' organizations and the placement of a wreath on the Tomb of the Unknown Soldier at Arlington National Cemetery in Arlington, Virginia, are hallmarks of this holiday.

Eid al-Adha (Feast of Sacrifice): Tenth through Thirteenth Day of the Twelfth Month of the Islamic Calendar

A three-day commemoration of Abraham's willingness to obey God by sacrificing his son, this Muslim holiday concludes the annual hajj (pilgrimage to Mecca). Animals are sometimes sacrificed and given to relatives or those in need to symbolize Abraham's sacrifice.

Thanksgiving Day: Fourth Thursday in November (Federal Holiday)

This holiday began in 1621 as a celebratory feast hosted by the colonists to thank Native Americans for their help with crops. Thanksgiving has become a favorite national tradition, marked by gatherings of family and friends, though many of the foods have changed over the years. Typical foods now enjoyed at the Thanksgiving table include roasted turkey, cranberry sauce, sweet potatoes, and pumpkin pie.

Hanukkah (Festival of Lights): Late November to December

Celebrated on the twenty-fifth day of Kislev in the Hebrew calendar, this festival lasts eight days and is associated with the lighting of candles in a menorah (candelabrum) for each day of the holiday, plus an additional candle, which is used to light the rest. The holiday was initiated by Judas Maccabeus in 165 BC to mark the rededication of the Temple of Jerusalem desecrated three years prior. It commemorates the miracle of the container of oil that, according to the Talmud, lit the Temple for eight days when there seemed to be only enough oil for one day.

Pearl Harbor Remembrance Day: December 7

Pearl Harbor Day recognizes the military personnel, numbering more than twenty-four hundred, who died during a surprise attack by Japanese forces on Pearl Harbor, Hawaii, on this date in 1941. This attack precipitated U.S. entrance into World War II.

Christmas Day: December 25 (Federal Holiday)

Christmas is a Christian holiday celebrating the birth of Jesus Christ. Secular traditions now associated with Christmas include erecting and decorating Christmas trees, decorating homes and yards with lights, and giving gifts (among many others).

WHITE HOUSE TOURS

Arrangements for White House Tours

Free tours of the White House are available to the public. Tour requests must be submitted through one's member of Congress. The number for the congressional switchboard is (202) 334-3121. Tours are scheduled on a first-come, first-served basis, and limited space is available. Thus, advance planning is necessary. White House tours are subject to last-minute cancellation. For the most current information regarding tours, a twenty-four-hour line is available at (202) 456-7041.

Those who are citizens of foreign countries should contact their embassies in Washington, D.C., for information and assistance in submitting tour requests.

The White House Visitor Center, located at the southeast corner of Fifteenth and E streets, provides much information related to the White House. A visit to the center prior to or following a tour of the White House is certain to enhance the tour, as the center offers a thirty-minute video and exhibits relating to a myriad of interesting aspects of the White House.

Suitable Attire for the White House

It is important to dress appropriately when visiting the White House for any tour. Men need not wear a suit, nor women dressy clothes; however, attire should be in good taste. Comfortable footwear should be worn. It is good to remember that the White House is the United States' most important historical working house. Visitors should dress accordingly and treat the building with respect.

Chapter 17

Embassy Names and
Other Office Information

AFGHANISTAN
Islamic Republic of Afghanistan
Embassy of Afghanistan
Chancery: 2341 Wyoming Avenue, NW
Washington, DC 20008
(202) 483-6410
Fax: (202) 483-6488

AFRICAN UNION
Delegation of the African Union
Chancery: 1919 Pennsylvania Avenue, NW
Washington, DC 20006
(202) 293-8006
Fax: (202) 429-7130

ALBANIA
Republic of Albania
Embassy of the Republic of Albania
Chancery: 2100 S Street, NW
Washington, DC 20008
(202) 223-4942
Fax: (202) 628-7342

ALGERIA
People's Democratic Republic of Algeria
Embassy of the People's Democratic Republic of Algeria
Chancery: 2118 Kalorama Road, NW
Washington, DC 20008
(202) 265-2800
Fax: (202) 667-2174

AMERICAN SAMOA**
Territory of American Samoa
An unincorporated, unorganized territory of the United States

ANDORRA
Principality of Andorra
Embassy of Andorra
Chancery: Two United Nations Plaza
27th Floor
New York, NY 10017
(212) 750-8064
Fax: (212) 750-6630

ANGOLA
Republic of Angola
Embassy of the Republic of Angola
Chancery: 2100–2108 Sixteenth Street, NW
Washington, DC 20009
(202) 785-1156
Fax: (202) 785-1258

ANTIGUA AND BARBUDA
Antigua and Barbuda
Embassy of Antigua and Barbuda
Chancery: 3216 New Mexico Avenue, NW
Washington, DC 20016
(202) 362-5122
Fax: (202) 362-5225

Argentina
Argentine Republic
Embassy of the Argentine Republic
Chancery: 1600 New Hampshire Avenue, NW
Washington, DC 20009
(202) 238-6400
Fax: (202) 332-3171

Armenia
Republic of Armenia
Embassy of the Republic of Armenia
Chancery: 2225 R Street, NW
Washington, DC 20008
(202) 319-1976
Fax: (202) 319-2982

Australia
Commonwealth of Australia
Embassy of Australia
Chancery: 1601 Massachusetts Avenue, NW
Washington, DC 20036
(202) 797-3000
Fax: (202) 797-3168

Austria
Republic of Austria
Embassy of Austria
Chancery: 3524 International Court, NW
Washington, DC 20008-3035
(202) 895-6700
Fax: (202) 895-6750

Azerbaijan
Republic of Azerbaijan
Embassy of the Republic of Azerbaijan
Chancery: 2741 Thirty-fourth Street, NW
Washington, DC 20008
(202) 337-3500
Fax: (202) 337-5911

BAHAMAS
Commonwealth of The Bahamas
Embassy of the Commonwealth of The Bahamas
Chancery: 2220 Massachusetts Avenue, NW
Washington, DC 20008
(202) 319-2660
Fax: (202) 319-2668

BAHRAIN
Kingdom of Bahrain
Embassy of the Kingdom of Bahrain
Chancery: 3502 International Drive, NW
Washington, DC 20008
(202) 342-0741
Fax: (202) 362-2192

BANGLADESH
People's Republic of Bangladesh
Embassy of the People's Republic of Bangladesh
Chancery: 3510 International Drive, NW
Washington, DC 20008
(202) 244-0183
Fax: (202) 244-5366

BARBADOS
Barbados
Embassy of Barbados
Chancery: 2144 Wyoming Avenue, NW
Washington, DC 20008
(202) 939-9200
Fax: (202) 332-7467

BELARUS
Republic of Belarus
Embassy of the Republic of Belarus
Chancery: 1619 New Hampshire Avenue, NW
Washington, DC 20009
(202) 986-1604
Fax: (202) 986-1805

BELGIUM
Kingdom of Belgium
Embassy of Belgium
Chancery: 3330 Garfield Street, NW
Washington, DC 20008
(202) 333-6900
Fax: (202) 333-3079

BELIZE
Belize
Embassy of Belize
Chancery: 2535 Massachusetts Avenue, NW
Washington, DC 20008
(202) 332-9636
Fax: (202) 332-6888

BENIN
Republic of Benin
Embassy of the Republic of Benin
Chancery: 2124 Kalorama Road, NW
Washington, DC 20008
(202) 232-6656
Fax: (202) 265-1996

BHUTAN*
The Kingdom of Bhutan and the United States have no formal relations.
Contact is handled though the U.S. Embassy in New Delhi, India.

BOLIVIA
Plurinational State of Bolivia
Embassy of Bolivia
Chancery: 3014 Massachusetts Avenue, NW
Washington, DC 20008
(202) 483-4410
Fax: (202) 328-3712

BOSNIA AND HERZEGOVINA
Bosnia and Herzegovina
Embassy of Bosnia and Herzegovina
Chancery: 2109 E Street, NW
Washington, DC 20037
(202) 337-1500
Fax: (202) 337-1502

BOTSWANA
Republic of Botswana
Embassy of the Republic of Botswana
Chancery: 1531–1533 New Hampshire Avenue, NW
Washington, DC 20036
(202) 244-4990
Fax: (202) 244-4164

BRAZIL
Federative Republic of Brazil
The ambassador is addressed: The Brazilian Ambassador.
Brazilian Embassy
Chancery: 3006 Massachusetts Avenue, NW
Washington, DC 20008
(202) 238-2700
Fax: (202) 238-2827

BRUNEI
Brunei Darussalam
Embassy of Brunei Darussalam
Chancery: 3520 International Court, NW
Washington, DC 20008
(202) 237-1838
Fax: (202) 885-0560

BULGARIA
Republic of Bulgaria
Embassy of the Republic of Bulgaria
Chancery: 1621 Twenty-second Street, NW
Washington, DC 20008
(202) 387-0174
Fax: (202) 234-7973

Burkina Faso
Burkina Faso
Embassy of Burkina Faso
Chancery: 2340 Massachusetts Avenue, NW
Washington, DC 20008
(202) 332-5577
Fax: (202) 667-1882

Burma
Union of Burma
Embassy of the Union of Burma
Chancery: 2300 S Street, NW
Washington, DC 20008
(202) 332-3344
Fax: (202) 332-4351

Burundi
Republic of Burundi
Embassy of the Republic of Burundi
Chancery: 2233 Wisconsin Avenue, NW
Suite 212
Washington, DC 20007
(202) 342-2574
Fax: (202) 342-2578

Cambodia
Kingdom of Cambodia
Royal Embassy of Cambodia
Chancery: 4530 Sixteenth Street, NW
Washington, DC 20011
(202) 726-7742
Fax: (202) 726-8381

Cameroon
Republic of Cameroon
Embassy of the Republic of Cameroon
Chancery: 2349 Massachusetts Avenue, NW
Washington, DC 20008
(202) 265-8790
Fax: (202) 387-3826

CANADA
Canada
Embassy of Canada
Chancery: 501 Pennsylvania Avenue, NW
Washington, DC 20001
(202) 682-1740
Fax: (202) 682-7726

CAPE VERDE
Republic of Cape Verde
Embassy of the Republic of Cape Verde
Chancery: 3415 Massachusetts Avenue, NW
Washington, DC 20007
(202) 965-6820
Fax: (202) 965-1207

CENTRAL AFRICAN REPUBLIC
Central African Republic
Embassy of Central African Republic
Chancery: 1618 Twenty-second Street, NW
Washington, DC 20008
(202) 483-7800
Fax: (202) 332-9893

CHAD
Republic of Chad
Embassy of the Republic of Chad
Chancery: 2002 R Street, NW
Washington, DC 20009
(202) 462-4009
Fax: (202) 265-1937

CHILE
Republic of Chile
Embassy of the Republic of Chile
Chancery: 1732 Massachusetts Avenue, NW
Washington, DC 20036
(202) 785-1746
Fax: (202) 887-5579

CHINA
People's Republic of China
Embassy of the People's Republic of China
Chancery: 3505 International Place, NW
Washington, DC 20008
(202) 495-2000
Fax: (202) 495-2138

COLOMBIA
Republic of Colombia
Embassy of Colombia
Chancery: 2118 Leroy Place, NW
Washington, DC 20008
(202) 387-8338
Fax: (202) 232-8643

COMOROS
Union of the Comoros
Embassy of the Union of Comoros
Chancery: 866 United Nations Plaza
Suite 418
New York, NY 10017
(212) 750-1637
Fax: (212) 750-1657

CONGO (DRC, KINSHASA)
Democratic Republic of the Congo
Embassy of the Democratic Republic of the Congo
Chancery: 1726 M Street, NW
Suite 601
Washington, DC 20036
(202) 234-7690
Fax: (202) 234-2609

CONGO (RC, BRAZZAVILLE)
Republic of the Congo
Embassy of the Republic of the Congo
Chancery: 4891 Colorado Avenue, NW
Washington, DC 20011
(202) 726-5500
Fax: (202) 726-1860

COSTA RICA
Republic of Costa Rica
Embassy of Costa Rica
Chancery: 2114 S Street, NW
Washington, DC 20008
(202) 234-2945
Fax: (202) 265-4795

CÔTE D'IVOIRE
Republic of Côte d'Ivoire
Embassy of the Republic of Côte d'Ivoire
Chancery: 2424 Massachusetts Avenue, NW
Washington, DC 20008
(202) 797-0300
Fax: (202) 462-9444

CROATIA
Republic of Croatia
Embassy of the Republic of Croatia
Chancery: 2343 Massachusetts Avenue, NW
Washington, DC 20008
(202) 588-5899
Fax: (202) 588-8936

CUBA*
Republic of Cuba
Diplomatic representation is conducted by an interests section of the
Swiss embassy in the United States and the Swiss embassy in Cuba.

Cyprus
Republic of Cyprus
Embassy of the Republic of Cyprus
Chancery: 2211 R Street, NW
Washington, DC 20008
(202) 462-5772
Fax: (202) 483-6710

Czech Republic
Czech Republic
Embassy of the Czech Republic
Chancery: 3900 Spring of Freedom Street, NW
Washington, DC 20008
(202) 274-9100
Fax: (202) 966-8540

Denmark
Kingdom of Denmark
Royal Danish Embassy
Chancery: 3200 Whitehaven Street, NW
Washington, DC 20008
(202) 234-4300
Fax: (202) 328-1470

Djibouti
Republic of Djibouti
Embassy of the Republic of Djibouti
Chancery: 1156 Fifteenth Street, NW
Suite 515
Washington, DC 20005
(202) 331-0270
Fax: (202) 331-0302

Dominica
Commonwealth of Dominica
Embassy of the Commonwealth of Dominica
Chancery: 3216 New Mexico Avenue, NW
Washington, DC 20016
(202) 364-6781
Fax: (202) 364-6791

DOMINICAN REPUBLIC
Dominican Republic
Embassy of the Dominican Republic
Chancery: 1715 Twenty-second Street, NW
Washington, DC 20008
(202) 332-6280
Fax: (202) 265-8057

ECUADOR
Republic of Ecuador
Embassy of Ecuador
Chancery: 2535 Fifteenth Street, NW
Washington, DC 20009
(202) 234-7200
Fax: (202) 667-3482

EGYPT
Arab Republic of Egypt
Embassy of the Arab Republic of Egypt
Chancery: 3521 International Court, NW
Washington, DC 20008
(202) 895-5400
Fax: (202) 244-4319

EL SALVADOR
Republic of El Salvador
Embassy of El Salvador
Chancery: 1400 Sixteenth Street, NW
Suite 100
Washington, DC 20036
(202) 265-9671
Fax: (202) 232-3763

EQUATORIAL GUINEA
Republic of Equatorial Guinea
Embassy of the Republic of Equatorial Guinea
Chancery: 2020 Sixteenth Street, NW
Washington, DC 20009
(202) 518-5700
Fax: (202) 518-5252

Eritrea
State of Eritrea
Embassy of the State of Eritrea
Chancery: 1708 New Hampshire Avenue, NW
Washington, DC 20009
(202) 319-1991
Fax: (202) 319-1304

Estonia
Republic of Estonia
Embassy of Estonia
Chancery: 2131 Massachusetts Avenue, NW
Washington, DC 20008
(202) 588-0101
Fax: (202) 588-0108

Ethiopia
Federal Democratic Republic of Ethiopia
Embassy of Ethiopia
Chancery: 3506 International Drive, NW
Washington, DC 20008
(202) 364-1200
Fax: (202) 686-9551

Fiji
Republic of the Fiji Islands
Embassy of the Republic of Fiji Islands
Chancery: 2000 M Street, NW
Suite 710
Washington, DC 20036
(202) 466-8320
Fax: (202) 466-8325

Finland
Republic of Finland
Embassy of Finland
Chancery: 3301 Massachusetts Avenue, NW
Washington, DC 20008
(202) 298-5800
Fax: (202) 298-6030

FRANCE
French Republic
Embassy of France
Chancery: 4101 Reservoir Road, NW
Washington, DC 20007
(202) 944-6000
Fax: (202) 944-6166

GABON
Gabonese Republic
Embassy of the Gabonese Republic
Chancery: 2034 Twentieth Street, NW
Suite 200
Washington, DC 20009
(202) 797-1000
Fax: (202) 332-0668

GAMBIA
Republic of The Gambia
Embassy of The Gambia
Chancery: 1424 K Street, NW
Suite 600
Washington, DC 20005
(202) 785-1379
Fax: (202) 785-1430

GEORGIA
Georgia
Embassy of the Republic of Georgia
Chancery: 2209 Massachusetts Avenue, NW
Washington, DC 20008
(202) 387-2390
Fax: (202) 387-0864

Germany
Federal Republic of Germany
Embassy of the Federal Republic of Germany
Chancery: 4645 Reservoir Road, NW
Washington, DC 20007
(202) 298-4000
Fax: (202) 298-4249

Ghana
Republic of Ghana
Embassy of Ghana
Chancery: 3512 International Drive, NW
Washington, DC 20008
(202) 686-4520
Fax: (202) 686-4527

Greece
Hellenic Republic
Embassy of Greece
Chancery: 2217 Massachusetts Avenue, NW
Washington, DC 20008
(202) 939-1300
Fax: (202) 939-1324

Guam**
Territory of Guam
Guam is a U.S. territory with diplomatic representation by the United
States.

Grenada
Grenada
Embassy of Grenada
Chancery: 1701 New Hampshire Avenue, NW
Washington, DC 20009
(202) 265-2561
Fax: (202) 265-2468

GUATEMALA
Republic of Guatemala
Embassy of Guatemala
Chancery: 2220 R Street, NW
Washington, DC 20008
(202) 745-4952
Fax: (202) 745-1908

GUINEA
Republic of Guinea
Embassy of the Republic of Guinea
Chancery: 2112 Leroy Place, NW
Washington, DC 20008
(202) 986-4300
Fax: (202) 986-3800

GUINEA-BISSAU
Republic of Guinea-Bissau
Embassy of the Republic of Guinea-Bissau
Chancery: P.O. Box 33813
Washington, DC 20033
(301) 947-3958

GUYANA
Cooperative Republic of Guyana
Embassy of Guyana
Chancery: 2490 Tracy Place, NW
Washington, DC 20008
(202) 265-6900
Fax: (202) 232-1297

HAITI
Republic of Haiti
Embassy of the Republic of Haiti
Chancery: 2311 Massachusetts Avenue, NW
Washington, DC 20008
(202) 332-4090
Fax: (202) 745-7215

Holy See
The Holy See or State of Vatican City
Apostolic Nunciature
Chancery: 3339 Massachusetts Avenue, NW
Washington, DC 20008
(202) 333-7121
Fax: (202) 337-4036

Honduras
Republic of Honduras
Embassy of Honduras
Chancery: 3007 Tilden Street, NW
Suite 4-M
Washington, DC 20008
(202) 966-2604
Fax: (202) 966-9751

Hungary
Republic of Hungary
Embassy of the Republic of Hungary
Chancery: 3910 Shoemaker Street, NW
Washington, DC 20008
(202) 362-6730
Fax: (202) 966-8135

Iceland
Republic of Iceland
Embassy of Iceland
Chancery: 2900 K Street, NW
Suite 509
Washington, DC 20007
(202) 265-6653
Fax: (202) 265-6656

India
Republic of India
Embassy of India
Chancery: 2107 Massachusetts Avenue, NW
Washington, DC 20008
(202) 939-7000
Fax: (202) 483-3972

INDONESIA
Republic of Indonesia
Embassy of the Republic of Indonesia
Chancery: 2020 Massachusetts Avenue, NW
Washington, DC 20036
(202) 775-5200
Fax: (202) 775-5365

IRAN*
Islamic Republic of Iran
The Swiss government assumed representation of U.S. interests in
Tehran. Iranian interests in the United States are represented by the
government of Pakistan.

IRAQ
Republic of Iraq
Embassy of the Republic of Iraq
Chancery: 3421 Massachusetts Avenue, NW
Washington, DC 20007
(202) 742-1600
Fax: (202) 462-5066

IRELAND
Ireland
Embassy of Ireland
Chancery: 2234 Massachusetts Avenue, NW
Washington, DC 20008
(202) 462-3939
Fax: (202) 232-5993

ISRAEL
State of Israel
Embassy of Israel
Chancery: 3514 International Drive, NW
Washington, DC 20008
(202) 364-5500
Fax: (202) 364-5607

ITALY
Italian Republic
Embassy of Italy
Chancery: 3000 Whitehaven Street, NW
Washington, DC 20008
(202) 612-4400
Fax: (202) 518-2151

JAMAICA
Jamaica
Embassy of Jamaica
Chancery: 1520 New Hampshire Avenue, NW
Washington, DC 20036
(202) 452-0660
Fax: (202) 452-0081

JAPAN
Japan
Embassy of Japan
Chancery: 2520 Massachusetts Avenue, NW
Washington, DC 20008
(202) 238-6700
Fax: (202) 328-2187

JORDAN
Hashemite Kingdom of Jordan
Embassy of the Hashemite Kingdom of Jordan
Chancery: 3504 International Drive, NW
Washington, DC 20008
(202) 966-2664
Fax: (202) 966-3110

KAZAKHSTAN
Republic of Kazakhstan
Embassy of the Republic of Kazakhstan
Chancery: 1401 Sixteenth Street, NW
Washington, DC 20036
(202) 232-5488
Fax: (202) 232-5845

KENYA
Republic of Kenya
Embassy of the Republic of Kenya
Chancery: 2249 R Street, NW
Washington, DC 20008
(202) 387-6101
Fax: (202) 462-3829

KOREA, NORTH*
Democratic People's Republic of Korea
The communist dictatorship of North Korea is not on friendly terms
with the United States. Talks are ongoing. There is no exchange of
ambassadors.

KOREA, SOUTH
Republic of Korea
Embassy of the Republic of Korea
Chancery: 2450 Massachusetts Avenue, NW
Washington, DC 20008
(202) 939-5600
Fax: (202) 387-0250

KOSOVO REPUBLIC
Republic of Kosovo
Embassy of the Republic of Kosovo
Chancery: 900 Nineteenth Street, NW
Suite 400
Washington, DC 20006
(202) 380-3581
Fax: (202) 380-3628

KUWAIT
State of Kuwait
Embassy of the State of Kuwait
Chancery: 2940 Tilden Street, NW
Washington, DC 20008
(202) 966-0702
Fax: (202) 966-0517

KYRGYZSTAN
Kyrgyz Republic
Embassy of the Kyrgyz Republic
Chancery: 2360 Massachusetts Avenue, NW
Washington, DC 20008
(202) 338-5141
Fax: (202) 338-5139

LAOS
Lao People's Democratic Republic
Embassy of the Lao People's Democratic Republic
Chancery: 2222 S Street, NW
Washington, DC 20008
(202) 332-6416
Fax: (202) 332-4923

LATVIA
Republic of Latvia
Embassy of Latvia
Chancery: 2306 Massachusetts Avenue, NW
Washington, DC 20008
(202) 328-2840
Fax: (202) 328-2860

LEBANON
Lebanese Republic
Embassy of Lebanon
Chancery: 2560 Twenty-eighth Street, NW
Washington, DC 20008
(202) 939-6300
Fax: (202) 939-6324

LESOTHO
Kingdom of Lesotho
Embassy of the Kingdom of Lesotho
Chancery: 2511 Massachusetts Avenue, NW
Washington, DC 20008
(202) 797-5533
Fax: (202) 234-6815

LIBERIA
Republic of Liberia
Embassy of the Republic of Liberia
Chancery: 5201 Sixteenth Street, NW
Washington, DC 20011
(202) 723-0437
Fax: (202) 723-0436

LIBYA
Great Socialist People's Libyan Arab Jamahiriya
Embassy of the Libyan Arab Jamahiriya
Chancery: 2600 Virginia Avenue, NW
Suite 705
Washington, DC 20037
(202) 944-9601
Fax: (202) 944-9606

LIECHTENSTEIN
Principality of Liechtenstein
Embassy of the Principality of Liechtenstein
Chancery: 2900 K Street, NW
Suite 602 B
Washington, DC 20007
(202) 331-0590
Fax: (202) 331-3221

LITHUANIA
Republic of Lithuania
Embassy of the Republic of Lithuania
Chancery: 2622 Sixteenth Street, NW
Washington, DC 20009
(202) 234-5860
Fax: (202) 328-0466

LUXEMBOURG
Grand Duchy of Luxembourg
Embassy of the Grand Duchy of Luxembourg
Chancery: 2200 Massachusetts Avenue, NW
Washington, DC 20008
(202) 265-4171
Fax: (202) 328-8270

MACEDONIA
Republic of Macedonia
Embassy of the Republic of Macedonia
Chancery: 2129 Wyoming Avenue, NW
Washington, DC 20008
(202) 667-0501
Fax: (202) 667-2131

MADAGASCAR
Republic of Madagascar
Embassy of the Republic of Madagascar
Chancery: 2374 Massachusetts Avenue, NW
Washington, DC 20008
(202) 265-5525
Fax: (202) 265-3034

MALAWI
Republic of Malawi
Embassy of Malawi
Chancery: 1029 Vermont Avenue, NW
Suite 1000
Washington, DC 20005
(202) 721-0270
Fax: (202) 721-0288

MALAYSIA
Malaysia
Embassy of Malaysia
Chancery: 3516 International Court, NW
Washington, DC 20008
(202) 572-9700
Fax: (202) 572-9882

MALDIVES
Republic of Maldives
Embassy of the Republic of Maldives
Chancery: 800 Second Avenue
Suite 400 E
New York, NY 10017
(212) 599-6195
Fax: (212) 661-6405

MALI
Republic of Mali
Embassy of the Republic of Mali
Chancery: 2130 R Street, NW
Washington, DC 20008
(202) 332-2249
Fax: (202) 332-6603

MALTA
Republic of Malta
Embassy of Malta
Chancery: 2017 Connecticut Avenue, NW
Washington, DC 20008
(202) 462-3611
Fax: (202) 387-5470

MARSHALL ISLANDS
Republic of the Marshall Islands
Embassy of the Republic of the Marshall Islands
Chancery: 2433 Massachusetts Avenue, NW
1st Floor
Washington, DC 20008
(202) 234-5414
Fax: (202) 232-3236

MAURITANIA
Islamic Republic of Mauritania
Embassy of the Islamic Republic of Mauritania
Chancery: 2129 Leroy Place, NW
Washington, DC 20008
(202) 232-5700
Fax: (202) 319-2623

MAURITIUS
Republic of Mauritius
Embassy of Republic of Mauritius
Chancery: 4301 Connecticut Avenue, NW
Suite 441
Washington, DC 20008
(202) 244-1491
Fax: (202) 966-0983

MEXICO
United Mexican States
Embassy of Mexico
Chancery: 1911 Pennsylvania Avenue, NW
Washington, DC 20006
(202) 728-1600
Fax: (202) 728-1698

MICRONESIA
Federated States of Micronesia
Embassy of the Federated States of Micronesia
Chancery: 1725 N Street, NW
Washington, DC 20036
(202) 223-4383
Fax: (202) 223-4391

MOLDOVA
Republic of Moldova
Embassy of the Republic of Moldova
Chancery: 2101 S Street, NW
Washington, DC 20008
(202) 667-1130
Fax: (202) 667-1204

MONACO
Principality of Monaco
Embassy of Monaco
Chancery: 3400 International Drive, NW
Suite 2K-100
Washington, DC 20008
(202) 234-1530
Fax: (202) 244-7656

MONGOLIA
Mongolia
Embassy of Mongolia
Chancery: 2833 M Street, NW
Washington, DC 20007
(202) 333-7117
Fax: (202) 298-9227

MONTENEGRO
Montenegro
Embassy of the Republic of Montenegro
Chancery: 1610 New Hampshire Avenue, NW
Washington, DC 20009
(202) 234-6108
Fax: (202) 234-6109

MOROCCO
Kingdom of Morocco
Embassy of the Kingdom of Morocco
Chancery: 1601 Twenty-first Street, NW
Washington, DC 20009
(202) 462-7980
Fax: (202) 462-7643

MOZAMBIQUE
Republic of Mozambique
Embassy of the Republic of Mozambique
Chancery: 1525 New Hampshire Avenue, NW
Washington, DC 20036
(202) 293-7146
Fax: (202) 835-0245

MYANMAR
Union of Myanmar
See *Burma*.

NAMIBIA
Republic of Namibia
Embassy of the Republic of Namibia
Chancery: 1605 New Hampshire Avenue, NW
Washington, DC 20009
(202) 986-0540
Fax: (202) 986-0443

NAURU
Republic of Nauru
Embassy of the Republic of Nauru
Chancery: 800 Second Avenue
New York, NY 10017
(212) 937-0074
Fax: (212) 937-0079

NEPAL
Federal Democratic Republic of Nepal
Embassy of Nepal
Chancery: 2131 Leroy Place, NW
Washington, DC 20008
(202) 667-4550
Fax: (202) 667-5534

NETHERLANDS
Kingdom of the Netherlands
Royal Netherlands Embassy
Chancery: 4200 Linnean Avenue, NW
Washington, DC 20008
(202) 244-5300
Fax: (202) 362-3430

NEW ZEALAND
New Zealand
Embassy of New Zealand
Chancery: 37 Observatory Circle, NW
Washington, DC 20008
(202) 328-4800
Fax: (202) 667-5227

NICARAGUA
Republic of Nicaragua
Embassy of the Republic of Nicaragua
Chancery: 1627 New Hampshire Avenue, NW
Washington, DC 20009
(202) 939-6570
Fax: (202) 939-6545

NIGER
Republic of Niger
Embassy of the Republic of Niger
Chancery: 2204 R Street, NW
Washington, DC 20008
(202) 483-4224
Fax: (202) 483-3169

NIGERIA
Federal Republic of Nigeria
Embassy of the Federal Republic of Nigeria
Chancery: 3519 International Court, NW
Washington, DC 20008
(202) 986-8400
Fax: (202) 362-6541

NORTHERN MARIANA ISLANDS**
Commonwealth of the Northern Mariana Islands
The Northern Mariana Islands have democratic representation in the
United States.

NORWAY
Kingdom of Norway
Royal Norwegian Embassy
Chancery: 2720 Thirty-fourth Street, NW
Washington, DC 20008
(202) 333-6000
Fax: (202) 337-0870

OMAN
Sultanate of Oman
Embassy of the Sultanate of Oman
Chancery: 2535 Belmont Road, NW
Washington, DC 20008
(202) 387-1980
Fax: (202) 745-4933

PAKISTAN
Islamic Republic of Pakistan
Embassy of Pakistan
Chancery: 3517 International Court, NW
Washington, DC 20008
(202) 243-6500
Fax: (202) 686-1544

PALAU
Republic of Palau
Embassy of the Republic of Palau
Chancery: 1701 Pennsylvania Avenue, NW
Suite 300
Washington, DC 20006
(202) 452-6814
Fax: (202) 452-6281

PANAMA
Republic of Panama
Embassy of the Republic of Panama
Chancery: 2862 McGill Terrace, NW
Washington, DC 20007
(202) 483-1407
Fax: (202) 483-8413

PAPUA NEW GUINEA
Independent State of Papua New Guinea
Embassy of Papua New Guinea
Chancery: 1779 Massachusetts Avenue, NW
Suite 805
Washington, DC 20036
(202) 745-3680
Fax: (202) 745-3679

PARAGUAY
Republic of Paraguay
Embassy of Paraguay
Chancery: 2400 Massachusetts Avenue, NW
Washington, DC 20008
(202) 483-6960
Fax: (202) 234-4508

PERU
Republic of Peru
Embassy of Peru
Chancery: 1700 Massachusetts Avenue, NW
Washington, DC 20036
(202) 833-9860
Fax: (202) 659-8124

PHILIPPINES
Republic of the Philippines
Embassy of the Republic of the Philippines
Chancery: 1600 Massachusetts Avenue, NW
Washington, DC 20036
(202) 467-9300
Fax: (202) 328-7614

POLAND
Republic of Poland
Embassy of the Republic of Poland
Chancery: 2640 Sixteenth Street, NW
Washington, DC 20009
(202) 234-3800
Fax: (202) 328-6271

PORTUGAL
Portuguese Republic
Embassy of Portugal
Chancery: 2012 Massachusetts Avenue, NW
Washington, DC 20036
(202) 328-8610
Fax: (202) 462-3726

Puerto Rico**
Commonwealth of Puerto Rico
This unincorporated organized U.S. territory has commonwealth status.

Qatar
State of Qatar
Embassy of the State of Qatar
Chancery: 2555 M Street, NW
Washington, DC 20037
(202) 274-1600
Fax: (202) 237-0061

Romania
Romania
Embassy of Romania
Chancery: 1607 Twenty-third Street, NW
Washington, DC 20008
(202) 332-4846
Fax: (202) 232-4748

Russia
Russian Federation
Embassy of the Russian Federation
Chancery: 2650 Wisconsin Avenue, NW
Washington, DC 20007
(202) 298-5700
Fax: (202) 298-5735

Rwanda
Republic of Rwanda
Embassy of the Republic of Rwanda
Chancery: 1714 New Hampshire Avenue, NW
Washington, DC 20009
(202) 232-2882
Fax: (202) 232-4544

SAMOA
Independent State of Samoa
Embassy of the Independent State of Samoa
Chancery: 800 Second Avenue
4th Floor
New York, NY 10017
(212) 599-6196
Fax: (212) 599-0797

SAN MARINO
Republic of San Marino
Embassy of Republic of San Marino
Chancery: 2650 Virginia Avenue, NW
Washington, DC 20037
(202) 250-1535

SÃO TOMÉ AND PRÍNCIPE
Democratic Republic of São Tomé and Príncipe
Embassy of São Tomé and Príncipe
Chancery: 1211 Connecticut Avenue, NW
Suite 300
Washington, DC 20036
(202) 775-2075
Fax: (202) 775-2077

SAUDI ARABIA
Kingdom of Saudi Arabia
Royal Embassy of Saudi Arabia
Chancery: 601 New Hampshire Avenue, NW
Washington, DC 20037
(202) 342-3800
Fax: (202) 944-3113

Senegal
Republic of Senegal
Embassy of the Republic of Senegal
Chancery: 2112 Wyoming Avenue, NW
Washington, DC 20008
(202) 234-0540
Fax: (202) 332-6315

Serbia
Republic of Serbia
Embassy of the Republic of Serbia
Chancery: 2134 Kalorama Road, NW
Washington, DC 20008
(202) 332-0333
Fax: (202) 332-3933

Seychelles
Republic of Seychelles
Embassy of the Republic of Seychelles
Chancery: 800 Second Avenue
Suite 400 C
New York, NY 10017
(212) 972-1785
Fax: (212) 972-1786

Sierra Leone
Republic of Sierra Leone
Embassy of Sierra Leone
Chancery: 1701 Nineteenth Street, NW
Washington, DC 20009
(202) 939-9261
Fax: (202) 483-1793

Singapore
Republic of Singapore
Embassy of the Republic of Singapore
Chancery: 3501 International Place, NW
Washington, DC 20008
(202) 537-3100
Fax: (202) 537-0876

SLOVAK REPUBLIC
Slovak Republic
Embassy of the Slovak Republic
Chancery: 3523 International Court, NW
Washington, DC 20008
(202) 237-1054
Fax: (202) 237-6438

SLOVENIA
Republic of Slovenia
Embassy of the Republic of Slovenia
Chancery: 2410 California Street, NW
Washington, DC 20008
(202) 386-6610
Fax: (202) 386-6633

SOLOMON ISLANDS
The Solomon Islands
Embassy of the Solomon Islands
Chancery: 800 Second Avenue
Suite 400 L
New York, NY 10017
(212) 599-6192
Fax: (212) 661-8925

SOUTH AFRICA
Republic of South Africa
Embassy of the Republic of South Africa
Chancery: 3051 Massachusetts Avenue, NW
Washington, DC 20008
(202) 232-4400
Fax: (202) 265-1607

SPAIN
Kingdom of Spain
Embassy of Spain
Chancery: 2375 Pennsylvania Avenue, NW
Washington, DC 20037
(202) 452-0100
Fax: (202) 833-5670

Sri Lanka
Democratic Socialist Republic of Sri Lanka
Embassy of the Democratic Socialist Republic of Sri Lanka
Chancery: 2148 Wyoming Avenue, NW
Washington, DC 20008
(202) 483-4025
Fax: (202) 232-7181

St. Kitts and Nevis
Federation of Saint Kitts and Nevis
Embassy of Saint Kitts and Nevis
Chancery: 3216 New Mexico Avenue, NW
Washington, DC 20016
(202) 686-2636
Fax: (202) 686-5740

St. Lucia
Saint Lucia
Embassy of Saint Lucia
Chancery: 3216 New Mexico Avenue, NW
Washington, DC 20016
(202) 364-6792
Fax: (202) 364-6723

St. Vincent and the Grenadines
Saint Vincent and the Grenadines
Embassy of Saint Vincent and the Grenadines
Chancery: 3216 New Mexico Avenue, NW
Washington, DC 20016
(202) 364-6730
Fax: (202) 364-6736

Sudan
Republic of the Sudan
Embassy of the Republic of the Sudan
Chancery: 2210 Massachusetts Avenue, NW
Washington, DC 20008
(202) 338-8565
Fax: (202) 667-2406

SURINAME
Republic of Suriname
Embassy of the Republic of Suriname
Chancery: 4301 Connecticut Avenue, NW
Suite 460
Washington, DC 20008
(202) 244-7488
Fax: (202) 244-5878

SWAZILAND
Kingdom of Swaziland
Embassy of the Kingdom of Swaziland
Chancery: 1712 New Hampshire Avenue, NW
Washington, DC 20009
(202) 234-5002
Fax: (202) 234-8254

SWEDEN
Kingdom of Sweden
Embassy of Sweden
Chancery: 2900 K Street, NW
Washington, DC 20007
(202) 467-2600
Fax: (202) 467-2699

SWITZERLAND
Swiss Confederation
Embassy of Switzerland
Chancery: 2900 Cathedral Avenue, NW
Washington, DC 20008
(202) 745-7900
Fax: (202) 387-2564

SYRIA
Syrian Arab Republic
Embassy of the Syrian Arab Republic
Chancery: 2215 Wyoming Avenue, NW
Washington, DC 20008
(202) 232-6313
Fax: (202) 234-9548

TAIWAN*
Taiwan
The United States has not recognized Taiwan as an independent country since the mainland People's Republic of China claimed the island nation. Unofficial relations are maintained through an unofficial instrumentality, the Taipei Economic and Cultural Representative Office.
4201 Wisconsin Avenue, NW
Washington, DC 20016-2146
(202) 895-1800
Fax: (202) 895-0825

TAJIKISTAN
Republic of Tajikistan
Embassy Republic of Tajikistan
Chancery: 1005 New Hampshire Avenue, NW
Washington, DC 20037
(202) 223-6090
Fax: (202) 223-6091

TANZANIA
United Republic of Tanzania
Embassy of the United Republic of Tanzania
Chancery: 2139 R Street, NW
Washington, DC 20008
(202) 939-6125
Fax: (202) 797-7408

THAILAND
Kingdom of Thailand
Embassy of Thailand
Chancery: 1024 Wisconsin Avenue, NW
Washington, DC 20007
(202) 944-3600
Fax: (202) 944-3611

TIMOR-LESTE
Democratic Republic of Timor-Leste
Embassy of the Democratic Republic of Timor-Leste
Chancery: 4201 Connecticut Avenue, NW
Suite 504
Washington, DC 20008
(202) 966-3202
Fax: (202) 966-3205

TOGO
Togolese Republic
Embassy of the Republic of Togo
Chancery: 2208 Massachusetts Avenue, NW
Washington, DC 20008
(202) 234-4212
Fax: (202) 232-3190

TONGA
Kingdom of Tonga
Embassy of the Kingdom of Tonga
Chancery: 250 E. Fifty-first Street
New York, NY 10022
917-369-1025
Fax: 917-369-1024

TRINIDAD AND TOBAGO
Republic of Trinidad and Tobago
Embassy of the Republic of Trinidad and Tobago
Chancery: 1708 Massachusetts Avenue, NW
Washington, DC 20036
(202) 467-6490
Fax: (202) 785-3130

TUNISIA
Tunisian Republic
Embassy of Tunisia
Chancery: 1515 Massachusetts Avenue, NW
Washington, DC 20005
(202) 862-1850
Fax: (202) 862-1858

TURKEY
Republic of Turkey
Embassy of the Republic of Turkey
Chancery: 2525 Massachusetts Avenue, NW
Washington, DC 20008
(202) 612-6700
Fax: (202) 612-6744

TURKMENISTAN
Turkmenistan
Embassy of Turkmenistan
Chancery: 2207 Massachusetts Avenue, NW
Washington, DC 20008
(202) 588-1500
Fax: (202) 588-0697

UGANDA
Republic of Uganda
Embassy of the Republic of Uganda
Chancery: 5911 Sixteenth Street, NW
Washington, DC 20011
(202) 726-0416
Fax: (202) 726-1727

UKRAINE
Ukraine
Embassy of Ukraine
Chancery: 3350 M Street, NW
Washington, DC 20007
(202) 349-2920
Fax: (202) 333-0817

UNITED ARAB EMIRATES
United Arab Emirates
Embassy of the United Arab Emirates
Chancery: 3522 International Court, NW
Washington, DC 20008
(202) 243-2400
Fax: (202) 243-2432

UNITED KINGDOM
United Kingdom of Great Britain and Northern Ireland
The ambassador is addressed: The British Ambassador.
British Embassy
Chancery: 3100 Massachusetts Avenue, NW
Washington, DC 20008
(202) 588-6500
Fax: (202) 588-7870

URUGUAY
Oriental Republic of Uruguay
Embassy of Uruguay
Chancery: 1913 I Street, NW
Washington, DC 20006
(202) 331-1313
Fax: (202) 331-8142

UZBEKISTAN
Republic of Uzbekistan
Embassy of the Republic of Uzbekistan
Chancery: 1746 Massachusetts Avenue, NW
Washington, DC 20036
(202) 293-6803
Fax: (202) 293-6804

VENEZUELA
Bolivarian Republic of Venezuela
Embassy of the Bolivarian Republic of Venezuela
Chancery: 1099 30th Street, NW
Washington, DC 20007
(202) 342-2214
Fax: (202) 342-6820

VIETNAM
Socialist Republic of Vietnam
Embassy of Vietnam
Chancery: 1233 Twentieth Street, NW
Suite 400
Washington, DC 20036
(202) 861-0737
Fax: (202) 861-0917

VIRGIN ISLANDS**
U.S. Virgin Islands
Diplomatic representation is conducted by the United States.

YEMEN
Republic of Yemen
Embassy of the Republic of Yemen
Chancery: 2319 Wyoming Avenue, NW
Washington, DC 20008
(202) 965-4760
Fax: (202) 337-2017

ZAMBIA
Republic of Zambia
Embassy of the Republic of Zambia
Chancery: 2419 Massachusetts Avenue, NW
Washington, DC 20008
(202) 265-9717
Fax: (202) 332-0826

ZIMBABWE
Republic of Zimbabwe
Embassy of Republic of Zimbabwe
Chancery: 1608 New Hampshire Avenue, NW
Washington, DC 20009
(202) 332-7100
Fax: (202) 483-9326

* No official diplomatic relations with the United States as of the printing of this book
** Territory of the United States

Chapter 18

──────────────○──────────────

Websites

www.cia.gov/library/publications/index.html

Official site of the Central Intelligence Agency (CIA), including the "World Factbook" (a reference site updated biweekly to provide information regarding the background, geography, people, government, economy, communications, transportation, military, and transnational issues of countries), "World Leaders" (a directory of chiefs of state and cabinet members of foreign governments listed alphabetically by country), maps, and other publications.

www.culturegrams.com

Concise cultural reports database for more than two hundred countries, all U.S. states, and all thirteen Canadian provinces and territories (may require subscription).

www.embassyworld.com

Directory and search engine of every nation's embassies and consulates.

www.protocolinternational.org

Protocol and Diplomacy International website. Protocol Officers Association's mission is to provide the highest level of collective expertise, training, information, and advice regarding internationally and nationally accepted rules of protocol.

www.state.gov/r/pa/ei/bgn

Website for the U.S. Department of State. Publications include facts about the land, people, history, government, political conditions, economy, and foreign relations of independent states, some dependencies, and areas of special sovereignty.

www.state.gov/s/cpr

U.S. Department of State, Office of the Chief of Protocol website. Provides information concerning the office and related links.

www.state.gov/s/cpr/rls/index.htm

Foreign embassy information and publications web page. This section of the Office of Protocol page includes two publications easily accessed online:

1. *Diplomatic List:* Complete list of the accredited diplomatic officers of foreign embassies within the United States. Includes national holidays for all countries listed and the order of precedence of all chiefs of mission.
2. *Foreign Consular Offices in the United States:* Complete list of foreign consular offices in the United States.

www.timeanddate.com/worldclock

Website for worldwide time zones.

National

www.house.gov

Official site of the U.S. House of Representatives.

www.mdw.army.mil

Website of the U.S. Army Military District of Washington.

www.members.cox.net/govdocs/govspeak.html

Web page providing an extensive list of government acronyms.

www.state.gov/www/about_state/diprooms/newh.html.

Web page describing the U.S. Department of State's diplomatic reception rooms. Includes tour and information about rooms.

www.senate.gov

Official site of the U.S. Senate.

www.state.gov/ofm

Links of interest to foreign missions: Diplomatic Security (DS), Office of Protocol (CPR), and the Bureau of Consular Affairs.

www.supremecourtus.gov

Official site of the U.S. Supreme Court.

www.usa.gov

"Government Made Easy": a resource for questions relating to the U.S. government. Includes links to official websites for all federal departments.

www.usflag.org/uscode36.html

Provides information on the U.S. Flag Code.

www.wassar.net/federal_flag_code.htm

Proper display of the U.S. flag: Federal Flag Code, Public Law 94-344.

www.whitehousehistory.org/whha_publications/_books-ebooks. html

To Be Preserved for All Time by Candace Shireman, a history of Blair House, the President's Guest House.

www.whitehouse.gov

Official site of the White House.

WASHINGTON, D.C., LOCAL

www.amtrak.com

Amtrak rail service website.

www.arlingtoncemetery.org

Arlington National Cemetery website.

www.dc.gov

Official site of the government of the District of Columbia.

www.meridian.org

Website of Meridian International Center, a nonpartisan nonprofit dedicated to strengthening international understanding.

www.metwashairports.com

Website of the Metropolitan Washington Airports Authority.

www.nationalcathedral.org

Website of Washington National Cathedral.

www.si.edu

Website of the Smithsonian Institution.

www.thisdiplomats.org

Website of the Hospitality and Information Service, a nonprofit that welcomes and assists diplomats and their families during their stays in Washington, D.C.

www.traffic.com

Provides traffic conditions locally and nationwide.

www.washdiplomat.com

The Washington Diplomat, a resource for the diplomatic community in Washington, D.C.

www.weather.com

Provides weather reports locally and worldwide.

www.wmata.com

Website of the Washington Metropolitan Transit Authority.

Glossary

Advance team: A team of individuals that literally goes in advance of the president and other high-ranking government officials. It is the responsibility of advance teams to make preparations for trips and public events for the president or other officials represented.

Agrément: The French word for "agreement," used to describe a procedure for ensuring that the person designated as an ambassador from one country to another is acceptable to the receiving state. For more information regarding *agrément*, see chapter 11, "Conduct of Diplomacy."

Air Force One: The air traffic control sign used to refer to any of the planes maintained by the U.S. Air Force to transport the president.

Ambassador, extraordinary and plenipotentiary: The highest-ranking diplomat sent by one country to another as the official representative of the sending country's sovereign or leader. (See chapter 11, "Conduct of Diplomacy.")

American service: A type of food service in which a waiter holds a platter while a guest uses utensils on the platter to serve his or her own plate.

Attire: The dress code for a particular occasion (i.e., the dress considered appropriate). Attire specifications such as "black tie" or "white tie" may appear at the bottom right-hand corner of official invitations. (See chapter 7, "Official Entertaining.")

Blair House: The official guesthouse of the U.S. president, located on Pennsylvania Avenue, across from the White House. Blair House is the official Washington residence for foreign chiefs of state and heads of government during state or official visits who may reside at Blair House at the invitation of the U.S. president. It is also used as a temporary residence for incoming U.S. presidents prior to their inauguration and for families of deceased former U.S. presidents while in Washington, D.C., for state funeral ceremonies.

Calling cards: Formerly used by U.S. government officials or their spouses when calling on superiors at superiors' homes. This practice is no longer considered mandatory, especially for the public at large. Diplomatic custom still prevails that the secretary of state or chief of protocol should leave cards when signing a condolence book at an embassy. The military has its own rules for the use of calling cards.

Career diplomat: Generally is a professional member of a government's diplomatic corps.

Catafalque: An elevated structure on which a decedent's body lies.

Chancery: The building or suite of offices where an ambassador and his or her staff work.

Chargé d'affaires: A diplomat in charge of the embassy temporarily when the ambassador is away or when the ambassadorial position is vacant (plural: chargés d'affaires).

Chief of protocol: The highest-ranking officer in the Office of Protocol, Department of State. The position is confirmed by the Senate Foreign Relations Committee.

Chief of state: The highest-ranking official and formal representative of a nation. The head of a constitutional monarchy, such as a king or queen, is a chief of state. In some republics, such as in the United States, a president is both a chief of state and a head of government.

Civil Service: Employees of the U.S. Department of State who are not members of the U.S. Foreign Service or presidential appointees.

Colors: Term used to refer to a flag and the colors of a flag. A joint service color guard refers to a line of units' flags with the U.S. flag in the place of honor, "to its own right."

Consul: A term used generally to describe a consular officer. Consuls provide consular services as opposed to carrying out diplomatic duties performed by diplomats at embassies or missions to international organizations.

Country desk: A term used to describe an office in the State Department that monitors and coordinates activities between the State Department and a foreign country and develops policies pertaining to the relationship between the two countries.

Courtesy title: A title given to an individual due to courtesy or custom rather than by right to an officeholder.

Dean of the diplomatic corps: The foreign ambassador who represents the entire diplomatic corps on occasions when it is not practical to invite all chiefs of mission. When the corps is assembled as a group, the dean precedes all others and, when necessary, speaks for the corps. In most countries today, the deanship automatically goes to the ambassador who has served longest in the host country. However, in some countries with a strong Roman Catholic tradition, the papal nuncio serves as dean.

Delegates: Those persons designated to act on behalf of or represent a political unit.

Delegations: The group of delegates selected to represent a political unit.

Diplomacy: Conduct relating to negotiations and relations between nations or the art of conducting international relations and negotiations.

Diplomat: A person appointed to establish and/or maintain political, economic, and social relations with another country or countries and to negotiate on behalf of a national government in said country or countries. Diplomats should not be confused with consular officers, who perform consular functions and often work with or through state or municipal authorities.

Diplomatic corps: The hundreds of diplomats working at their various governments' embassies in host countries. This term may also be used to refer only to the ambassadors and chargés d'affaires of foreign countries residing in a nation's capital. Generally speaking, *diplomatic corps* is taken to mean the chiefs of diplomatic missions residing in a given country.

Diplomatic security: The law-enforcement agency of the U.S. State Department. The Bureau of Diplomatic Security provides protection for the secretary of state, visiting foreign ministers, other high-ranking foreign officials, and royalty. Diplomatic Security operates globally to ensure a safe and secure environment for the conduct of U.S. foreign policy.

District of Columbia: Washington, D.C. As of July 16, 1790, it was unofficially referred to a "territory of Columbia." On May 6, 1796, it received the official name "District of Columbia," and on June 1, 1871, it became the District of Columbia by an act of Congress.

Embassy: The premises of a permanent diplomatic mission of one country in another country. The term *embassy* describes two types of buildings: the *chancery*, which is the building or suite of offices where an ambassador and staff work, and the *residence*, which is the home of the ambassador.

Espontoon: A type of spear carried during the Revolutionary era and now used by the Old Guard Fife and Drum Corps as a component of dress. The espontoon is used by the drum major to issue silent commands while performing.

Etiquette: The rules governing appropriate behavior or conduct in a given situation.

Finger bowls: Small bowls that may be used for formal dinners, including dinners at the White House. A finger bowl is used for dipping and cleansing fingertips prior to desert's being served.

First Gentleman: The unofficial title of the male spouse of many elected female leaders of foreign countries. This is also the unofficial title of male spouses of U.S. governors.

First Lady: The wife of the U.S. president. The wife of the governor of a state is referred to as the first lady of (state). "First Lady" is an unofficial title.

Foreign Service officer: A career member of a nation's diplomatic corps, as distinguished from a person who is appointed to a position from outside the career service or assigned temporarily from another government agency.

Forks: Forks may be held in two ways, either of which is correct: American (holding the fork tines up and keeping the fork in the right hand) and European or Continental (with fork tines down, keeping the fork in the left hand and the knife in the right throughout the meal).

French service: A type of food service in which a waiter holds a platter and serves food onto a guest's plate on the table.

Gilt: A thin layer of gold applied to a surface (such as the Steinway grand piano at the White House).

"Hail to the Chief": The song played by the U.S. Marine Band, The President's Own, upon the president's arrival at ceremonies, formal gatherings, or during presidential events.

Head of government: The highest official of a country who is the chief officer of the executive branch of a government. Prime ministers and chancellors typically hold the title "head of government."

Honorific: An appellation conveying the bearer's office title or rank, identifying his or her profession, or specifying gender and marital status.

Library: The White House room where books are kept and where some presidential press conferences have taken place. The library is the location of the only men's bathroom available to White House guests.

Lying in honor: The phrase used when a deceased is not a member of government and his or her body is on display for public viewing in a government building.

Lying in repose: Though funeral directors nationwide use the phrases "lying in repose" and "lying in state" interchangeably, lying in repose simply means that a body is on display for public viewing at a venue, other than the Rotunda, predetermined by the deceased or chosen by the deceased's family. Sitting presidents who die while in office may lie in repose in the East Room of the White House.

Lying in state: Though funeral directors nationwide use the phrases "lying in repose" and "lying in state" interchangeably, when one is referring to U.S. government funerals, lying in state refers to a deceased's body or the body of a former president on display in the Rotunda of the U.S. Capitol Building in Washington, D.C. The use of the Rotunda is controlled by concurrent action of Congress.

Marine One: The president's helicopter.

Napkins: If departing from the table during the meal but planning to return, one should place the napkin, lightly folded, in one's chair. When dinner concludes, the napkin should be lightly folded and placed where the plate was removed from the table or to the left of the plate if the plate remains on the table.

Nighthawks Two and Three: Helicopters that transport senior staff, Secret Service , other staff, and press when traveling with the president.

Office of Protocol: The federal office that works in conjunction with the White House in planning, hosting, and directing events for visiting chiefs of state and heads of government; managing the president's guesthouse (Blair House); and overseeing all protocol matters for the president, the vice president, and the secretary of state. The chief of protocol oversees the Office of Protocol.

Official entertaining: The presence of official guests of the United States for entertainment purposes. The White House, the State Department, government agencies, and private individuals may all entertain officially. Official entertaining is usually intended to develop relationships and strengthen bonds within and between the government, foreign nations, the diplomatic corps, the media, and business and social communities. This type of entertaining helps achieve U.S. objectives, both domestically and abroad.

Official gift: Gift given by one nation's leader to another's. Such gifts have enormous import because they may pave the way not only for the blossoming of friendships between leaders but for the formation or maintenance of diplomatic relations between countries. Thus, gifts must be selected carefully (see chapter 13, "Official Gift Giving").

Official gift giving is generally accomplished in private, between one nation's protocol official and another's.

Official visit: A visit to the United States by a foreign head of government at the invitation of the president. Official visits are marked by the highest level of formality and may include state dinners, official meetings, tours, and other entertainment.

Old Guard Fife and Drum Corps: Stationed at Fort Myer, Virginia, and part of the Third United States Infantry ("The Old Guard"). Members play musical instruments and wear uniforms inspired by those of the Continental army during the American Revolution. The corps performs at sporting events, abroad as ambassadors of the United States, for parades (such as inaugural parades) and historical celebrations, and at arrival ceremonies on the White House South Lawn.

Order of Precedence: Document setting forth the ranking of officials within the United States. Consulted to determine who has the right to precede others in ceremonies or during social formalities, the order is formulated by rank and hierarchy and dictates conduct related to seating at official dinners and standing in official receiving lines (see chapter 7), as well as at most other official ceremonies.

Pledge of Allegiance: An oath of loyalty to the United States of America. The Pledge of Allegiance, written in 1892 by Francis Bellamy, was officially adopted by Congress under the Flag Code on June 22, 1942. (See chapter 9, "Flag Etiquette.")

Presidential seal: A symbol of the U.S. presidency that appears on correspondence from the president to Congress, on the presidential flag, on official invitations from the White House, and in other circumstances to denote the presidency.

Protocol: Customs and rules associated with diplomatic formality, precedence, and etiquette.

Receiving line: A line of important persons waiting to receive greetings from guests. The order of those standing in the receiving line is found in chapter 7, "Official Entertaining."

Regrets only: A designation appearing on invitations indicating that guests should respond only if they do not plan to attend an event.

Residence: The home of a foreign ambassador in a country. It is one of the two buildings, the chancery being the other, that together comprise an embassy.

RSVP: An acronym borrowed from the French phrase *Répondez s'il vous plaît*, meaning "Respond, if you please" or "Please respond." "RSVP" may appear at the close of an invitation to an event, indicating that the invited guest *must* tell the host whether he or she plans to attend.

Ruffles and flourishes: Ruffles (played by drums) and flourishes (played by bugles) sounded to bestow personal honors. They precede the national anthem, the General's March, "Hail, Columbia," and the Flag Officer's March. The U.S. president receives four ruffles and flourishes (the highest honor) each time "Hail to the Chief" is played.

Secret Service: The federal law-enforcement agency headquartered in Washington, D.C., and mandated by Congress to protect the president, former presidents, the vice president, and presidential and vice presidential candidates and their families. The Secret Service also provides protection for visiting foreign chiefs of state and heads of government. Treasury services provided by the Secret Service aim to prevent counterfeiting and fraud.

South Lawn ceremony: A South Lawn ceremony at the White House for a state or official visit honors a chief of state or head of government. Other types of ceremonies are also conducted on the South Lawn.

State Department: The oldest cabinet agency in the U.S. government. Administered by the secretary of state, the U.S. State Department (or Department of State) is the branch of the U.S. government responsible for foreign affairs at the cabinet level.

State Dining Room: White House dining room used for state and official dinners, receptions, and luncheons. This room seats 140 guests and measures approximately 48 feet by 36 feet.

State dinner: Dinner given by the president to honor a visiting chief of state or head of government.

State visit: A state visit by a chief of state to another country at the invitation of that country's chief of state or head of government. State visits are marked by the highest level of formality and may include state dinners, meetings, tours, and other entertainment.

Strolling Strings: Divisions of the U.S. Army and Air Force musicians that play at official ceremonies and state dinners. (See chapter 7, "Official Entertaining.")

Taps: The most easily recognized military bugle call. These twenty-four notes invite listeners to remember patriots who have served the country with honor and valor.

The President's Own: The U.S. Marine Band, which honors presidents by playing "Hail to the Chief" and other music. "Hail to the Chief" marks the arrival of the president and is played for newly inaugurated presidents after they take the oath of office.

Toast: An honor and tribute paid to a guest or guests of honor. The toast is usually given at the beginning of a meal (before or after the first course is served); however, it can come after the dessert course. It is inappropriate to clink one's glass in order to signal a toast. Persons receiving a toast do not drink to themselves; instead, they should simply raise their glasses.

Union: The name for the portion of the U.S. flag consisting of the field of stars against a blue backdrop (also called "the canton" or "the field").

Vermeil Room: Pronounced "ver-MAY," a White House room located in the Lower Cross Hall. On display here are paintings of former first ladies. The only ladies' powder room available for White House guests is located in this area.

Vienna Convention on Diplomatic Relations: International law governing the conduct of diplomacy.

White House: The official residence of the U.S. president. Important positions among the executive residence staff of the White House and their accompanying responsibilities are listed:

> *White House chief floral designer*: Reports directly to the White House chief usher and is responsible for all floral décor

for the White House and the first family; this includes all floral arrangements for official and private entertaining, holidays, and so forth.

White House chief usher: Responsible for the operation and management of the White House and its executive staff and works with numerous organizations in executing these duties. The usher is also responsible for development and administration of the budget related to the operation, maintenance, and utilities of the White House.

White House executive chef: Reports directly to the White House chief usher and is responsible for all states of menu and meal planning, preparation, and management for the first family at the White House.

White House social secretary: Appointed by each administration, as head of the White House Social Office. The social secretary's responsibilities include the advance planning, coordination, and execution of White House social events.

Bibliography

Aikman, Lonnelle. *The Living White House*. Washington, DC: White House Historical Association, 1991.

Baldrige, Letitia. *Letitia Baldrige's Complete Guide to the New Manners for the '90s*. New York: Macmillan Publishing Company, 1990.

Freidel, Frank. *The Presidents of the United States of America*. 14th ed. Washington, DC: White House Historical Association, 1995.

Gonthier, Giovinella. *Rude Awakenings: Overcoming the Civility Crisis in the Workplace*. Chicago: Dearborn Trade Publishing, 2002.

Heck, Marlene. *Blair House: The President's Guest House*. Washington, DC: Blair House Restoration Fund, 1989.

Hickey, Robert. *Honor and Respect: The Official Guide to Names, Titles, and Forms of Address*. Columbia, SC: Protocol School of Washington, 2008.

Kennedy, Caroline. *A Patriot's Handbook*. New York: Hyperion Books, 2003.

Klapthor, Margaret Brown. *The First Ladies*. 6th ed. Washington, DC: White House Historical Association, 1989.

McCaffree, Mary Jane, and Pauline Innis. *Protocol: The Complete Handbook of Diplomatic, Official and Social Usage*. 1977. Reprint, Washington, DC: Devon Publishing Company, 1985.

McCaffree, Mary Jane, Pauline Innis, and Richard M. Sand. *Protocol: The Complete Handbook of Diplomatic, Official and Social Usage*. 2002. Reprint, Washington, DC: Devon Publishing Company, 1985, 1989, 1997.

Post, Peggy. *Emily Post's Etiquette*. New York: HarperCollins, 2004.

Shireman, Candace. To be Preserved for All Time: The Major and the President Save Blair House. Washington, DC: White House Historical Association, 2009. www.whitehousehistory.org/whha_publications/publications_documents/whha_publications-blair-house (accessed January 6, 2010).

White House Historical Association. *The White House: An Historic Guide*. 17th ed. Washington, DC: White House Historical Association. 1991.

Index

Abdullah, King, 206

Adams, Abigail, 185

Adams, John Quincy, 195

Adams, Louisa Catherine, 195

advance teams, 315–16; Bureau of Diplomatic Security, 166, 177, 324, 424; confidentiality, 322–23; correct forms of address, 318–19; dietary precautions, 325; at events, 323; flag etiquette, 324; flowers, 326; foreign embassies, 317; gifts, 325; guidance for, 319–26; hotels, 323; lead advance, 316; Order of Precedence, 318; protocol, 318; Secret Service, 324; team members, 316–17; volunteers, 316

Agency for International Development (AID), 20

Albright, Madeleine K., *179*, 197

Allen, Lew Jr., 363

ambassadors, 279–87; agrément, 280–81; credentials, presentation of, 281–82; representational responsibilities of, 284–86; role of, 282–84; spouse of, role of, 286–87. *See also* American ambassadors

American ambassador-designate, 20

American ambassadors, 11, 16, 20

American flag, 237–53; on automobiles, 245; on boats, 245; on caskets, 244; clean, keeping of, 244; dipping the colors, 238; displaying of, alone in front of building, 240; displaying of, alone over sidewalk, 241; displaying of, alone over street, 240; displaying of, with another flag, 238–39; displaying of, in church, 250; displaying of, in classroom, 249; displaying of, with crossed staffs, 240; displaying of, in inclement weather, 239–40; displaying of, indoors, 240; displaying of, in front of building, 246; displaying of, at night, 239; displaying of, with other nations' flags, 241; displaying of, in open area, 247;

About the Author and Contributing Writers

Meet the Author

Ambassador Mary Mel French was appointed by President William Jefferson Clinton and confirmed by the U.S. Senate as the chief of protocol for the United States. During her years as the top protocol officer for the White House and Department of State, Ambassador French worked directly with former president Clinton and former secretary of state Madeleine Korbel Albright, advising them in fulfilling the U.S. government's obligations relating to national and international protocol. Ambassador French managed the protocol logistics of all official foreign affairs events, which included several presidential summits, Israeli/Palestinian peace negotiations, and the NATO Fiftieth Anniversary Summit. During President Clinton's official trips abroad, Ambassador French worked with foreign governments on all matters related to protocol in the countries to which the president traveled. Ambassador French began work in the U.S. protocol office in 1993 as Assistant Chief of Protocol for Visits.

Ambassador French also spent many years in the political arena, first as a state volunteer coordinator for President Clinton during his years as governor of Arkansas and eventually as administrative director of the Clinton for President Campaign. After Clinton won the election,

French was appointed co–executive director of the Fifty-second Presidential Inaugural Committee.

Ambassador French holds an associate of arts degree from Stephens College in Columbia, Missouri, and a bachelor of arts in international studies from the University of Arkansas, Little Rock.

MEET THE CONTRIBUTING WRITERS

Lawrence Dunham served as U.S. assistant chief of protocol from 1989 until 2005, heading Protocol's Diplomatic Affairs Division, which oversees the State Department's day-to-day relations with over 180 foreign embassies in Washington, D.C., and the diplomatic community throughout the United States. He began his career in the Protocol Office in 1983. In addition to his primary responsibilities, he was involved in many of the major events coordinated by the office, including Presidential inaugurals, state funerals, the visits of foreign leaders, entertaining by presidents and secretaries of state, and presidential travel. He has been featured in television and radio broadcasts, provided guidance and insight to authors and journalists, and spoken to a variety of groups and organizations on a broad range of protocol-related subjects. He is a graduate of the Catholic University of America and the George Mason University School of Law.

Michelle Snyder Brady served in the U.S. Office of Protocol for five years, as a visits officer and as the special assistant to the U.S. chief of protocol. In these positions, she was involved in every aspect of the Office of Protocol. This included the official visits of chiefs of state and heads of government, during which she was responsible for coordinating activities involving the participation of foreign ambassadors; senior White House staff; Department of State officials; federal, state and municipal authorities; and private organizations. She served as a protocol officer supporting the president and the secretary of state for the United Nations Millennium Summit and the Fifty-fifth United Nations General Assembly, as well as at the NATO Fiftieth Anniversary Washington Summit Meetings.

Brady also held the position of development director for special events at Meridian International Center, where she managed all aspects of the annual Meridian Ball and worked closely with the embassies and diplomatic community in Washington.

She holds a bachelor of science in foreign service from Georgetown University's School of Foreign Service and a master's in intercultural relations from New York University.

MEET THE CONTRIBUTING EDITOR AND WRITER

Erin Snow Pennington served as a contributing writer to, and general editor of, this book prior to its submission to the publisher. Pennington is a freelance editor, creative writer, grant writer, and writing instructor living in Little Rock, Arkansas. As an undergraduate at Duke University, she earned her bachelor of arts in English with a minor in psychology. After attending law school, she practiced construction, general commercial, and trademark litigation in Atlanta, Georgia, before deciding to return to her home state of Arkansas to pursue a master's in professional and technical writing with a nonfiction writing focus at the University of Arkansas, Little Rock (UALR). She teaches in the First-Year Writing Program at UALR and leads workshops in professional writing at the Clinton School of Public Service. Pennington has recently completed a personal essay collection entitled *Storied Things: A Memoir in Possessions*, which details the stories behind objects of personal importance to her. Her essays have been broadcast on National Public Radio's *Tales from the South*, and her essays, fiction, and poetry have appeared in various publications.

Pennington holds a bachelor of arts in English from Duke University (2000), a juris doctorate from Georgia State University College of Law (2005), and a master's in professional and technical writing from the University of Arkansas, Little Rock (2009).